D1525763

THE ECOLOGY OF VISION

THE ECOLOGY OF VISION

J. N. LYTHGOE

Clarendon Press · Oxford · 1979

Oxford University Press, Walton Street, Oxford OX2 6DP

OXFORD LONDON GLASGOW
NEW YORK TORONTO MELBOURNE WELLINGTON
KUALA LUMPUR SINGAPORE JAKARTA HONG KONG TOKYO
DELHI BOMBAY CALCUTTA MADRAS KARACHI
NAIROBI DAR ES SALAAM CAPE TOWN

British Library Cataloguing in Publication Data

Lythgoe, John Nicholas
The Ecology of Vision
1. Animal ecology   2. Vision
I. Title
591.1'823   QH541   79–40411
ISBN 0–19–854529–0

*Published in the United States
by Oxford University Press, New York*

*Set, printed and bound in Great Britain by
Fakenham Press Limited, Fakenham, Norfolk*

Preface

A book about all ways that the ecology of animals is in some way shaped by the sense of vision would need to be rather longer than this one. Many and various are the animals that have eyes, but whether they are insects or cephalopods, fishes or man, the visual sense must work within performance limits set by the physical nature of light and by their own physiological performance.

The laws of physics are, of course, the same for all animals; physiological processes are more varied but they, too, show basic similarities throughout the animal kingdom. Between them, physics and physiology set the stage for all visual performances. In it we can begin to glimpse themes common to all animals and in this book I hope to identify some of them.

In outline, the book has three parts. The first two chapters deal with the physical nature of the light environment and the underlying physiological processes that animals have in common. The second part consists of four chapters on the way that particular aspects of the light climate make some visual tasks easy, or difficult, or impossible, and hence influence the lifestyle of the whole animal. The final part is an attempt to bring together the themes that have been taken separately in the previous chapters to try and get some insight into one of the much more complex problems of natural history.

The first two chapters on the physical nature of the light environment and the physiology of the eye are the foundations on which much of the rest is based. Several of the topics such as Rayleigh scattering and the spectral absorption of visual pigments are relevant to more than one aspect of visual ecology and help to avoid repetition if they are described only once. In fact I have failed to banish repetition altogether, for, at the risk of irritating the reader who starts the book at the beginning and reads it through to the end, I have tried to cater also for those who may sample the book on a specific question and who needs each section to be reasonably comprehensible in its own right.

The middle section of the book is concerned with the problems of seeing through scattering media such as fog or water, vision in very dim light, colour vision in environments with a pronounced colour bias, and environments where the directional distribution of light is important. The length of each chapter reflects more the extent of our present knowledge rather than its importance. For example, the visual difficulties encountered in light-scattering media are some of the most incapacitating and intractable that an animal has to face, yet there is little known about how the visual system makes the best of a bad situation.

The final chapter explores the ways that the coloration and visual physiology of various organisms, all functioning within much the same confines of physics and physiology, have evolved particular relationships according to the need to be noticed or to remain hidden. It has been accepted for many years that one of the prime interests in animal and plant coloration is what it can tell us about the vision of the animals concerned. Until recently the gap between physiology and natural history has been too wide for this to be really useful; it may still be premature to consider coloration in relation to the visual process, but perhaps the effort is now worth making.

This book could not have been written without the help and encouragement of my colleagues at every stage: from first introducing me to the animals in the field; through many discussions; and in helping me with unfamiliar literature. I should particularly like to thank: M. A. Ali; D. J. Bellamy; J. K. Bowmaker; F. W. Campbell; C. J. Chapman; H. J. A. Dartnall; E. J. Denton; W. M. Hamner; C. C. Hemmings; R. G. Jaeger; A. Knowles; M. F. Land; J. S. Levine; E. R. Loew; W. N. McFarland; G. R. Martin; N. R. Merrett; J. Mollon; W. R. A. Muntz; D. P. M. Northmore; J. C. Ogden; G. W. Potts; P. J. Scoones; P. H. Silver; F. Talbot; and S. Young.

J.N.L.

Bristol 1978

for Gillian

Contents

List of plates

1 The light environment

Introduction

Ours is a fortunate planet with its huge diversity of animals and plants clothed in a seemingly endless variety of colours and patterns. Only rarely can we imagine that some detail of coloration such as the mother-of-pearl inner face of an oyster shell has no visual significance. More often we know, or suspect, that colour and pattern has some special role to play in behaviour and ecology.

The diversity of coloration is rivalled by the diversity of techniques that animals use to find their food and to avoid being eaten themselves. Vision is so often an essential sense in these processes that it is tempting to think that the visual sense is infinitely versatile. Yet the physical laws that govern the behaviour of light encompass every aspect of vision; every animal has to function within the same set of rules, and the variation in vision and associated coloration is confined to the permutation of those rules.

Most of the light used in vision is generated by the sun and it is the ways that sunlight is modified in quantity and quality by selective absorption, reflection, and scatter that shape the photic environment. Various optical phenomena, such as the scattering of light by particles of molecular size, and the refraction of light at the air–water interface, have consequences that can be recognized in quite different areas of ecology and physiological optics. To reiterate these phenomena each time they become relevant would be quite wearisome; instead, most of them are described in the first chapter. Logically, also, it is easier to present the necessary physical information in one piece by tracing the fate of the sun's rays as they are reflected from the moon, absorbed and scattered in the atmosphere and by foliage, refracted at the water surface, and absorbed and scattered by water. At night, or in the depths of the sea where little sunlight penetrates, many organisms generate their own light and must, therefore, be treated as primary light sources.

The nature of light

Many optical phenomena such as dispersion refraction and interference can be explained by assuming that light behaves as a wave-form, but this description does not explain the way that light interacts with matter. For example, if a photographic plate is exposed for a suitable length of time to very dim light and then developed, it is found that the emulsion has not darkened uniformly over the entire surface, but rather in a series of dark points scattered at random over the surface. The dark points mark the places where a unit of electromagnetic energy has been absorbed. This unit of energy is called a quantum, or in the special case of visible electromagnetic energy, a photon. A description of light that combines the two ideas is that it is a form of energy that travels as a wave-form, but that the energy can only be transferred to matter at particular loci in time and space.

As a parcel of energy, a photon cannot be subdivided. It is either totally absorbed and all its energy is passed over to a molecule with which it coincides, or it is not absorbed and is in no way diminished in energy. The actual energy of a photon is proportional to the frequency of light with which it is associated, frequency being proportional to the reciprocal of the wavelength. Thus blue light, which is of high frequency (i.e. short wavelength) has photons of higher energy than red light. The energy, E, of a photon can be calculated from the following formula:

$$E = hv = hc/\lambda, \tag{1.1}$$

where h is Planck's constant and has a value of $6\cdot62517 \times 10^{-34}$ J S, c is the velocity of light and is $2\cdot99793 \times 10^8$ m s^{-1}, λ is the wavelength of light, and v is the frequency.

A distinction has to be drawn between processes where the energy of the photon is converted to vibrational movement of the molecules, i.e. as heat, when it is the total energy of the light that is important, and photochemical processes such as vision where the energy goes to change the electronic configuration of the molecule.

Assessing the visual effectiveness of light

Many of the measurements of natural light are rather unhelpful to the animal ecologist because they use psychometric units that relate only to humans. The most common of these human-related units are the lux, phot, and foot-candle for illuminance, and the lambert and candela for luminance. Luminance and illuminance are the psychometric equivalents of radiance and irradiance (see pp. 7 and 9). Integral to each of them is the spectral sensitivity of the human eye, usually for photopic (bright-light) vision (see p. 82). In this way the luminance of any light can be described by just one number; for example the illuminance of sunlight at midday on the earth's surface is about 10 000 foot-candles. The basic problem is that psychometric units contain no information about the spectral distribution of the light, so that even if the spectral sensitivity of the animal is known, the visual effectiveness of the light cannot be assessed. Human psychometric units do have their uses for the animal ecologist for they do, for example, give information about changes in relative light levels, provided these are not accompanied by too great changes in the spectral distribution of the light.

The visual ecologist therefore has little alternative but to make both spectral radiance measurements of the incident light and spectral sensitivity measurements of his animal. These measurements contain most, or all, the information that is needed, but can still be misleading if used in the wrong way.

The most common, and potentially the most misleading, method of assessing the efficiency with which a particular radiance will stimulate a particular visual system is to compare by eye the spectral radiance curve of the one against the spectral absorption (or spectral sensitivity) curve of the other. The difficulty is that it is the number of photons that are absorbed, rather than the energy, that modulates the strength of the visual signal. Most measurements of the spectral distribution of natural radiation have been made on an energy per unit wavelength interval basis. However, the energy carried by a photon is proportional to $1/\lambda$ (the frequency) of the light. Thus, to calculate the relative number of photons present within a narrow wavelength band, it is necessary to multiply the measured energy by λ. This procedure has the effect of shifting the wavelength of maximum apparent effectiveness to longer wavelength. Where the spectral energy curve is broad, for example, sunlight at the earth's surface, the shift is large; where the curve is narrow, for example, bioluminescent light, the shift is small. A similar correction is not made to spectral absorption or reflection curves since these are a measure of the proportions of the incident light at particular wavelengths that is absorbed or transmitted. The result is the same whether it is energy or the number of photons that is measured.

It is sometimes convenient to make a further adjustment to the form of the spectral radiance data before conclusions are drawn from them. The shape of the spectral absorption curve of the visual pigments is more closely similar when plotted on a frequency rather than a wavelength basis (see p. 52). Thus radiances plotted on an equal-frequency bandwidth basis can be directly compared to the absorption of a range of visual pigments in assessing which visual pigments are best fitted to a particular visual task. Because frequency is proportional to $1/\lambda$, a unit-wavelength bandwidth is narrower, as compared to a unit-frequency bandwidth, at long wavelengths than at short.

Dartnall (1975) has given procedures for calculating the visual efficiency of natural radiations on the basis of the absolute number of photons per unit time per unit wavelength (or frequency) interval per unit area. Dartnall has used as a model Moon's (1940) values for the energy of sunlight at the earth's surface. In Fig. 1.1 Moon's original data are expressed on an energy and equal wavelength basis ($dP/d\lambda$), but Dartnall has plotted these data also on the basis of the number of photons per unit wavelength

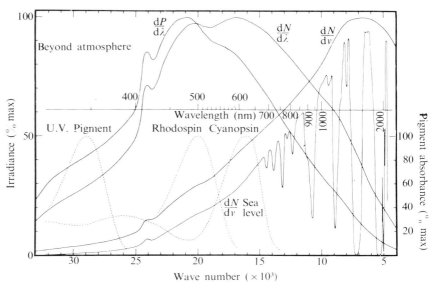

Fig. 1.1. The spectral irradiance of the sun beyond the earth's atmosphere presented in three ways: $dP/d\lambda$ (watts per wavelength interval), $dN/d\lambda$ (quanta per second per wavelength interval), and $dN/d\upsilon$ (quanta per second per frequency interval), and the irradiance at sea level on the $dN/d\upsilon$ basis. Also shown are the absorbance spectra for rhodopsins of λ_{max} 345 nm and 500 nm and a porphyropsin ('cyanopsin') of λ_{max} 620 nm. (From Dartnall 1975.)

($dN/d\lambda$) and per unit frequency ($dN/d\upsilon$). A similar exercise has also been independently completed by Govadovskii (1972, 1976). Dartnall remarks that the three curves are so different that it is hard to believe that they refer to the same data.

Astronomical light sources

Sunlight

Overwhelmingly the strongest source of light in the daylight hours is the sun. It has a surface temperature of about 6000 °C and the colour of its light is similar to that of a black body of this temperature. In its passage through the atmosphere, much of the sun's energy is absorbed, particularly in the infrared, by water vapour and in both the infrared and ultraviolet by ozone.

Moonlight

The moon owes its radiance to reflected sunlight, but since the moon's spectral reflectance is about the same throughout the spectrum, the spectral distribution of moonlight is similar to that of direct sunlight. Overall, the night sky, including the full moon, is about 6 log units less bright than full sunlight and is slightly richer in longer wavelengths (Richardson 1969; Munz and McFarland 1973, 1977).

Starlight

The unobscured starry sky with no moon is about 3 log units less bright than full moonlight (see Munz and McFarland 1973 for a review). The low intensity of starlight makes spectral irradiance measurements difficult, but there is general agreement that starlight is redder than moonlight (Figs. 1.2 and 1.3).

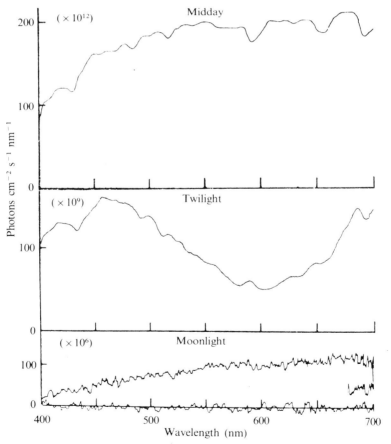

Fig. 1.2. Spectral irradiance during midday, twilight, and moonlight at Einewetok Atoll, summer 1970. (From McFarland and Munz 1975*a*, *b*.)

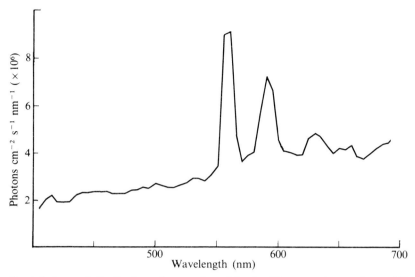

Fig. 1.3. Spectral distributions of a moonless night sky. The auroral green line at 590 nm and a second lower peak is clearly shown. 04·30 hr, 23 October 1974, elevation 1650 m. (For details see Munz and McFarland 1977.)

At night, the airglow from the earth's own atmosphere becomes relatively more important (Chamberlain 1961 for a review). Barbier (1955) found that airglow varies from 20 per cent to 54 per cent of the total night sky emission. In particular, one component of this earthlight, the green aurora line at 558 nm, which results from oxygen activation in the atmosphere, is very prominent. (Fig. 1.3). Rayleigh (1930) estimates that about 7 per cent of the light perceived by the dark-adapted human eye comes from the green line.

Optics of air and water

The underlying principles that control the transmission of light are the same in both air and water. There are two basic processes: absorption, where the energy from light is transferred to matter, and scatter where light is deflected from its original path but suffers no loss in energy. Absorption and scatter jointly control the quantity of light available for vision and the quality of the images that the eye can form.

Absorption

There is scarcely any process in visual ecology that does not involve absorption at some stage. Rarely are all the light wavelengths absorbed to an equal extent, and therefore the light that is not absorbed is generally richer in some wavelengths than in others. Absorption by air is perhaps not visually significant except that it may save living tissue from the effects of ionizing radiation. The absorption of light by water is, however, of profound importance to aquatic organisms because daylight is so reduced in intensity that at depths of 1000 m or so even in the clearest waters on the brightest of days insufficient light remains for vision (p. 104). At shallower depths, the wavelength-selective absorption of natural water effectively removes everything but a narrow waveband of light.

When a beam of light is shone through air or water, it is reduced in intensity partly by absorption and partly by being scattered into other directions by the molecules of the medium itself and by larger particles in the light path. An instrument that measures the intensity of a narrow beam of light is made up to include only light from the direction of the source (Fig. 1.4). The quality it measures is radiance (L) which is defined as radiant flux per unit solid angle per unit projected area of surface.

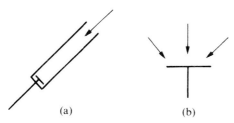

(a)   (b)

Fig. 1.4. The arrangement of the photocell used to measure (a) radiance and (b) irradiance.

If the radiance of the beam is reduced by half when it has travelled a unit distance, the residue will be again reduced by half after it has travelled a further unit distance. Conventionally, this type of exponential reduction is described thus:

$$L_r = L_0 e^{-ar}, \tag{1.2}$$

where e is the root of natural logarithms, a is the beam-attenuation coefficient, and r is the pathlength through the medium. Losses by both absorption and scatter are included in a. Absorption is strongly wavelength-dependent. In the atmosphere it is only for very long pathlengths where sunlight passes through the entire thickness of the atmosphere that it is visually significant. In water, pathlengths of a metre or so can alter the spectral distribution of light enough to be noticeable to our eyes. At even moderate depths selective absorption is so strong that water acts as an efficient monochromator (Tyler 1959).

Scatter

It is hard to overstate the importance of scattered light. The scattering of light rather than its absorption is usually the limiting factor in underwater visibility. On land, absorption is quite small and poor visibility is almost always due to scattering particles in the atmosphere. Furthermore, scattering from very small particles is wavelength-selective, the blue end of the spectrum being scattered more than the red. The familiar sight of the red setting sun with the blue sky overhead is an example of the effects of selective scatter. The deep-blue colour of the open seas owes a significant part of its blueness to selective scatter. As if this were not enough, light scattered from small particles is also plane-polarized, a fact that terrestrial invertebrates and possibly aquatic animals use for orientation and navigation (Waterman 1972, 1975).

When the particles that scatter light are much smaller than the wavelength of light, the intensity of the scattered light is proportional to the reciprocal of the fourth power of the wavelength $(1/\lambda^4)$ and is known as Rayleigh scattering (Fig. 1.5). (See Born and Wolf (1970) for a detailed

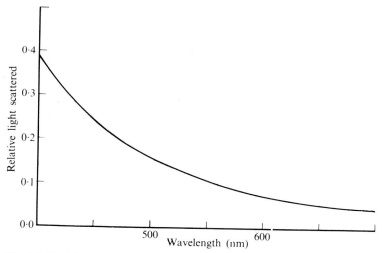

Fig. 1.5. Rayleigh scattering from very small particles is proportional to $1/\lambda^4$.

physical description.) The scattered light from the setting sun, therefore, looks blue, whereas the unscattered light travelling its original path will become relatively richer in long-wavelength red light.

The origin of blue colours in nature from scattered light was apparently first shown by Tyndall (1869), but the physical basis of the phenomenon was worked out by Rayleigh and published first in 1871. Even now physicists tend to refer to Rayleigh scatter, and biologists to Tyndall blues. Larger particles, such as sand grains and water droplets, scatter all wavelengths about equally, which is why a rough sea near a sandy beach can look milky and a misty sky is white.

It is often important to have information about the total light incident on the environment, including both scattered (diffuse) light and directional (image-forming) light. The instrument that measures this is an irradiance meter. It has a flat photosensitive surface which collects light from a $180°$ solid angle. Irradiance (E) is defined as the radiant flux incident on an infinitesimal element of surface containing the area under consideration divided by the area of that element.

The attenuation of irradiance at a particular wavelength is similar to that for radiance and can approximately be written:

$$E_z = E_o e^{-Kz}, \tag{1.3}$$

where K is the diffuse attenuation coefficient and z is the depth of water or atmosphere that the light traverses. K is always smaller than a at any particular wavelength because radiance measurements used to compute a do not include scattered light, whereas irradiance measurements used to compute K include light scattered in the forward direction.

Daylight

Phases of daylight

In their passage through the atmosphere, the sun's rays are scattered out of their original path by particles that vary in size from molecules to snowflakes. As we have already seen, it is this scattered light that gives radiance to the sky. The blue colour of the clear sky is a result of Rayleigh scattering. The white and grey colours of a misty, cloudy, or overcast sky are a result of scattering from larger particles, such as water droplets, dust, and ice crystals. The relation between daylight colour, solar altitude, and cloud and haze cover has been discussed by Sastri and Das (1968), Condit and Grum (1964), and McFarland and Munz (1975a and b). In general, the colour temperature of the daylight is reduced when the sky is cloudy. At twilight the sun's rays pass through a thicker layer of atmosphere before reaching the earth and the specific absorption of ozone in the yellow–orange part of the spectrum becomes significant (Rozenberg 1966; Munz and McFarland 1973). This relative reduction of yellow–orange light is called the Chappuis effect. It is often marked by a slight magenta cast to the sky, especially when clouds are present. The onset of the Chappuis effect is variable. At sunset in the Caribbean it may be noticeable anything from 4 to 30 minutes before sunset, but once sunset has occurred the spectral irradiance declines at a more or less constant rate independent of wavelength. At dawn, the Chappuis effect becomes noticeable 5–10 minutes before sunrise (McFarland, personal communication).

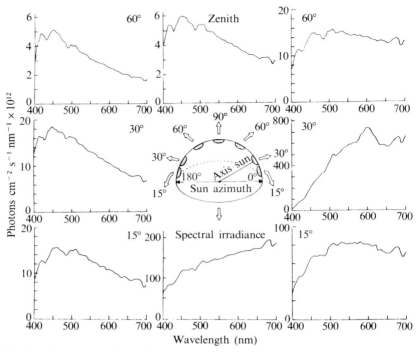

Fig. 1.6. Spectral irradiance (bottom centre) and spectral radiance (all other curves) for noon daylight at Ithaca, New York. Sun altitude was 30° and there was a cloudless sky. Values are photons cm^{-2} nm^{-1} × 10^{12}. The acceptance angle of the light meter for the radiance measurement was 15°. (From McFarland and Munz 1975a.)

Temporal changes in daylight intensity

During the time that the sun's altitude is 30 ° or more above the horizon, there is little variation in the intensity of daylight. However, between the time that the sun moves from 20 ° above the horizon to 20 ° below, there is a luminance change of around 7 log units, provided there is no moon. Heavy storm clouds will reduce the daytime irradiance by 1 log unit and average cloud cover reduces it by perhaps 0·3 log units or about 1 photographic stop.

Polarized skylight

The light from blue sky is plane polarized (Fig. 1.7), which, like the blueness itself, is a result of light scatter from small particles in the atmosphere. The direction of the *e*-vector is at right-angles to the sun's rays and thus an animal that can detect the *e*-vector is able to orientate itself to the sun provided only that a small patch of blue sky is visible. In the sky, the direction of the *e*-vector is at right-angles to the plane that contains the

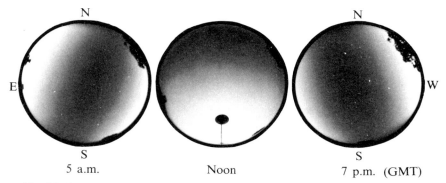

Fig. 1.7. Pattern of plane-polarized light on a cloudless day, 3 August, at Lewes, Sussex, taken with a 'fish-eye' lens. The object at the bottom of the middle picture shields the sun from the camera lens. (Photographs by courtesy of M. F. Land.)

observer, the point observed, and the sun. The percentage polarization (i.e. the percentage of light vibrating in one plane to the total light) may reach 70 per cent during the day and as much as 90 per cent in the zenith sky just before dawn (Waterman 1975). The water droplets of cloud, mist, and fog have a depolarizing effect and on an overcast day the skylight is no longer polarized.

The air–water interface

The way that light is reflected and refracted at the interface between air and water has several important consequences for animals that need to look down into the water or up out of it. The problem may be most relevant to a predatory seabird searching for fish through the water surface, but a fisherman standing on the river bank is also well aware that a fish can see him. Of at least equal importance is the effect of refraction at the water surface on the directional distribution of underwater light and consequent strategies of predation (see Chapter 6).

Part of the daylight incident on the water surface is reflected back into the air whilst the remainder passes through the surface. In passing through a flat water surface, a light ray is refracted according to Snell's law:

$$\frac{\sin i}{\sin j} = n, \tag{1.4}$$

where i and j are the angles that the incident ray and refracted ray make with the normal and n is the refractive index of water relative to air. It has a value of 1·333 for fresh water and 1·341 for sea water.

The water surface from above

The radiance from the water surface is made up of light reflected from the sun and sky, and from the inherent radiance reflected back from the water volume itself (see Austin (1974) for a review). On looking down at a calm sea the brightest feature is the reflection of the sun. As the wind ruffles the surface, this reflection fragments into a myriad of glitter points as the sun is reflected from the facets of the waves. The rougher the water the wider the glitter pattern, a relation that has been used to estimate the roughness of the sea from satellite photographs (Cox 1974). For a flat, calm sea, the reflection from the sun can be calculated from Fresnel's equations, but the sea is rarely flat calm and if there is any disturbance of the surface direct measurements are needed. Because reflection is greater at oblique angles of incidence, the reflected skylight is brighter near the horizon than when

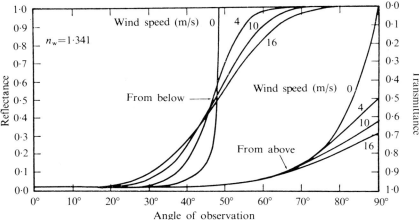

Fig. 1.8. The reflection of light from various angles from the water surface as seen from above, looking down on the surface, and from below, looking up. Surface state varies with wind speed. (From Austin 1974.)

looking directly downwards. On a clear day the sky is not equally bright in all directions, there being an area of minimum brightness at zenith angles 20–40° away from the sun. It is, therefore, safe to conclude that surface glare will be at a minimum when the angle of view is 20–40° from the vertical away from the sun.

Spectral radiance

The spectral radiance of the sea has been measured directly by satellites and compared with simultaneous measurements of the upwelling light made in the sea just beneath the surface, and the transmittance of the atmosphere (Austin 1974). The spectral distribution of the upwelling light is clearly related to the spectral absorption of the water (see pp. 134–5) and shows the water cut-off at 575 nm. The spectral radiance of the reflected skylight is, of course, related to the spectral radiance of the sky and does not show the 575-nm cut-off. Over most of the spectrum for downward-directed sensors, the upwelling light is brighter than the reflected light, but at wavelengths longer than the water cut-off point, the reflected sky-light may be brighter than the upwelling light, especially in clear deep-blue and blue–green water.

The water surface from below

A view of the water surface as seen from below is shown in Plate 1. The prime feature is that, owing to refraction at the water surface, the entire 180° dome of land and sky above the water is compressed into a cone of half-angle 48·5° (Fig. 1.9). At angles greater than 48·5°, the underwater

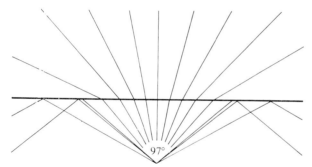

Fig. 1.9. Diagram illustrating the refraction of light at the surface of calm water. The diagram has been calculated from Snell's law assuming the refractive index is 1 for air and 1·33 for water. A fish looking upwards will see the entire hemisphere above the water condensed into a solid angle of 97°.

scene is totally reflected back into the water from the surface. On looking upwards, therefore, there is a circular window which always subtends a solid angle of 97° (48·5° × 2) through which the above-water world can be seen. Because this window is predicted by Snell's law, it is usually referred to as Snell's window.

On a calm day the boundary of Snell's window is distinct and sharp. But wind ruffle and wavelets break up the outline so that areas of bright sky and dark reflected bottom are jumbled together. On a still day, but with a large swell moving across the surface, the edges of the window are less broken up but the round window is continually distorted. Objects on land remain recognizable in quite rough conditions, but the images seen through the window are continually distorted and fragmented, especially near the edge of the window.

The angle subtended by Snell's window does not increase as the observer sinks deeper into the water, which means that the area of surface silhouetted against the sky gets larger. However, the sharp boundary of the window is degraded by scattered light at anything from a metre or so beneath the surface in very turbid water to, say, 40 m in clear ocean water. The direction of the sun, which must necessarily be within 48·5 ° of the vertical, can be detected by radiance measurements to at least 275 m in clear Mediterranean water and 66 m in clear lake water (Jerlov 1976).

Radiance distribution in water

The directional distribution of underwater light has a profound influence on the directions that different objects are most easily seen, or indeed, whether they can be seen at all. Not surprisingly the hunting strategies of pelagic animals are adapted the better to see their prey, whilst both predator and prey are likely to shade their camouflage colours to be as invisible as possible against the background scene.

Most of the information about the radiance distribution in different directions and at different depths has been reviewed by Jerlov (1976).

Near the surface the angular distribution of radiance is complex, but it is dominated by Snell's window and the position of the sun. The sun's rays are refracted by waves and ripples at the water surface which act as a series of concave and convex lenses focusing the light into a ripple pattern of intense light. The higher frequency light ripples are focused into the top metre or so of water, and lower frequency ripples can be detected on a light, sandy bottom down to depths of perhaps 5–10 metres. The dancing rays of the sun are a striking feature of the light environment in shallow water, but their visual significance has not yet been assessed.

The radiance distribution curves are gradually transformed into a more uniform shape as the depth increases, their shape being the result of the joint effects of absorption and scatter. If there were absorption but no scatter, a depth under water would be reached where light was visible only from directly above, since that is the shortest route from the surface. If scatter but no absorption were present, a depth would be reached where the light came equally from all directions. The combined effects of absorption and scatter give radiance distributions of the kind shown in Fig. 1.10. The curves are gradually transformed into a shape that remains constant as the depth increases. The exact shape depends upon the relative values for absorption and scatter in that particular body of water.

As already mentioned on pp. 7 and 9, there are two kinds of measure-

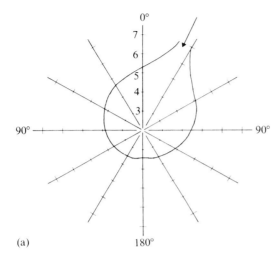

(a)

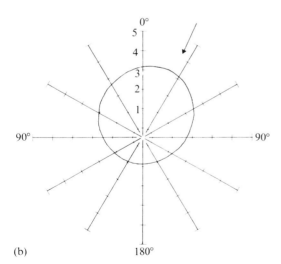

(b)

Fig. 1.10. Polar distribution of underwater spacelight (log scale) at two depths ((a) 4·24 m,
(b) 41·3 m) on a sunny day in a freshwater lake.
The measurements are in the plane of the sun; the
arrows indicate the sun's direction. Note how the
dominating effect of the sun is reduced at the
deeper station. (Data from Tyler and Preisendorfer
1962.)

ment of light reduction in the sea. The narrow-band attenuation coefficient α measures the reduction in radiance and includes losses from both absorption and light scattered out of the light beams. The broad-beam attenuation coefficient K measures the reduction of irradiance, and in this case light scattered in the forward direction is not lost. Thus α is always more than K and the ratio K/α is an indication of the relative importance of absorption and scatter in the water. The greater the ratio K/α, the clearer is the water (Table 1.1).

Table 1.1

	λ (nm)	K/α	Reference
Baltic Sea	535	0·35	Jerlov and Nygård (1968)
Mediterranean Sea	465	0·5–0·6	Lundgren (1976) ex Jerlov (1976)
Sargasso Sea	475	0·85	Lundgren and Højerslev (1971)

Transfer to the asymptotic state occurs deeper in clear water (Table 1.2) and Timofeeva (1971) has calculated the asymptotic radiance distribution for different values of K/α. On an overcast day when the radiance distribution above water is more uniform anyway, the asymptotic state is reached in shallower water. In very clear ocean water, where scattering is small compared to absorption, the upwelling light is so dim relative to downwelling light that existing instrumentation is not adequate to measure it at the 400-m or so depth where the asymptotic state is attained. In fact, the curves have almost reached their final form at about half the asymptotic depth, except that the direction of maximum radiance is still tilted in the direction of the sun.

Table 1.2 Depth of asymptotic state

	Data from	Depth	Estimate by
Lake Pend	Tyler (1960)	100 m	Duntley (1963)
Baltic Sea	Jerlov and Lilje-quist (1938)	100 m +	Jerlov (1976)
West Mediterranean Sea	Lundgren (1976) ex Jerlov (1976)	275 m	Jerlov (1976)
Sargasso Sea	Jerlov (1976)	400 m	Jerlov (1976)

Polarized light

The scattered light in the sea, like that in the atmosphere, is polarized. This was originally observed and measured by Waterman in the first of a series of scuba studies (Waterman 1954, 1955; Waterman and Westell 1956) and has been later reviewed by Ivanoff (1974), Timofeeva (1974), Waterman (1974), and Jerlov (1976). A large number of animals, mostly invertebrates with rhabdomeric eyes, have been shown to respond to the e-vector direction (Waterman, 1975), but most of these are land animals and the evidence that aquatic animals do the same is at present less strong.

The plane of polarization is normal to the direction of the light ray. On an overcast day or in deep water the plane of polarization is perpendicular to the direction of greatest light flow and is thus more nearly horizontal. In clear surface waters on a sunny day, polarization may approach 60 per cent and reaches an asymptotic value of nearly 40 per cent (Ivanoff and Waterman 1958). However, in more turbid water where the Secchi disc is visible at about 15 m or less, polarization falls to practically zero.

Spectral absorption of water

The oceans, lakes, and rivers make a first-rate natural laboratory for investigating the evolutionary adaptations of colour vision. The wave-length-selective light-filtering action of the water means that at depth the natural light is about as efficient a monochromator as a good quality coloured glass filter, whilst in very shallow water downwelling daylight is not greatly modified (Plate 1).

Viewed obliquely from land or from the deck of a ship, an expanse of water assumes much the same colour as the sky it reflects. Underwater, the colour of water varies dramatically from the deep blue of clear tropical oceans (Plate 2) to the red-brown colour of peat-laden inland lakes. Within broad limits, each body of water has its characteristic colour. The English Channel (Plate 4), for example, may vary from blue–green after a cold, dry spell in winter to yellow–green after a warm, wet spell in summer. At no time is it likely to be indigo blue or orange–brown.

The colour of natural water has four main components, two of which are an inherent property of pure water and two are of biological origin. These components are as follows.

1. *Rayleigh scatter*

The clearest ocean water owes part of its blue colour to Rayleigh scatter (Fig. 1.5, p. 8). This is demonstrated by the increased proportion of short wavelengths in upwelling light compared to downwelling light at the same depths (see Jerlov (1976) for a review).

2. *Selective absorption of pure water*

Pure distilled water is most transparent to 475-nm blue light (Clarke and James 1939). It absorbs light more strongly at both shorter and longer wavelengths. In particular, there is a rapid increase in absorption at around 575 nm. Some bodies of natural water are so clear that their spectral absorption is similar to that of distilled water. An example of such exceptionally pure water is shown in Fig. 1.11(a).

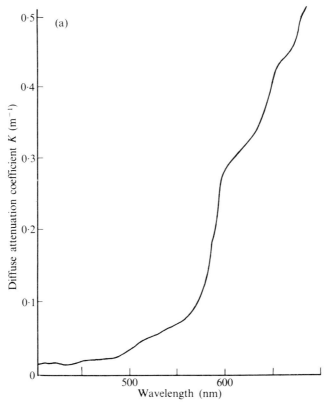

Fig. 1.11. Three of the major colouring agents in natural water are the water itself (a) *Gelbstoffe* (b), and chlorophyll (c). (a) The attenuation coefficient K for the exceptionally pure and unstained water of Crater Lake. (Data averaged from Tyler and Smith 1970.) (b) Relative absorption of *Gelbstoffe*. (From Kalle 1937.) (c) Chlorophyll-dominated attenuation spectrum of a suspension of the green alga *Nannochloris atomus*. (After Yentsch 1962.)

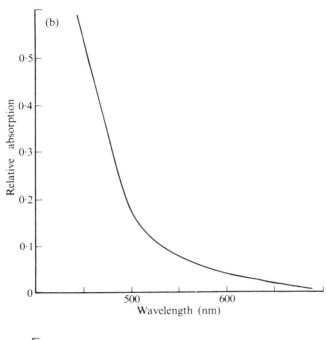

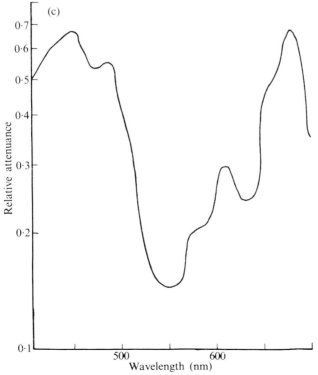

3. *Chlorophyll*

Water that is rich in nutrients and receives sufficient light for photosynthesis may support a rich crop of phytoplankton. The chlorophyll that this contains can dominate the colour of natural water (Yentsch 1960) especially in freshwater lakes (Plate 5) and reservoirs (Fig. 1.11 (b)). When chlorophyll *a* is added to clear water the band of greatest transparency approaches 560–750 nm (Morel and Smith 1974) for it is in this region of the spectrum where chlorophyll has minimum absorption and where absorption due to water begins to increase rapidly.

4. *Yellow substance*

Persistent yellow or yellow–brown humus-like substances dissolved in the water significantly affect the colour of the sea (Kalle 1938, 1966). These substances are known either as *Gelbstoffe* or, in English translation, 'yellow substances'. The yellow substances in fresh water are somewhat browner than those in the sea, but both show a progressive increase in absorption as the wavelength shortens (Fig. 1.11 (c)). The production of yellow substances is associated with the breakdown of plant chloroplasts (Yentsch and Reichert 1962).

Yellow substances absorb short-wavelength light; pure water absorbs long wavelengths. When both are present in a balanced amount, both the blue light and the orange and red light are absorbed, leaving the mid-spectrum green light to be transmitted. When yellow substance is present in high concentration, especially where they are leached from humus-rich soil by the rain, the water transmits most strongly at longer wavelengths.

The geography of water colours

The blue colour of pure water derived from Rayleigh scatter and selective absorption is an inherent property that remains the same whether the water is tropical or polar, fresh or salt. The clearest known freshwater lakes such as Crater Lake in Oregon and Lake Tahoe in California, are deep blue in colour (Smith, Tyler, and Goldman 1973). Clear tropical seas and the Mediterranean are also deep blue in colour. Like the clearwater lakes, the blue oceans retain their inherent blue colour because they are too poor in nutrients to support much phytoplankton growth and are remote from large, fertile land masses whose rivers bring down quantities of yellow substances from the soil.

The seas that wash the coasts of the fertile continents, such as northwest Europe, North America and southern Asia, are usually green in colour. Greenness results from either yellow substances or phytoplankton in the water and it is not always certain which agent is the most important. In oceanic areas made fertile by the upwelling of nutrients from deep water (Morel and Smith 1974) there is little doubt that the phytoplankton growth that this induces is responsible; whereas in the Baltic, encircled by fertile land, it seems probable that yellow substances are the most important.

The optical characteristics of fresh water are similar to those of sea water for the dissolved salts are transparent in the visible spectrum. The purest fresh water like that in Crater Lake is rare. Lakes and rivers are by their very nature surrounded by land and are constantly replenished by nutrients and yellow substances leached into them. In general, therefore, fresh waters are redder than sea water. The water colour varies from lake to lake and river to river, each having its characteristic colour (see, for instance, Spence 1972). In peat-laden water and water fed by swampy land, there may be such a concentration of yellow substances that its transparency is greatest in the red part of the spectrum and when seen underwater has a red-brown appearance.

The time of year has an important influence on the colour of inland water and, to a lesser extent, on ocean water as well. Water covered by ice tends to be more blue than at warmer seasons. This is partly because the water is too cold and the days are too short for phytoplankton to grow, and partly because there is no drainage from the land. Even when the landscape is not frozen, the restricted daylight and low temperatures of winter inhibit phytoplankton growth. However when the days lengthen and the winter gets warmer there is an increase in growth that reaches a peak in spring and early summer. Thereafter the nutrients become exhausted and the phytoplankton crop declines.

Apart from seasonal changes in water colour, there are sometimes colour changes that are completed within hours rather than weeks. For example, the water in tropical tidal lagoons and mangrove swamps are often coloured green or brown (Plate 6), whereas the ocean water outside the reef barrier is blue (Plate 3). On the ebb tide the swamp and lagoon water flows back through the reef channels, dramatically changing the water colour. Another example is provided by the sea lochs of Scotland. The peat-stained fresh water flowing off the surrounding hills, floats on top of the salt water, making a sharply discrete upper layer of yellow water on top of the green.

Optical classification of water

In 1951 Jerlov performed a signal service to biologists when he published his optical classification of ocean water based on the spectral transmittance of downward irradiance. Jerlov's scheme has since been revised in points of detail as more data became available (Jerlov 1976) and is reproduced here in Fig. 1.12 and Table 1.3. Strictly, the classification applies only to the open ocean, coastal water, and brackish (Baltic) water. The oceanic

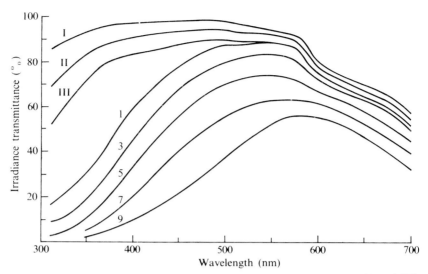

Fig. 1.12. Jerlov's classification of types of natural water, Oceanic types, I, II, and III, and coastal types 1, 3, 5, 7, and 9, are shown. (From Jerlov 1976.)

water is now divided into five categories (I, IA, IB, II, III) and the coastal and brackish water into a further five (1, 3, 5, 7, 9). It is possible that fresh water also fits this classification, but Jerlov considers that waters more turbid than type 9 cannot be classified in this way.

The greater absorption of short-wavelength light by the clearest coastal water derives from the higher proportion of yellow substance near coasts. Type III ocean water is characteristic of the highly fertile areas, chiefly associated with the west coasts of continents (Fig. 1.13), where nutrient-rich upwelling water feeds the vigorous growth of phytoplankton. The nutrient-poor regions such as the eastern Mediterranean and the Sargasso Sea have the clearest water; indeed, the Sargasso Sea can be slightly clearer than type I.

Table 1.3 Downward irradiance attenuation coefficient K_d at 0–10 m (expressed as 10^2 m^{-1})

Water type	Wavelength (nm)															
	310	350	375	400	425	450	475	500	525	550	575	600	625	650	675	700
I	15	6.2	3.8	2.8	2.2	1.9	1.8	2.7	4.3	6.3	8.9	23.5	30.5	36	42	56
IA	18	7.8	5.2	3.8	3.1	2.6	2.5	3.2	4.8	6.7	9.4	24	31.5	37	43	57
IB	22	10	6.6	5.1	4.2	3.6	3.3	4.2	5.4	7.2	9.9	24.5	31.5	37.5	43.5	58
II	37	17.5	12.2	9.6	8.1	6.8	6.2	7.0	7.6	8.9	11.5	26	33.5	40	46.5	61
III	65	32	22	18.5	16	13.5	11.6	11.5	11.6	12.0	14.8	29.5	37.5	44.5	52	66
1	180	120	80	51	36	25	17	14	13	12	15	30	37	45	51	65
3	240	170	110	78	54	39	29	22	20	19	21	33	40	46	56	71
5	350	230	160	110	78	56	43	36	31	30	33	40	48	54	65	80
7		300	210	160	120	89	71	58	49	46	46	48	54	63	78	92
9		390	300	240	190	160	123	99	78	63	58	60	65	76	92	110

Source: Jerlov (1976).

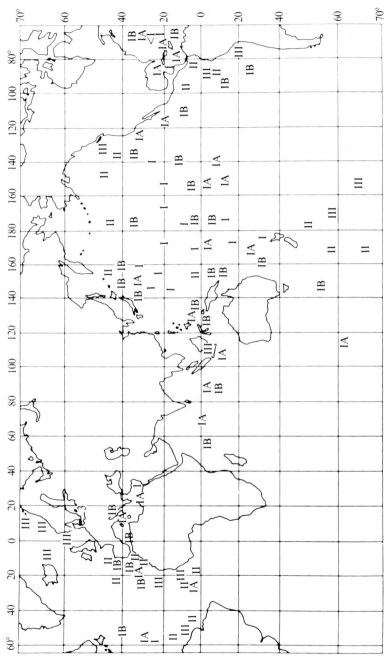

Fig. 1.13. World-wide distribution of oceanic water types. Note the common occurrence of productive, relatively turbid, type III water near the west coast of continents. (From Jerlov 1976.)

In-water measurements

Some spectral irradiance measurements in different natural waters are listed in Table 1.4 and some examples are shown in Figs. 1.14, 1.15, and 1.16. It is a prerequisite of these measurements that the daylight should remain stable and this normally means that they were conducted at high solar elevation on a clear day. Some useful measurements of the diffuse attenuation coefficient, K, are also listed (Table 1.4).

Table 1.4 Some spectral irradiance measurements in natural water

Water	Measurement[1]	Reference
Eastern Mediterranean	Ed	Jerlov (1951)
Caribbean	Ed	Jerlov (1951)
Japan	Ed	Sasaki et al. (1958a)
Baltic	Ed	Ahlquist ex Jerlov (1976)
Caribbean	Ed	Smith ex Jerlov (1976)
Crater Lake	K Ed	Smith and Tyler (1967)
Blelham Tarn	K	Talling (1970)
Coniston Water	K	Talling (1970)
Buttermere	K	Talling (1970)
Bermuda	Ed	Kampa (1961)
Banyuls sur Mer	Ed	Kampa (1961)
San Diego	Ed	Kampa (1961)
Loch Croispol	K	Spence et al. (1971)
Loch Uanagan	K	Spence et al. (1971)
Loch Leven	K	Spence et al. (1971)
Lake Tahoe	K Ed	Smith et al. (1973)
Crater Lake	K Ed	Smith et al. (1973)
Crater Lake	K Ed	Tyler and Smith (1970)
Gulf Stream	K Ed	Tyler and Smith (1970)
Tongue of Ocean, Bahamas	K Ed	Tyler and Smith (1970)
Isla Tres Marias, Mexico	K Ed	Tyler and Smith (1970)
Gulf of California	K Ed	Tyler and Smith (1970)
San Vicente Reservoir	K Ed	Tyler and Smith (1970)
Eniwetok	Ed	Munz and McFarland (1975)
South Pacific	K Ed	Morel and Caloumenos (1974)
Galapagos current	K Ed	Morel and Caloumenos (1974)
Mauritanian upwelling	K Ed	Morel and Caloumenos (1974)
Mauritania	K Ed	Morel and Caloumenos (1974)
Senegal	K Ed	Morel and Caloumenos (1974)
Sargasso Sea	K Ed	Morel and Caloumenos (1974)

[1]Ed: Downwelling irradiance;   K: diffuse attenuation coefficient.

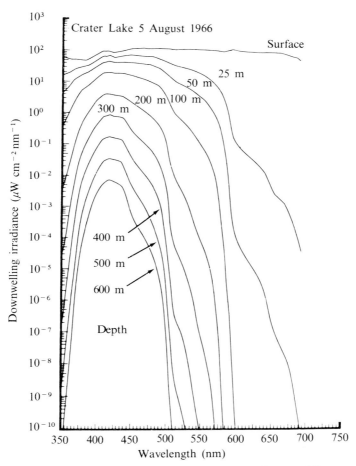

Fig. 1.14. Downwelling irradiance in the pure, natural water of Crater Lake. These are calculated values based on actual measurements at 10 m. Note how the spectral bandwidth becomes narrower as the depth increases. (From Tyler and Smith 1970.)

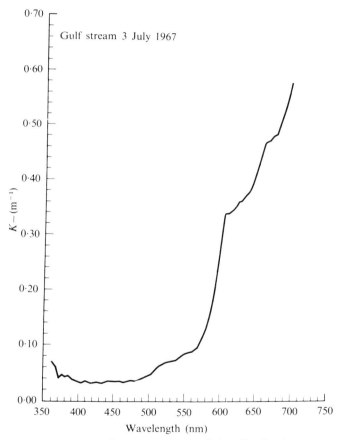

Fig. 1.15. Average diffuse attenuation coefficient $K-$ for clear blue Gulf Stream water. (From Tyler and Smith 1970.)

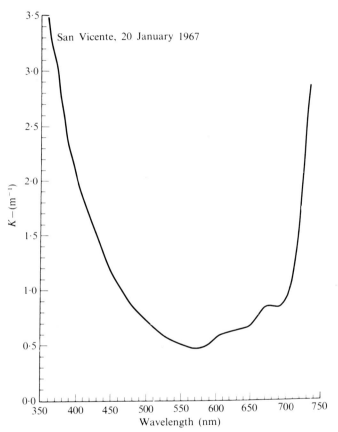

Fig. 1.16. Average diffuse attenuation coefficient $K-$ for green phytoplankton rich fresh water. (From Tyler and Smith 1970.)

Colours of living organisms

Addition radiances

Bioluminescence

On a dark night or in deep water, the strongest light is no longer the light from the sun or moon but the bioluminescent light manufactured by living organisms. In clear ocean water, bioluminescent background light becomes significant relative to daylight at depths greater than 500 m in the daytime (Jerlov 1968) and 100 m on a moonlight night. In turbid inshore water bioluminescence can be the only visible source of light at depths of less than 30 m even in the middle of the day (Hemmings and Lythgoe 1964).

Bioluminescence is an extremely widespread phenomenon occurring in ~ll the major animal phyla, in bacteria, protozoa, and fungi, although for some reason it is rare in freshwater life. It is an enzyme-catalysed reaction; various enzymes, collectively known as luciferases, catalyse the oxidation of specific substrates, collectively known as luciferins. The energy that is released is emitted as light.

There is a considerable amount of information about the colour (to humans) of bioluminescence in different organisms (Harvey 1952, 1955; Nicol 1962; Swift, Biggley, and Napora 1977). According to Harvey (1955) the most common colours for animal lights are 'white', blue, or blue–green; less common are green, yellow–green, and yellow; orange and red are comparatively rare. Spectral emission curves for various organisms are given in Fig. 1.17. It should be noted that these curves are plotted on the basis of energy per unit area per wavelength interval (see pp. 3 and 4) although in this case plotting them on a photon basis will have an only marginal influence on the shape of the curves.

Luminescence may either be produced intracellularly within special effector cells (photocytes), or luminous secretions may be discharged to the exterior, or it may be produced by symbiotic bacteria that are often confined to discrete areas in the body. Continuous luminescence is infrequent except in animals that harbour luminous bacteria. There is sometimes a diurnal periodicity; or a series of flashes as in some fireflies, which may have specific signalling functions (Lloyd 1975; Buck and Buck 1976). It is probable also that the intensity of luminescence can be modified to match the radiance of the spacelight against which it is seen in order to disguise the animal's silhouette (see pp. 175–6).

Fluorescence

Fluorescence is a related phenomenon to bioluminescence, but from the biological display viewpoint is of less importance. When some molecules

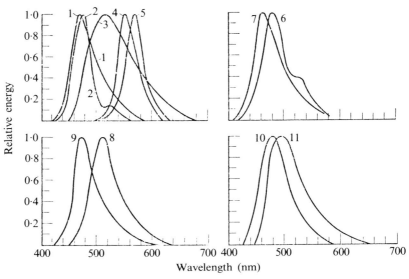

Fig. 1.17. The relative spectral emission curves for the bioluminescent light of various animals: (1) *Noctiluca miliaris;* (2) *Euphausia pacifica;* (3) Polynoid worms; (4) *Photuris pennsylvanica;* (5) *Photinus pyralis;* (6) *Pyrosoma atlanticum;* (7) *Chaetopterus variopedatus;* (8) *Pennatula phosphorea;* (9) *Myctophum punctatum;* (10) *Gonyaulax polyedra;* (11) *Pholas dactylus.* (Data from various authors collected by Lythgoe 1972.)

absorb a photon, they pass to a more excited state. There follows a transition back to a less excited state that is accompanied by the emission of a photon. The peak of the absorption and emission spectra do not coincide. The emission spectra is displaced to lower frequencies (longer wavelengths) compared to the absorption spectrum, although the two curves overlap. The total light emitted in a fluorescent system always contains less energy than the light absorbed but it is possible for the emitted light to be brighter than the incident light at the long wavelength end of the spectrum (Clayton 1970). On land, fluorescence seems to have little visual impact and may confidently be dismissed as irrelevant to our present interest here. Underwater, it may be different for here some animals, especially some corals and sea anemones that live in a predominantly blue environment, show up vividly because they emit green, yellow–green, orange, or red light (Limbaugh and North 1956). At present, however, the function of these fluorescent colours is obscure.

Subtraction radiances

Bioluminescent and fluorescent organisms actually emit light, although in the case of fluorescence the energy to do this comes from light of shorter wavelength incident on the organism. In both cases, the light energy emitted at particular wavelengths can exceed the light incident on the organism at that wavelength. All other organisms owe their radiance to the reflection or transmission of the incident light and the reflected or transmitted light at every wavelength is always less than the incident light.

It is convenient to divide subtraction colours into two classes, namely pigment colours and structural colours.

Pigment colours

It is usually possible to extract the pigments (biochromes) responsible for selective absorption. The biochemistry of naturally occurring biochromes has been extensively treated by D. L. Fox (1976) and their biology by H. Munro Fox and Vevers (1960). By far the most important plant biochrome is chlorophyll which gives the green colour to a fertile landscape, and gives a green bias to light in forest and dense stands of vegetation. The colours of purple, blue, and many red flowers are often due to anthocyanins which also tint the green colour of foliage. Another important class of colouring agent in plants are the carotenoids that give red, orange, and yellow colours to fruits and many flowers.

There are many different animal biochromes. The most important are probably the carotenoids and melanin. Carotenoids give the same range of orange, red, and yellow colours as in plants and when conjugated with proteins may also give blues and greens. It is doubtful whether any animals can synthesize carotenoids; they obtain them by eating plants. Melanins are not common in plants, but in animals they are chiefly responsible for black, brown, and occasionally orange and red pigmentation.

Amongst the enormous variety of naturally occurring colours, the yellows, oranges, and reds merit special mention. The pigments responsible for nearly all of them are so-called cut-off filters (Fig. 1.18); that is wavelengths shorter than a certain value are absorbed, whilst the longer wavelengths are transmitted or reflected. The transmission curves for the red, orange, and yellow oil droplets in the bird retinas are typical (Fig. 2.19, p. 57) and so are the reflection curves for yellow and red fish fins (Fig. 7.12, p. 186), or yellow, orange, and red plants (Fig. 1.18). These characteristic cut-off curves have also been measured from building paints and building materials (see Wyszecki and Stiles (1967) for a review). The most obvious exceptions are the yellow of low-pressure sodium lights that have two very close emission lines at 589 and 590 nm, and the yellow band of the rainbow. Only one of these is 'natural' and neither can have had much influence on the evolution of vision.

These generalizations are certainly defensible when applied to human vision in daylight, but they have to be made with some discretion for other animals and visual environments. For example, the flowers of the celan-

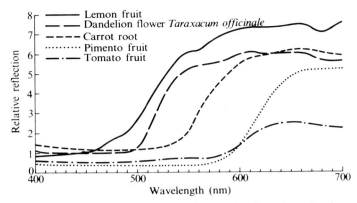

Fig. 1.18. Spectral reflectance curves of parts of various plants that have colours belonging to the yellow–orange–red family.

dine, *Ranunculus ficaria*, look uniformly yellow to our eyes, but to an insect which can see into the ultraviolet, the centre of the flower cup will have a different colour from the rim (see pp. 191–2).

The changed spectral distribution of the ambient light in water can completely alter the appearance of colours. Taking a simple view, one would expect that red objects would appear black because at depths greater than about 25 m in blue water, all red light has been absorbed. In reality, objects usually take on a colour other than black because the strong reflections in the red no longer swamp the reflections at shorter wavelengths. Blood is a good example; many a diver has been concerned to note that a cut finger bleeds green rather than the usual red. Of more biological significance is the colour of fishes that look red near the surface, but in deeper water assume a greyish-blue colour that blends well with the background light (Plate 7).

Structural colours

Pigment colours owe their appearance to the selective absorption of parts of the spectrum. Structural colours are formed by diverting different light wavelengths along separate optical paths. With pigment colours, the reflected and transmitted rays are the same colour, but with structural colours the wavelengths that are not transmitted are reflected and the transmitted and reflected rays differ in colour. A further point of difference is that structural colours are sorted not only by wavelength, but by plane of polarization as well, so that reflections from structural colours are often plane-polarized.

Very small particles scatter short-wave blue light more than longer wavelengths. The effect is responsible for the blue of the sky, some of the blue of water, and for the diffuse blue reflections from certain animals. As explained on p. 8), physicists tend to refer to the phenomenon as Rayleigh scattering and biologists refer to the colour as Tyndall blues.

Tyndall blues are characterized by a diffuse reflection that does not change greatly with viewing angle; the reflected light is plane-polarized and, of course, no blue pigment is extractable. Amongst vertebrates many non-iridescent blue colours are due to Tyndall scattering; amongst invertebrates Tyndall blues are less common but are found in dragonflies, at least one cephalopod, and some coelenterates (see Fox 1976 for a review). Tyndall blues are often backed with a dark layer of melanin granules which prevent reflection of transmitted light back through the scattering layer. Such transmitted light is pinkish or yellowish and would degrade the blue of the scattered light.

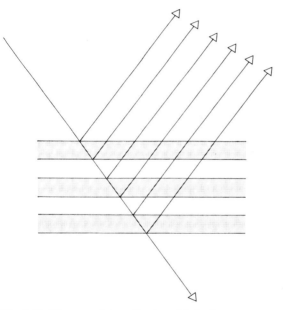

Fig. 1.19. Diagram of the reflection of light from an iridescent multilayer. The layer consists of a stack of plates of the order of a quarter of a wavelength in thickness, interleaved with plates of comparable thickness but of different refractive index. Light incident on the multilayer is reflected at the interface separating each layer and suffers a phase delay. When the reflected rays are in phase, there is constructive interference and reflection is enhanced; when the reflected rays are out of phase there is destructive interference and reflections are suppressed. The wavelengths that are reflected depend upon the refractive index and thickness of each layer and upon the angle of incidence of the light. The multilayers in corneas or in fish scales will be transparent at some angles of incidence, but reflect iridescent colours at others.

When the scattering particles are relatively large compared to the wavelength of light, the degree of scattering is no longer wavelength-dependent and the resulting reflections are white. The white opalescence of many animals is probably due to a combination of scatter of this sort and iridescence, which is characteristic of a more ordered structure.

When light penetrates a thin layer of material that is transparent but different in refractive index from its surrounding medium, some light is reflected from the upper and lower surface. If the layer is of the order of a light wavelength in thickness, then light of particular wavelengths reflected from each surface will emerge in phase and the two waveforms will augment each other. The resulting reflection is highly coloured; the remainder of the light is transmitted through the layer. In most biological systems there is a stack of thin plates which increases the efficiency of the system (Fig. 1.19). These interference colours have qualities that give them their characteristic iridescent appearance. The reflections are from flat plates so there is often a mirror-like quality and at particular angles of incidence very bright local light sources, such as the sun, are reflected directly to the observer and look very bright. The wavelengths of light best reflected depend in part upon the angle of view, the thickness of the layers, and their refractive index. The distribution and optics of interference colours in animals has been reviewed by Land (1972).

Iridescent colours are often violet, blue, or blue–green and less often orange and red. I can think of no purely optical reason why this should be for it is presumably possible to selectively reflect radiation of any required wavelength. It is amongst the fishes and insects, particularly the latter, where iridescence is most conspicuous and striking.

2 Mechanisms of vision

Introduction

During the long process of evolution, an animal may have evolved a visual mechanism that is particularly suited to some specific visual task. For example, it may function well in dim light, be able to detect subtle differences in colour, or be able to detect small and distant objects. However, there are often well-defined limits beyond which improvement is impossible, or adaptation for one type of visual task involves unacceptable penalties for others.

In dim light, the basic limit to vision is set by the number of photons that are present, for even if every available photon is captured and if each initiates a visual signal, there may still be insufficient photons to form an image (Fig. 2.1). An analogy that is useful if it is not taken too far is that of raindrops falling on a warm dry pavement; and the wet patch left by each raindrop represents the absorption of one photon. Suppose a car is parked on the pavement; no raindrops will fall on the pavement beneath the car and its outline will be marked by a dry area. If the shower is heavy, there will be no difficulty in deciding the contour of the car, but if the raindrops are very sparse, then an area of raindrop-free pavement may either mark the position of the car or it may simply be chance that no raindrop has fallen on that particular area. To decide whether an area of pavement was sheltered from the rain is a matter of statistical probability rather than certainty. The appropriate measure of raindrop fall would be for a defined area, and a defined time, and the units of measurements might be in drops per square metre per minute.

Suppose now that the car is not stationary, but moving; an area of pavement will be sheltered from the rain only at the time when the car is directly overhead. Before the car arrives, and after it has gone, the raindrops will fall with the same frequency as everywhere else. The passing of the car can thus only be detected if the sampling time is short and the rain sufficiently heavy to allow enough drops to fall for a statistical judgment to be made. If the car is moving too fast, or it shades too small an area, or the raindrops are too infrequent, then the presence of the car cannot be detected by the raindrop method.

Returning to vision; the appropriate measure of light intensity is number of photons per unit area per unit time per unit frequency (or wavelength interval) (see pp. 2–4). If too few photons are registered, then the visual mechanism does not have enough information to make the essentially statistical decision whether two adjacent areas of the retina have different

Fig. 2.1. The ultimate sensitivity of an imaging system is governed by the number of photons available. These photographs are of the output tube of a channel image intensifier television system, exposure time 1/8th second: (a) starlight illumination, brightness gain $\times 10^5$; (b) full moonlight, brightness gain $\times 10^4$. (From Schagen 1977.)

intensities of light incident upon them, or whether the incident light on a single area has changed in intensity. At low light intensities, the more photons that can be counted the smaller is the differences between two radiances the eye can reliably detect. There are two kinds of ways that the eye can increase the number of photons counted. First, the anatomy of the eye can be designed so that the image on the retina is as bright as possible, and that the greatest possible percentage of photons incident on the retina are absorbed by visual pigment. Secondly, the physiology of the eye may be so arranged that more photon hits are included in each sample. This is is achieved both by increasing the area of image that is sampled (with a resulting loss of image detail), and by lengthening of time over which each sample is taken (with a resulting loss in movement perception). If there is to be colour vision, different wavelength bands in the spectrum must be individually sampled and compared with each other. This necessarily reduces the number of photon hits in each sample and it is significant that colour vision is rare, or perhaps even absent, in animals active at very low light intensities.

Optical mechanisms

The process of vision falls naturally into three stages: first is the optical stage when an image of the outside world is projected on to the retina; second is the transduction stage when the light-sensitive visual cells absorb photons and respond by generating electrical signals; and third is the physiological stage when these primary signals are analysed. Possibly there is a further, fourth, stage that marks the conscious awareness of a visual display.

The more photons that go to form the image of the visual scene on the retina, the more finely it can be analysed in terms of detail, contrast, movement, and colour. It is only the photons that are actually received into the eye that can be used in this analysis and the geometry and optics of the eye are obviously important in forming an image that is most favour-able for analysis. However, the nature of the visual display that is brought into focus also affects the brightness of the image. The geometry of the eye required to form a bright image of a point source of light, such as a distant star, is different from that of the extended bright field that normally is encountered by diurnal animals (Rodieck 1973, pp. 269–72; Kirschfeld 1974). The reader might also like to be aware that a comprehensive review on the comparative optics of animal eyes, both vertebrate and invertebrate, and the ecological implications of the various designs, has been written by Dr M. F. Land and will appear in a forthcoming volume (VII 6 B) of the *Handbook of sensory physiology*.

Sensitivity

Kirschfeld (1974), in considering point sources of light, such as a star or perhaps a small bioluminescent animal, shows that the point source will not, in fact, be focused at a point on the retina but, because of diffraction effects at the edges of the entrance pupil, will form an Airy pattern which has a bright central disc with concentric bright and dark rings surrounding it. The number of photons per unit time incident at the lens surface will be distributed over the Airy pattern and the smaller the Airy pattern the brighter the image. The diameter D of Airy's disc will vary thus:

$$D \propto f/A, \tag{2.1}$$

where f is the focal length of the lens and A is the diameter of the pupil aperture (Fig. 2.2). f/A is, in fact, the 'f-number' used by photographers to indicate the brightness of the image at the focal plane. Thus all eyes of the same f-number produce Airy's discs of the same size.

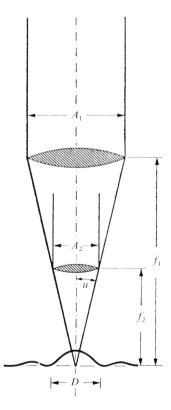

Fig. 2.2. The absolute diameter D of Airy's disc depends on the ratio of pupil diameter A to focal length f irrespective of the absolute size of A. The number given by f/A is the 'f-number' used by photographers. (After Kirschfeld 1974.)

The number of photons per unit time, q, distributed over Airy's pattern will increase by the square of the pupil diameter:

$$q \propto A^2. \tag{2.2}$$

This means that eyes with large pupils are much more sensitive to point sources of light than are eyes with small entrance pupils such as apposition compound eyes that are made up of a number of optically isolated facets.

Most animals look not only at stars or bright points of bioluminescence, but at an extended visual scene reflecting photons from every point. In the case of a light source extending over a wide area, the brightness of a small area of the image dq is proportional to the solid angle of the cone of light illuminating dq. In other words, the brightness of the image is proportional to the aperture of the lens and its focal length:

$$dq \propto A^2/f^2. \tag{2.3}$$

For viewing extended light sources it makes no difference what the diameter of the lens aperture might be so long as the f-number is kept the same by a corresponding change in focal length.

Animals that need to be most sensitive to bright points of light against a dark background may thus evolve large pupil apertures, whereas animals that require to see extended light sources in dim light, and this probably includes the majority of nocturnal animals, may evolve eyes with f-numbers as small as possible. Table 2.1 compares pupil apertures and f-numbers of various animals.

Kirschfeld (1974) and Blest and Land (1977) have shown how these principles have particular interest in the study of faceted invertebrate

Table 2.1 Pupil aperture and f-number of various animals

Animal	Pupil aperture (mm)	f-number	Reference
Net-casting spider *Dinopis subrufus*	1·325	0·58	Blest and Land (1977)
Cat	14	0·89	Vakkur and Bishop (1963)
Flour moth *Ephestia*	2×10^{-2}	1·2	Kirschfeld (1974)
Tawny owl, *Strix aluco*	13·3	1·3	Martin (1977)
Jumping spider, *Phidippus johnsoni*	$3·8 \times 10^{-1}$	1·72	Land (1977)
Housefly, *Musca*	$2·5 \times 10^{-2}$	2·0	Kirschfeld (1974)
Man	8	2·1	Martin (1977)
Bee	$2·5 \times 10^{-2}$	2·4	Kirschfeld (1974)
Man	7	3·3	Kirschfeld (1974)
Pigeon, *Columba livia*	2·0	4·0	Marshall *et al.* (1973)

The animals are arranged in order of f-number. The net-casting spider, cat, and owl are nocturnal; the bee and pigeon are diurnal.

eyes. In the classical apposition eye (Fig. 2.4(a)), such as that of the bee, the light entering each facet is primarily channelled to the visual pigment in the rhabdome of the same ommatidium. The ratio of pupil area in man to a single facet in the bee is about 10^5:1. This means that all apposition eyes will be 10^5 times less sensitive to points of light such as stars. Kirschfeld estimates that the planet Venus should be invisible to a bee providing its receptor sensitivity is similar to man's. However, a comparison of sensitivity to an extended visual display shows that on optical grounds the bee and man should have about the same sensitivity because the ratio of focal length to pupil aperture is about the same, and the receptors have nearly the same diameter.

Nocturnal insects, such as the moth *Ephestia* (Fig. 2.3), possess super-

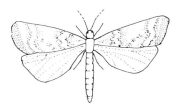

Fig. 2.3. The flour moth *Ephestia*.

position eyes (Fig. 2.4(b)). In this type of eye, parallel light that enters a group of facets is focused onto a single rhabdome. Thus the effective aperture area is increased by roughly the number of facets that focus light onto one rhabdome. Since in *Ephestia* there are approximately 100 facets, the sensitivity to a point source is increased by 100. Even so, *Ephestia* is still 10^3 times less sensitive to point sources than the human eye, but may just be able to see the brightest stars.

(a)   (b)

Fig. 2.4. (a) The apposition compound eye and (b) the optical superposition (clear-zone) eye. (From Kirschfeld 1974.)

For extended light sources, *Ephestia* is considerably more sensitive than either man or bee, since the pooling of light from several facets makes for a larger effective aperture without altering the focal length, and Kirschfeld calculates that the number of photons per area in the plane of the receptors is approximately 25 times that of man or bee.

Tapeta

Many animals, both vertebrate and invertebrate, enhance the light-catching power of the visual cells by placing light-reflecting material near the light-sensitive cells in such a way that light that has already passed through a cell without being absorbed is directed back again into it, thus giving a further chance for absorption. Well-developed tapeta are mostly present in nocturnal animals or those that live in very deep or dark water (Walls 1942). There are many different types of reflecting layer; probably most of them owe their reflectivity to interference effects (Land 1972; Nicol 1974; Nicol, Arnott, and Best 1973).

Resolving power

The resolution of an eye ultimately depends upon the wavelength of the light, and the best resolution of a small eye cannot match the best resolution of a large one. It is undoubtedly true that compound eyes are more common than lens eyes in small animals and there are few animals larger than a lobster that have compound eyes.

There are two basic limits to the resolving power of the eye. First, diffraction effects at the entrance aperture limit the quality of the image. Secondly the size of the photoreceptor cells determines the grain of the retinal mosaic and hence the detail of the image, however sharp, that can be analysed. The optical and biological consequences of these wavelength-related limitations have been reviewed by Kirschfeld (1976). It has been mentioned in the previous section that as a result of diffraction, a point does not form a point image on the retina but rather an Airy pattern of concentric dark and light rings. The diameter of the Airy pattern limits the resolution of an eye. The angular size of the pattern is related to the entrance aperture of the single-lens eye (or a single facet of a compound eye) according to the relation

$$\Delta r = 1.22 \, \lambda/A \text{ (radians)}, \tag{2.4}$$

where Δr is the radius of Airy's disc in angular units and A is the aperture of the (circular) lens. For man the optimum pupil aperture for resolution is 2·4 mm and the diameter of Airy's disc is then 1·30 arc minutes.

Because the angular size of Airy's disc depends upon the pupil aperture, it follows that the overall size of an eye can be reduced without affecting its resolution, provided the smaller eye can still house a lens of the same diameter. The problem is that the actual diameter (in mm) of Airy's disc and the actual size of the image depends upon the focal length of the lens as well as upon its diameter. It requires smaller visual cells to give the finer retinal grain in order to get the same amount of information from the smaller image in the smaller eye.

The size of the visual cells cannot be reduced indefinitely because when the diameter of the visual-pigment-containing part of the cell gets smaller than about 1 or 2 μm, the light is guided down the outside of the cell. Two adverse consequences of this are that less light is absorbed by the visual pigment molecules, and light passing along one visual cell may be absorbed by its neighbour. The two cells cannot then act independently of each other. The 1 or 2 μm value is set by the refractive index difference between the visual cell and its surrounding medium, and by the wavelength of light. To get all the information potentially available to it, Kirschfeld has calculated that it requires approximately five receptors to scan the diameter of Airy's disc, or approximately 20 receptors to scan its area to get all the angular information that is available (Fig. 2.5).

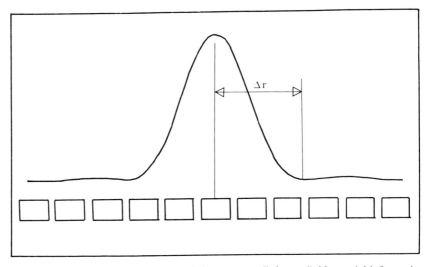

Fig. 2.5. The number of receptors needed to extract all the available spatial information from Airy's disc is $\Delta r/2\cdot44$, where Δr is the radius of Airy's disc. (After Kirschfeld 1976.)

As one might expect, in many animals the optical resolution of the eye set by the diameter of Airy's disc, and the anatomical resolution set by the grain of the retina, are about the same since the one limits the effectiveness of the other. This is true for man (Campbell and Green 1965*b*; Green 1970) and for the goldfish (Northmore 1977). In the house-fly, *Musca* (Fig. 2.6), Kirschfeld finds that the resolution limit set by the packing of the retinular cells is worse by a factor of two than the optical resolution. This discrepancy is not large and could be accounted for if the fly gets

Fig. 2.6. The house-fly *Musca domestica*.

information by the change of image with time as the eye scans across the visual scene.

In a diffraction-limited lens eye, the best resolution obtainable is proportional to eye size. But in the compound eye the geometrical arrangement of the facets around the periphery of the eye (Fig. 2.7) means that resolution increases only with the square root of eye size. Indeed, Kirschfeld calculates that the smallest possible compound eye that has the same resolution as the human eye would be 1 m in diameter.

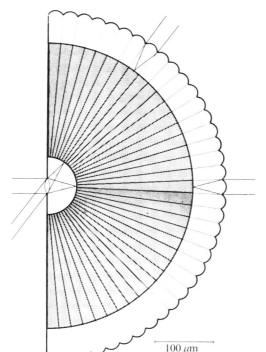

100 μm

Fig. 2.7. The comparison of a lens eye and a compound eye, both having the same angular resolution of a fly's compound eye. In both cases the size of the eye is basically governed by the size of the photoreceptors (stippled areas). (From Kirschfeld 1976.)

Eyes of such size would be ridiculously incommodious even for an earth-bound creature like man (Fig. 2.8). For a flying insect the 400-kg weight of such an eye would be impossible. Pennycuick (1972) remarks that on energetic grounds no flying animal is likely to weigh more than 20 kg. Animals with compound eyes are, therefore, excluded from a lifestyle that requires them to see small objects at a distance, no matter how fast they can move.

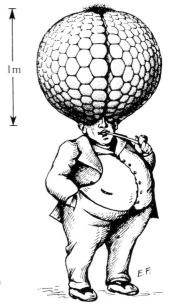

Fig. 2.8. A man would need a compound eye of at least 1 m diameter to get the same angular resolution as his lens eye. (From Kirschfeld 1976.)

For any animal, except perhaps modern man, there is a distance beyond which events in the surrounding scene are of no practical interest. This reaction distance depends on the lifestyle of the animal, how fast and how far it can move, and how its enemies can move. If an animal relies chiefly on vision to gather information about distant events, we can expect that the resolution of its eyes will be appropriate to its reaction distance. It is often true that larger animals have a greater reaction distance than small ones and Kirschfeld has shown that there is a simple first-order relationship between visual resolution and body height (Fig. 2.9). The interest of such a relationship is that one is able to recognize animals such as the bat, *Myotis*, and the jumping spider, *Metaphidippus*, that have eyes that are better (the spider) or worse (the bat) than would be generally expected from the size of the animal. If it is better, the animal is clearly visually orientated; if worse, there are probably other senses that take the place of vision.

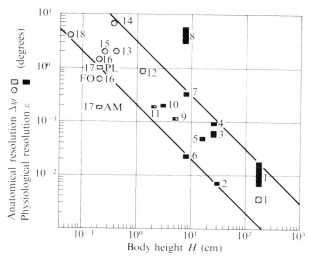

Fig. 2.9. Resolution of the eyes of various animals measured physiologically and deduced from anatomical criteria compared to body height: (1) man; (2) peregrine falcon; (3) hen; (4) cat; (5) pigeon; (6) chaffinch; (7) rat; (8) bat (*Myotis*); (9) frog; (10) lizard; (11) minnow; (12) dragonfly (*Aeschna*); (13) bee (*Apis*); (14) *Chlorophanus*; (15) housefly (*Musca*); (16) hover fly (*Syrrita*), frontal region FO; (17) jumping spider (*Methaphidippus*), anteromedian eye AM, postero-lateral eye PL; (18) fruit fly, *Drosophila*. (From Kirschfeld 1976.)

Areas of acute vision

Some parts of the visual image may be better served than others in the investment of visual cell numbers and neural circuitry. These are areas of particularly acute vision and can be recognized by an increased number of visual cells packed more closely together and by a corresponding increase in the number of retinal ganglion cells that serve them. These regions are known as *areae retinae* or more simply as areas (pp. 149–51).

They are found in most or all vertebrate groups, particularly in mammals and birds, and their distribution has been reviewed by Walls (1942), Rochon Duvigneau (1943), and, in more detail for birds, by Meyer (1977), and for mammals by Hughes (1977).

Areas seem to be so contoured and positioned in the retina that they scan those parts of the visual scene that are most important to the animal (see Chapter 6). It is also worth remembering that the acuity of the retina can only be as good as the dioptrics serving it. In the single-lens eye the oblique ray suffers more optical aberrations than the one closer to the optic axis. In this, the single-lens eye differs from the compound eye, which should be able to provide an equally sharp image from all directions (Kirschfeld 1976). In some animals, particularly in primates, some fishes, and birds, there is a much restricted domain within the area called the fovea that has exceptionally densely packed visual cells and is often formed into a pit or groove.

Photochemical mechanisms

Chemistry of visual pigments

In all eyes that have been examined, both vertebrate and invertebrate, the light-sensitive materials that absorb light and, in response, initiate the process that leads to a nerve impulse, are chemically very closely related and have similarly shaped absorbance spectra (Fig. 2.10). These are the

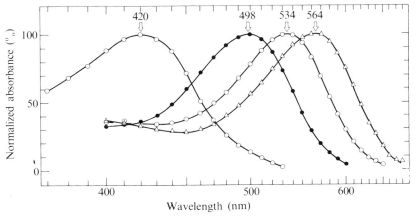

Fig. 2.10. Absorbance spectra of the four visual pigments in man (see also Plate 10). Filled circles, rods; open symbols, cones. These data were obtained by microspectrophotometry by Bowmaker and Dartnall (MSS. in preparation). Note that the abscissa is calibrated by wavelength, but a unit length on the abscissa represents an equal frequency interval.

visual pigments and they occupy a pivotal position in visual science. Their structure and chemistry have been reviewed from time to time (Rodieck 1973; Dartnall 1957; Morton 1972; Knowles and Dartnall 1977) and only the briefest of accounts is given here.

The visual pigments are chromoproteins consisting of a chromophoric group related either to vitamin A_1 (retinol) or vitamin A_2 (dehydroretinol) joined to a protein molecule (opsin). The retinols are derived from β-carotene ingested in the food. The chromophoric group is the aldehyde of vitamin A_1 (retinal) or vitamin A_2 (3-dehydroretinal) Fig. 2.11(a)). Retinal and 3-dehydroretinal can exist in several isomeric forms, of which only two, 11-*cis* and all-*trans*, are important in the visual process (Fig. 2.11(b)).

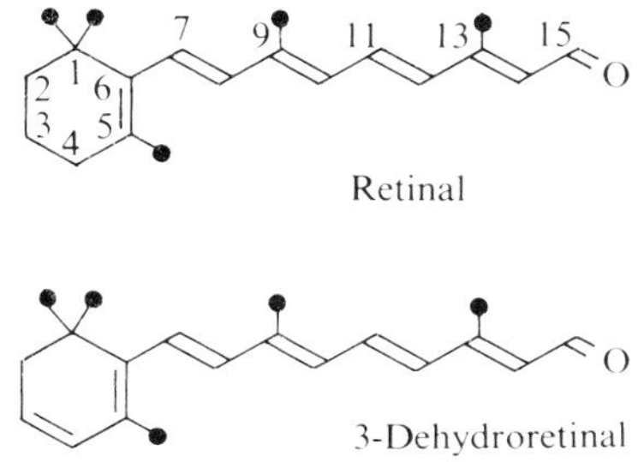

Retinal

3-Dehydroretinal

Fig. 2.11(a). The structure of retinal and 3-dehydro-retinal.

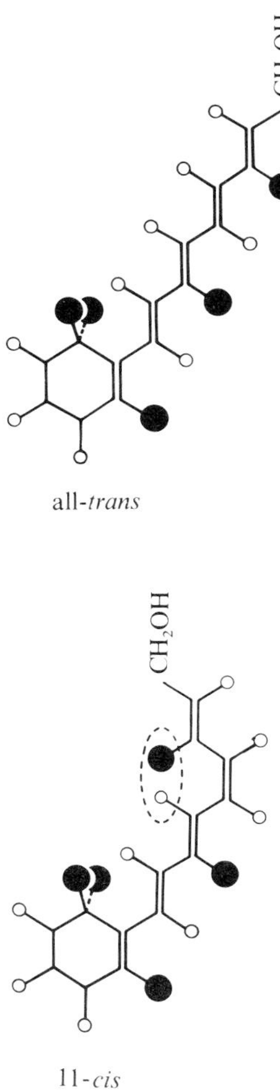

all-*trans*

Fig. 2.11(b). The isomeric configurations of retinal.

11-*cis*

The initial stage of photoactivation appears to be the same in all animals. Before a photon is absorbed, the chromophoric group is in the 11-*cis* configuration and fits snugly into the opsin molecule (Fig. 2.12(a)). On the absorption of a photon, the chromophore changes to the all-*trans* configuration, thus becoming 'unlatched' from the opsin molecule (Fig.

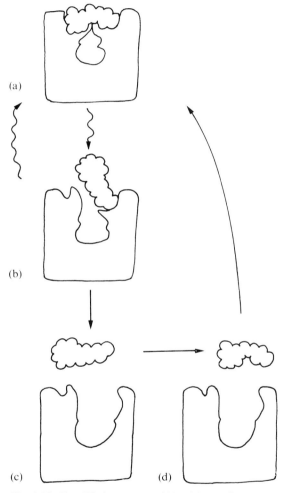

Fig. 2.12. Simplified sequence of bleaching and regeneration of rhodopsin: (a) rhodopsin molecule; (b) metarhodopsin; (c) opsin plus all-*trans* retinal; (d) opsin plus 11-*cis* retinal. The wavy arrows represent changes induced by the absorption of a photon. Straight arrows represent thermal changes not requiring light. In mammals the main sequence of bleaching and regeneration is a–b–c–d–a. In vertebrates it is a–b–a.

2.12(b)). This isomerization is virtually instantaneous, but there follows a slower and spontaneous detachment of the chromophoric group from the opsin. At some intermediate stage of detachment, coloured compounds called metarhodopsins are formed. In invertebrates the process stops at metarhodopsin but in vertebrates the opsin and chromophore become completely detached (Fig. 2.12(c)). The whole process is called bleaching. In vertebrates, where bleaching was first described, the final products are only faintly coloured. In invertebrates, light converts one coloured pigment into another coloured pigment and the term 'bleaching' becomes somewhat misleading.

Invertebrate metarhodopsin when it itself absorbs a photon is converted back to rhodopsin. Since metarhodopsin and rhodopsin have different absorption spectra, the two pigments may be present together in an equilibrium mixture that depends upon the colour of the irradiating light. The regeneration of vertebrate rhodopsin is a chemical one and involves first the isomerization of the chromophore group back from the all-*trans* to the 11-*cis* configuration Fig. 2.12(d) followed by the spontaneous recombination of the opsin molecule with the chromophore to form the rhodopsin or porphyropsin molecule.

Nomenclature

The tortuous evolution of visual pigment nomenclature has been well reviewed by Dartnall (1962) and by Crescitelli (1972). The visual pigments can be described by the colour they appear, i.e. the colour they transmit most strongly; or by the opposite description of the colour to which they are most sensitive. Naming by colour fails because there are now more visual pigments known than there are unambiguous colour names to describe them. Instead of colour names, the wavelength of maximum absorption (λ_{max}) gives a much more precise description. Visual pigments can further be described by whether the chromophore group is retinal (vitamin-A_1 aldehyde) or 3-dehydroretinal (vitamin-A_2 aldehyde). At the present time it is not certain that the visual pigments in rods, cones, and invertebrate receptors differ systematically from each other and in this book there is no attempt to name them separately.

Thus I call all retinal-based visual pigments rhodopsins; all 3-dehydroretinal pigments porphyropsins. More precisely, a visual pigment may be referred to as, for example, VP 523_2 which means that it has a λ_{max} of 523 and is based on vitamin A_2 (3-dehydroretinal).

The spectral absorption of visual pigments

There are two major factors that influence the spectral absorption of the visual pigment. The first is whether the chromophoric group is retinal or 3-dehydroretinal. The second is the detailed nature of the electronic linkage between the chromophore and the opsin. The precise nature of this linkage is not yet known (see Knowles and Dartnall (1977) for a review) but it is clear that the differences lie at the binding site between the opsin and chromophore group. There may be about a score of opsin types, each of which can bind to either retinal or 3-dehydroretinal. In all, therefore, we may expect to find perhaps 40 different visual pigment species which may nevertheless show some slight variation in λ_{max}, say about $\pm$ 3 nm.

It is desirable to have some way of characterizing visual pigments that is independent of pigment concentration, and this is provided by presenting the absorption data as absorbance spectra. (For a more detailed exposition see Knowles and Dartnall (1977) pp. 56–9.)

Absorbance (A_λ) is defined as

$$A_\lambda = \log (I_{inc}/I_{trans}), \tag{2.5}$$

where I_{inc} and I_{trans} are the incident and transmitted fluxes. A_λ is sometimes also called the 'optical density' or 'density' or 'extinction' of the solution. Absorbances are additive. That is, if the pathlength is doubled, the absorbance is also doubled. A measure of absorbance independent of concentration or pathlength is obtained by plotting each spectral absorbance curve as a percentage of the maximum absorbance of that curve. It is curves of this form that are used to compare the shapes of visual pigment absorbances.

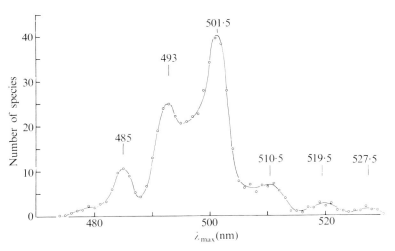

Fig. 2.13. The cluster points for rhodopsins appear at approximately regular intervals through the spectrum. The cluster points of the porphyropsin analogue is related to the rhodopsin points according to the formula $\lambda_1 = 0.60\lambda_2 + 186$ (Dartnall and Lythgoe 1965b). Note that the difference in λ_{max} between a rhodopsin and its porphyropsin analogue is greatest for red-sensitive visual pigments, and negligible or even reversed for blue-sensitive pigments. The interval between each rhodopsin cluster point is 8·5 nm.

A histogram of the λ_{max} of all known rhodopsins against the number of species in which they have been found shows evidence that the rhodopsins cluster around particular preferred positions in the spectrum (Fig. 2.13). (Dartnall and Lythgoe 1965a, b). A similar histogram of the porphyropsins (Bridges 1964, 1965) shows that these too display the clustering phenomenon, but the cluster points are shifted to longer wavelengths and the wavelength interval between each cluster point is greater. Both Dartnall and Lythgoe and Bridges realized that there was a relationship between the λ_{max} of the rhodopsin and its porphyropsin analogue. This is shown in Fig. 2.14. It is evident that the difference in λ_{max} which is due to the

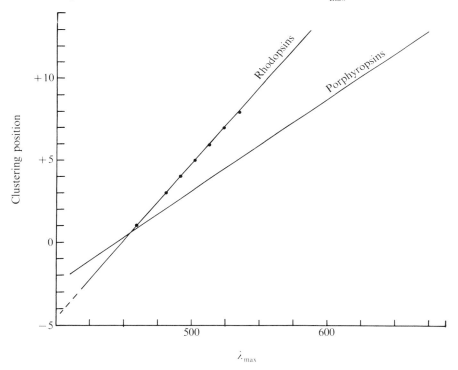

Fig. 2.14. Relation between the λ_{max} of the clustering positions of rhodopsins (see Fig. 2.13) and the clustering positions of their porphyropsin analogues.

presence of either a retinal or 3-dehydroretinal chromophore is going to be significant for the more red-sensitive visual pigments, but much less important for the more blue-sensitive pigments.

Amphibia and fishes often have a mixture of rhodopsin and porphyropsin in the retina. The proportion in an individual animal sometimes varies with daylength, its stage of metamorphosis and whether the animal is living in fresh or salt water or on land (see pp. 87–9). In at least one case—a freshwater fish named the rudd (Fig. 2.15)—the change in the proportion of rhodopsin and porphyropsin in the rods is accompanied by a corresponding change in the cones (Loew and Dartnall 1976). It is the more red-sensitive cones that will change most in spectral sensitivity as a result of the rhodopsin–porphyropsin shift.

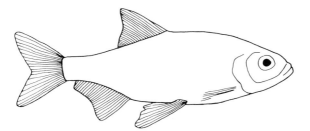

Fig. 2.15. The rudd
Scardinius erythropthalmus.

It was mentioned earlier that the spectral absorption curves of all visual pigments have very much the same shape, when plotted on a frequency rather than on a wavelength basis. Dartnall, who first noticed this, pointed out that a single curve would fit all the known rhodopsins provided that the λ_{max} was known. This led him to construct his celebrated nomogram (Dartnall 1953) for deducing the absorption characteristics of any rhodopsin. The absorption curve of porphyropsin is superficially similar to that of rhodopsin but is somewhat broader (Bridges 1967).

Much more recently it has been realized that the longer-wave pigments in both series are narrower than the shorter-wave pigments (see, for example, Harosi 1976) and Fig. 2.10, a fact that has led Ebrey and Honig (1977) to construct nomograms for long-, intermediate-, and short-wave rhodopsins and porphyropsins.

The visual-pigment nomogram has proved its value over many years. However, for numerical calculations it is more useful to present the standard visual-pigment curves in numerical form. This has been done by Knowles and Dartnall (1977, p. 76) and their data are reproduced here in Table 2.2.

Visual pigments *in situ*

There is a fundamental difference in the arrangement of visual pigment in vertebrates and invertebrates. In vertebrates, the chromophores lie randomly in the planes of flat lamellae which are themselves arranged perpendicular to the direction of the incident light. Rods and cones, therefore, exhibit no dichroism. In invertebrates, the membranes are 'rolled' into microvilli and the microvilli are arranged into bundles, each having their microvilli arranged in parallel lines, but the microvilli in adjacent bundles

Table 2.2 The standard shapes of absorbance spectra for visual pigments

Absorbance as % maximum	Wave-number separation from peak				
	Rhodopsin	Porphyropsin	Chicken red cone pigment	Frog green rod pigment	Cyanopsin
30	+3736	—	—	—	+2850
40	+2940	+3866	+3080	+3960	+2460
50	+2442	+2905	+2408	+3100	+2120
60	+2020	+2353	+1890	+2480	+1810
70	+1620	+1880	+1480	+2013	+1490
80	+1224	+1445	+1105	+1535	+1180
90	+ 796	+ 985	+ 720	+ 995	+ 860
95	+ 545	+ 670	+ 480	+ 650	+ 600
100	0	0	0	0	0
95	− 520	− 621	− 520	− 675	− 500
90	− 732	− 869	− 690	− 920	− 660
80	−1031	−1213	− 970	−1255	− 880
70	−1275	−1476	−1195	−1505	−1050
60	−1492	−1707	−1390	−1725	−1200
50	−1705	−1924	−1600	−1935	−1360
40	−1930	−2142	−1803	−2150	−1520
30	−2178	−2372	−2025	−2383	−1700
20	−2460	−2638	−2290	−2670	−1910
10	−2850	−2999	−2720	−3075	−2210

The table shows, for example, that a rhodopsin of λ_{max} 480 nm, corresponding to a wave-number of 20833 cm^{-1} $(1/\lambda$ cm$^{-1})$ has an absorbance that is 50 per cent of the maximum on the long-wave side at a wave-number of $20833 - 1705 = 19128$ cm^{-1}, which is equivalent to 523 nm. At the short-wave end of the spectrum, the absorbance curves are somewhat broader than the standard rhodopsin and porphyropsin curves. Therefore, the green rod pigment of the frog (a rhodopsin of λ_{max} 433 nm), the red cone pigment of the chicken (a rhodopsin of λ_{max} 569 nm), and the synthetic cyanopsin (a porphyropsin of λ_{max} 620 nm) are included. (From Knowles and Dartnall 1977.)

are oriented at an angle to each other. The entire rhabdome, which is usually composed of several bundles, has the potential to act as a polarization analyser (Goldsmith 1975).

The arrangement of the microvilli into directionally opposed bundles in some invertebrate rhabdomes is responsible for the invertebrates' sensitivity to polarized light. However, the sensitivity of the animal to polarized light is frequently greater than might be expected from the fine structure and the probable arrangement of the rhodopsin molecules in the microtubules. At the time of writing, there seems to be no generally agreed reason for the discrepancy, although it is postulated that the orientation of the rhodopsin molecules is incorporated in the walls of the microvilli (Goldsmith 1975; Laughlin, Menzel, and Snyder 1975). Or perhaps optical effects due to reflection in superposition eyes could be responsible.

The orientation of the visual pigment chromophores in most vertebrate rods and cones is such that the absorption per μm (specific absorbance) of the outer segments measured with plane-polarized light having the e-vector

Table 2.3 Specific absorbance of vertebrate outer segments

Animal	Photoreceptor	Length (μm)	Specific absorbance	Reference
Leopard frog,	Red rod	50	0·018	Liebman (1972)
Rana pipiens	Red rod		0·018	Harosi and MacNichol (1974)
Tiger Salamander,				
Ambystoma tigrinum				
Larva	Red rod	26	0·012	Harosi (1975)
	Green rod	24	0·012	Harosi (1975)
Adult	Red rod	31	0·018	Harosi (1975)
Tcad (adult),	Red rod	51	0·016	Harosi (1975)
Bufo marinus	Green rod	33	0·014	Harosi (1975)
Mudpuppy,	Rod	28	0·013	Harosi (1975)
Necturus mandosus	Cone		0·016	Liebman (1972)
Goldfish	Cone	40–50	0·013	Liebman (1972)
Carassius auratus	Cone		0·012	Harosi and MacNichol (1974)
Chicken,	Rod	25	0·023 ± 0·003	Bowmaker and Knowles (1977)
Gallus domesticus	Cone	20	0·015 ± 0·003	Bowmaker and Knowles (1977)
Squirrel,	Rod	10	0·017 ± 0·003	Bowmaker (unpublished)
Sciurus leucotis	Cone	3	0·014 ± 0·003	
Rhesus monkey,	Rod	25	0·019 ± 0·004	Bowmaker et al. (1978)
Macaca mulatta	Cone	35	0·015 ± 0·004	

at right-angles to the disc, gives the same value as for unpolarized light travelling the length of the outer segment. The specific absorbance for rods and cones in various species is given in Table 2.3. The mean of all rod data in Table 2.2 gives a specific absorption of 0·016 and for cones a specific absorption of 0·014.

In vertebrates, at least, it does not seem to be necessary to consider the wavelength-selective effects of waveguiding down narrow cylinders (cf. Snyder 1975). For example, the spectral sensitivity of the human red and green mechanisms and the scotopic mechanism are about those that would be predicted from the length and specific (lateral) absorbance of the red and green sensitive cones and the rods of the Rhesus monkey (Bowmaker, Dartnall, Lythgoe, and Mollon 1978).

There are fewer systematic data for the specific absorbance of inverte-brate rhabdomes. There is little doubt that the visual pigment is packed less densely in the rhabdome than in rods and cones. For example, spider crab (*Libinia emarginata*) rhabdomes absorb 1·3 per cent of unpolarized light per μm length (Hays and Goldsmith 1969) which corresponds to a specific absorption of 0·0057. A similar value has been found for the fly (Kirschfeld 1969). More recently Bruno *et al.* (1977), have obtained a value of 0·0029 for the lobster *Homarus*.

It is often necessary to know how much light is absorbed in its passage through some light-absorbing material such as a cell containing visual pigment or coloured oil droplets. The actual amount of light absorbed at any particular wavelength depends upon the concentration of the pigment and upon the path length through the cell.

The amount of light absorbed by the solution is given as

$$I_{abs} = I_{inc} - I_{trans}. \tag{2.6}$$

A graph plotting I_{abs} against wavelength is called an absorptance spec-trum. The shape of the absorptance spectrum depends upon the con-

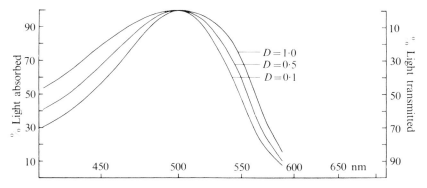

Fig. 2.16. The percentage of light absorbed by a rhodopsin at various densities.

centration of the absorbing material and upon the length of the path that the light travels through it. If the material is either very thick or very concentrated, then most of the light at all wavelengths will be absorbed and the percentage difference in light absorbed between the most and the least absorbed wavelengths will be reduced. That is, the absorptance curve becomes flatter (Fig. 2.16) provided, of course, that the outer segment is equally effective throughout its length. This could be a consideration in the study of colour vision, because it is the difference in the sensitivity of each visual pigment at each wavelength that leads to the perception of hue differences. If the sensitivity of the eye is increased by making the visual cells longer, there will be some sacrifice of colour discrimination.

Coloured oil droplets

A sheet of fresh retina laid on a microscope slide generally appears greyish-yellow by transmitted light (the visual pigment having bleached away), but sometimes the light microscope shows a field of red, yellow, and pale-green highly refractive spheres. These are the oil droplets that are lodged in the cone ellipsoid and through which the light must pass before being absorbed by the visual pigment (Fig. 2.17). Oil droplets have been seen in

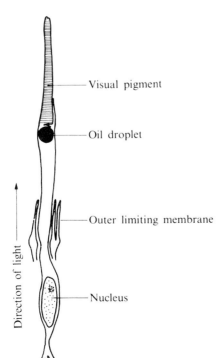

Fig. 2.17. Diagram of a cone in a bird. To reach the visual pigment the light must first pass through the coloured oil droplet. (After Morris and Shorey 1967.)

the retinas of chondrosteans, dipnoans, amphibians, reptiles, birds, monotremes, and marsupials (Walls 1942). Nearly always they occur only in the
cones, but Walls has seen them in the rods of the tuatara (*Sphenodon*)
(Fig. 2.18) and some geckoes. It is only in amphibia, reptiles, and birds

Fig. 2.18. The tuatara *Sphenodon*.

that brightly coloured oil droplets have been seen and only in turtles and
birds have red droplets (Plate 8) been reported.

Oil droplets, at least the coloured ones, all appear to contain carotenoids (see Muntz 1972 and Rodieck 1973 for reviews). The characteristic
three-peaked absorption curve of carotenoids is not usually seen in absorption spectra measured *in situ* (Fig. 2.19) since the optical densities reach

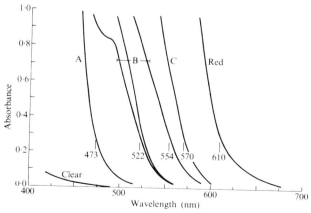

Fig. 2.19. Absorbance spectra of oil droplets in the cones in the
red sector of the pigeon retina. The wavelengths are the 50 per
cent transmission points of the droplets. (From Bowmaker 1977.)

the enormous values of around 20 or 30 (Bowmaker and Knowles 1977)
The optical consequence is that the coloured oil droplets act as simple cut-
off filters; the shorter wavelengths being almost totally absorbed and the
longer wavelengths transmitted.

The apparent colours of small refractile objects like oil droplets seen
through a microscope by transmitted light are a notoriously bad guide to
their spectral absorption. Generally, however, the spectral cut-off of red
objects is at longer wavelengths than for the yellow and yellow–green ones.
Neither is the eye very good at distinguishing the number of different types
of oil droplets present in a retina. For instance, it is difficult to discern
more than three droplet colours in the chicken retina although microspectrophotometry shows there to be at least five (Bowmaker and Knowles
1977).

The occurrence of different coloured oil droplets in different cones has
naturally led to speculation about the role of oil droplets in colour vision.
For instance, Roaf (1933) thought that each cone that had a coloured oil
droplet might be individually most sensitive to that colour and together
the cones containing the different droplet colours could provide the sensation of colour. Walls (1942) argues somewhat forcefully that this could not
constitute a universal theory of colour vision chiefly because colour vision
can occur in the absence of differently coloured oil droplets and, indeed, of
any droplets at all. Much more recently King-Smith (1969) has argued
that the known characteristics of the colour vision of the domestic fowl
could be explained by the presence of a single cone pigment (iodopsin)
screened by three types of oil droplet.

A theory that colour vision is mediated by two or more visual pigments
when oil droplets are absent and by two or more colours of oil droplet
when only a single cone pigment is present has an appealing simplicity but
cannot be universally true. In one of the earliest investigations using
microspectrophotometry, Liebman and Granda (1971) have shown that
in the turtle, *Chelonia mydas* (Fig. 2.20) there are four types of oil droplet:

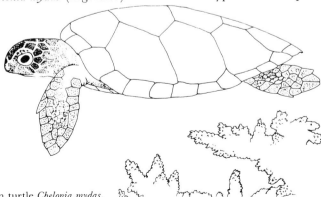

Fig. 2.20. The green turtle *Chelonia mydas*.

orange, two types of yellow, and colourless. In another turtle, *Pseudemys scripta* (Fig. 2.21) they are red, orange, yellow, and colourless. In the

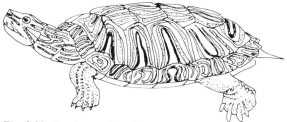

Fig. 2.21. *Pseudemys scripta elegans.*

chicken, Bowmaker and Knowles have described five types of oil droplet screening two types of cone. The pigeon (Fig. 2.22) has at least five types of oil droplet screening at least three types of cone (Bowmaker 1977).

It is clear from Liebman's (1972) work on the turtle *Chelonia* and the work by Bowmaker and Knowles on the chicken and the pigeon that although there may be only two or three visual pigments in the cones of a

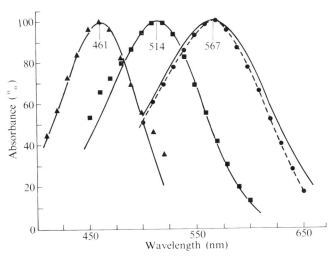

Fig. 2.22. Absorbance curves of the three cone visual pigments in the pigeon retina. The solid lines are the Dartnall nomogram curves. (From Bowmaker 1977.)

particular retina, each may be screened by one of a set of differently coloured oil droplets. It is unlikely that any cones have visual pigments sensitive only to wavelengths totally absorbed by the oil droplet that screens them. In *Chelonia*, for instance, it is unlikely that the 460, rhodopsin occurs in a cone with a red oil droplet. However, cones certainly exist where the oil droplet cuts off at wavelengths near or even longer than the λ_{max} of the visual pigment.

Vertebrates that have no coloured oil droplets, such as fishes and mammals, have to analyse the visual world in terms of the signals received from two to four types of cone and one type of rod. Birds, on the other hand, may have only two cone visual pigments but, due to teaming with specific oil droplets, have at least six types of cone, each with its own spectral sensitivity characteristics (Fig. 2.23). The presence of a coloured

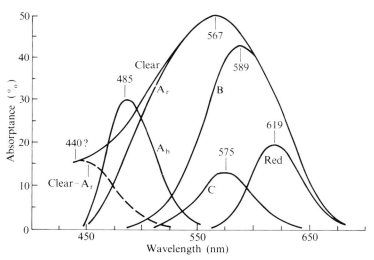

Fig. 2.23. Calculated absorptance for the pigment–oil-droplet combination in the six recognized cone types in the red sector of the pigeon retina: Clear (pigment- 567 and clear oil droplet); Ar (type A droplet with pigment 567); Ab (type A droplet with pigment 461); B (B type droplet (λ_{50} 554 nm) with pigment 567); C (type C droplet with pigment 514); and Red (red droplet with pigment 567). The dashed line indicates the possible response, maximal at about 430–40 nm, derived by interaction between the 'Clear' and 'Type A' cones. (From Bowmaker 1977.)

oil droplet in a cone narrows the spectral sensitivity curve of the cone, particularly at short wavelengths, and will presumably have the effect of sharpening hue discrimination (Martin and Muntz 1978) although at the expense of sensitivity.

Photoreceptor damage

There is growing evidence that the alternation of dark and light periods corresponding to day and night are essential for maintaining normal visual function. Rats, monkeys, and rabbits kept in constant light of about the intensity found in well-lit animal rooms show photoreceptor degeneration (see Loew (1976) for references). Intense light sufficient to bleach away all the visual pigment leads to no permanent damage and this has led Gorn and Kuwabara (1967) to postulate that the prolonged presence of visual pigment photoproducts are responsible for the degeneration. More recently (Marshall, Mellerio, and Palmer 1972) it has been shown that pigeons also show a similar degeneration.

Amongst invertebrates light-induced photoreceptor damage is well illustrated in the commercially important Norway lobster, *Nephrops norvegicus*. These live in holes that they excavate in soft muddy bottoms of the European continental shelf and in nature only emerge in subdued light (see pp. 98–100). Loew (1976) was led to investigate the damaging effects of light on these creatures when he noticed that those that had never been exposed to daylight at the surface had a beautiful, clear, golden-orange eyeglow, but animals that had been exposed to daylight soon developed a grey and diffuse reflection from their eyes—scarcely an eyeglow at all.

Eyeglow is a characteristic feature of dark adapted clear zone eyes. It results from the reflection of incident light out of the eye. It is most often seen in the eyes of certain night-flying moths that are resting on the window glass of a lighted room and seen from inside the room. In *Nephrops*, the eyeglow, as seen by a hand torch, is very obvious before the light-induced degeneration has time to set in. The golden colour of the eyeglow in normally sighted animals is probably due to the photoproducts of bleaching. The change to a fuzzy grey appearance some 10 hours after exposure to light is thought to be a result of thermal decay of the photo-product and the change from a specular to diffuse type of reflection to a disorganization of the tapetal surface.

The disorganization of the tapetum appears to be due to the total degeneration of the rhabdomes. Post-light changes were first noticeable under the electron microscope when the normally orderly and parallel microvilli became thrown into loops and swirls. Loew (1976) estimates that light only 3 log units brighter than the natural level for *Nephrops* is sufficient to cause degeneration. In Loch Torridon, where these *Nephrops* were caught, this light level is equivalent to that at a depth of 30 m at mid-day. An animal at the upper limit of its range and stranded outside its hole would become blinded, in all probability permanently, after only two or three hours in the middle of the day. The damaging effects of light obviously has important ecological consequences that are discussed in the next chapter.

Unrelieved darkness may also be harmful. There is good evidence that the eyes of the rudd (Fig. 2.15), kept in total darkness for a year or more, although looking natural from an external view, nevertheless have a severely dystrophic retina and almost total loss of function as judged by a nearly absent electrical response to light (Heath 1977). There is also the case of Ogneff's (1911) goldfish. After three years in the dark, these had lost their skin pigment, had degenerate eyes and apparently complete loss of visual function. The eyes of some cave-dwelling animals degenerate only when they are deprived of all light, as they are in deep caves. When they are exposed to light sufficiently early in development, the eyes do not degenerate (see p. 108).

It is open to speculation how important the blinding effects of continuous light and continuous darkness are in nature. Is there, for instance, any barrier to migration with regions of 24-hour daylight in the polar summer? The bottom of deep turbid lakes must receive virtually no light whatever. How long can an animal living at these depths retain a functioning eye? It is possible that some animals that are able to survive in a light-free environment become permanently confined there because to stray outside would make them certain victims to normally sighted predators.

Limits of spectral sensitivity

The spectral absorption characteristics of the visual pigments set the limits to visual sensitivity at both ends of the visible spectrum. At the longer

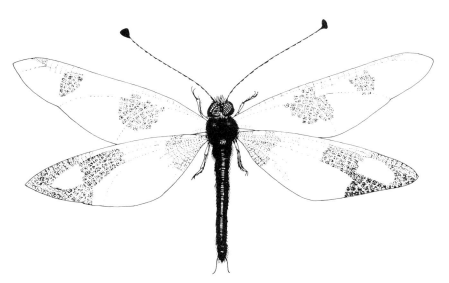

Fig. 2.24. The lacewing *Ascalaphus macaronius*.

wavelengths, the individual quanta do not possess sufficient energy to cause electronic excitation and the acquisition of the energy from the quantum only results in enhanced intra-atomic vibration and rotation of the molecules manifest as a rise in temperature. At higher frequencies the quanta possess so much energy that they can damage the complex molecules of living tissue (Dartnall 1975). Visual pigments are known that range in λ_{max} from the 345 pigment of the Lacewing, *Ascalaphus macaronius* (Fig. 2.24) (Schwemer, Hamdorf, and Gogola 1971), to the 625 porphyropsin of the perch (p. 72).

It is technically difficult to measure absorption at long wavelengths owing to the very low absorption of the pigment. At short wavelengths the problem is finding suitable light sources and optics transparent to ultraviolet light. At the long wavelength end of the spectrum a human observer can detect an intense radiation source of at least 1000 nm. However, no fixed limit for vision into the infrared can be defined since it depends upon the intensity of the radiation. In normal life, a longer limit of perhaps 750–850 nm might be an acceptable if ill-defined value. Freshwater fishes possessing 625 nm λ_{max} porphyropsin in many of their cones may well be able to see further into the infrared than we can.

In vertebrates the short-wavelength limits of vision are not in practice set by the absorption characteristics of the visual pigments. Apart from the main absorption band (the α-band) there is also the shorter-wavelength *cis*-peak (the β-band) and in the ultraviolet a strong protein absorption band (Fig. 2.25). The spectral position of the protein band at about 280 nm is chiefly set by the presence of aromatic amino acids, principally

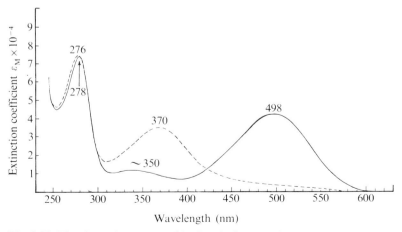

Fig. 2.25. The absorption spectra of bovine rhodopsin before bleaching (solid line) showing the main absorption band at 498 nm and the protein band at 278 nm. After bleaching (dashed line), the main peak has disappeared, but the metarhodopsin shows up as a peak at 370 nm. (From Shichi *et al.* 1969.)

tryptophan in the protein molecule (Collins, Love, and Morton 1952). Apparently electromagnetic energy absorbed by the protein can be transferred to the attached chromophoric group with a result identical to the normal light-induced isomerization (Kropf 1967). Indeed, in the frog *Rana temporaria* Govardovskii and Zueva (1974) found that in the isolated retina light at 280 nm evoked 60 per cent of the electrical potential produced by the most efficient wavelength of 500 nm. This high sensitivity was only achieved when the visual cells were illuminated from the back of the retina. When the light had first to pass through the neural retina in the normal way, there was little response below 300 nm. In invertebrates, Kirschfeld, Franceschini, and Minke (1977) have suggested that in the housefly, *Musca* (Fig. 2.6), and possibly in the blowfly, *Calliphora* (Fig. 2.26), sensitivity in the ultraviolet is due to a photostable pigment that absorbs ultraviolet light and transfers the energy to the visual-pigment chromophore.

Fig. 2.26. The blowfly *Calliphora*.

The absorption characteristics of proteins below about 300 nm seem to play an important part in setting the short-wavelength limit for vision in vertebrates. Protein is an important constituent of the cornea, lens, and neural retina, and all these tissues will absorb short-wavelength light without any possibility that the electromagnetic energy will be transferred to a visually active molecule. The potential sensitizing effect of the protein of the visual pigment opsin is, in fact, never realized since other protein molecules in the eye absorb all the relevant light before it reaches the visual pigment.

The electronic absorption spectrum of a molecule can be calculated provided its structure is known. On such grounds, Blatz and Liebman (1973) consider that no retinal-based pigment can exist in nature with a λ_{max} longer than 582 nm. The addition of the double bond that changes the pigment from a rhodopsin to a porphyropsin should extend the wavelength by about 62 nm, and thus it is unlikely that a porphyropsin of λ_{max} longer than around 644 nm will be found. The longest λ_{max} rhodopsin presently known is the 582 pigment in some monkey cones (Bowmaker, personal communication) and the longest porphyropsin is the 625 pigment of the perch.

If we consider sensitivity alone, it is unlikely that any animal has eyes that can make much use of electromagnetic radiation below about 280 nm or above 1000 nm. These are limits set by the absorption of aromatic amino acids at the short wavelengths and by the visual pigment chromophore at the long. There are reptiles, notably the pit vipers, that are able to 'see' infra-red radiation from their prey. The sensitive organ is the pit that lies midway between the eye and nostril. Vipers of the subfamily Crotalidae are sensitive to rises in temperature of 0·003 °C. It is thought that the organ is sensitive to local heating that results from the absorption of infrared radiation (Barrett, Maderson, and Meszler (1970)).

Neural mechanisms

An eye with but a single visual cell can signal only that it has absorbed a quantity of photons and the time during which the absorption took place. It can give no unequivocal information about spectral distribution of the light, its direction and its intensity since a change in signal strength may be due to a change in intensity, direction, or spectral composition of the light. To get information about the direction of a light source and whether it is moving or simply fluctuating in intensity, at least two cells that are maximally sensitive in different directions are needed. To get information about spectral distribution (coded in our brain as 'colour') there must be two kinds of visual cell that differ in their spectral sensitivity. It is by comparing the signals from an array of visual cells that the retina and the brain builds up a picture of the colour, shape, and brightness of the outside world.

Receptor area and summation

If absorptance and length are the same, it is evident that a visual cell with a large cross-sectional area will capture more photons and will thus be more sensitive than a visual cell smaller in cross-section. However, it is likely that the reception of a single photon by a vertebrate rod is potentially enough to trigger a response (Hecht, Shlaer, and Pirenne 1942; Ashmore and Falk 1976). In that case, the neural circuitry of the retina may be so arranged that the responses from a group of cells are summed together. In man, for example, as many as 300 rods may contribute to one pool (Pirenne 1967). Where summation of this kind occurs, the retina is functionally divided into fewer individual receptor areas, but each has greater sensitivity (Rodieck 1973, pp. 452–6; Arden 1976).

Another strategy that may be connected with summation is shown by some deep-sea fishes which possess in some areas of the retina tight bundles of rods optically isolated from neighbouring bundles by screening

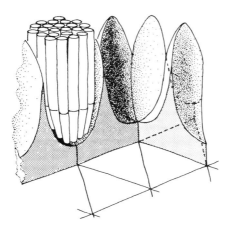

Fig. 2.27. One type of retinal organization that is an adaptation to dim light in deep-sea fish: discrete groups of rods within cups of reflecting tapetum. (From Locket 1977.)

pigments (Fig. 2.27). Some examples are *Scopelarchus guentheri* (Fig. 2.28), *S. sagax* (Locket 1971), and *Scopelosaurus lepidus*, *Evermanella indica*, *Ahliesaurus berryi* (Munk 1977).

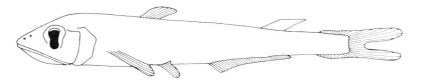

Fig. 2.28. The pearleye *Scopelarchus guentheri*.

Neural summation seems to be less developed in cones (Walls 1942), but since summation improves sensitivity at the expense of acuity, this is perhaps not surprising. However, there is currently an impression amongst workers in the field (for example, Munz and McFarland 1977) that fishes that are crepuscular predators have adapted their cone vision for the low light intensities at dawn and dusk by the enlarged cross-sectional area of their cones. It may also be that the two members of double cones (Fig. 2.29) of fishes (Plate 9), amphibians, reptiles, birds, monotremes, and

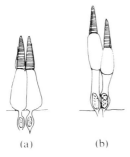

(a)   (b)

Fig. 2.29. Paired cones in teleost fishes: (a) equal doubled (*Pleuronectes*) and (b) unequal doubles (*Leuciscus*). (After Engstrom 1963.)

marsupials, but not of placental mammals (Walls 1942), are either optically or neurally coupled together and function as a single cone of large cross-sectional area. Such doubles would have increased sensitivity and it may be significant in this context that the visual pigments of teleost doubles often appear to match the colour of the ambient light which further enhances sensitivity (see pp. 141–2).

Amongst invertebrates there is also some evidence that the cross-sectional area of the rhabdomes are larger in nocturnal than in diurnal species (Kirschfeld 1974; Blest and Land 1977). Thus in the diurnal bee and housefly (*Musca*) the rhabdomes have a diameter of 1–2 μm and in the diurnal jumping spider, *Phidippus* (Fig. 2.30), they are 2 μm. By comparison, in the eyes of the nocturnal net-casting spider, *Dinopis*, and the

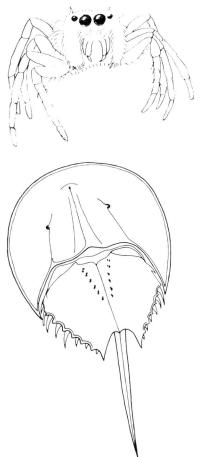

Fig. 2.30. The jumping spider *Phidippus* sp.
Fig. 2.31. The horseshoe crab (or king crab) *Limulus polyphemus*.

nocturnal moth, *Ephestia*, they are 20 μm and 8 μm in diameter respectively.

There is a further intriguing likelihood mentioned by Blest and Land (1977) that the size of the visual-pigment rhabdomes in *Dinopus* increase in volume at night and reduce again in the daytime. A process of this kind is known to occur in the lateral eyes of the Horseshoe crab, *Limulus* (Fig. 2.31), (Behrens and Krebs 1976) where the rhabdome may increase fourfold in thickness from about 1 μm to 4 μm as a result of dark adaptation. At present, however, it is uncertain what happens to the visual pigment lost from the rhabdomes during light adaptation or where it comes from when the rhabdomere is rebuilt in the dark.

Retinal memory and movement perception

The number of photons that are absorbed may not be sufficient for the nervous system to make reliable judgments about the nature of the image on the retina. Enlarging the area that is sampled increases the number of photons absorbed, but at the expense of the perception of spatial detail (see p. 37). The increase of the sampling time is the alternative strategy although, in this case, at the expense of temporal detail. The consequence of this is that fast-moving retinal images will not be seen and this is, of course, true whether it is the observer, or the display, or both that are moving. This is illustrated in Fig. 2.32 where a child on a swing has been photographed with an exposure time of 4 seconds, made possible by using a neutral-density filter that cuts out 99·9 per cent of the light. The moving child and the swing on which she is sitting are invisible in the photograph, whilst her mother, who is relatively stationary, is visible.

The sampling time (which is variously called the memory time, integration time, or summation time) is estimated by taking advantage of the fact that for periods less than the sampling time an increase in the photon flux can be compensated for by a decrease in the exposure time (see Ripps and Weale 1976). Thus up to a certain exposure time sensitivity increases as the flash duration increases, but beyond that an increase in flash duration results in no further increase in sensitivity. It is this critical time that is a measure of the sampling time. For human scotopic vision, the sampling time is about 0·1 second, but for photopic vision it drops to 0·035–0·06 second.

Flicker fusion frequency measurements are a convenient way of estimating the retinal sampling time, at least in a relative sense. Fast-moving diurnal animals such as bees have exceedingly fast flicker-fusion frequencies of around 300 Hz (Autrum and Stocker 1950) which compares to the slow-moving, chiefly nocturnal, cricket that has a flicker-fusion frequency of 45 Hz (Autrum 1948). Man has a rather low flicker fusion frequency of 50–60 Hz in bright lights but less than 10 Hz at near threshold

Fig. 2.32. Child on a swing being pushed by her mother. (a) Photograph at 1/250th of a second. The child and swing are clearly visible. (b) The same scene but with a neutral filter of density 3 on the camera lens. In compensation for the consequent 99·9 per cent loss of illumination on the film, the exposure time was increased to 4 seconds. The child and swing, which are moving, are no longer visible but the stationary objects in the photographs, and the mother (who was asked to keep as still as possible), show up clearly.

intensities (Hecht and Verrijp 1933). Fishes range from about 67 Hz in the sand smelt *Atherina hepsetus*, to 14–18 Hz in the goldfish (Protasov 1964).

Spatial information

The signals from individual rods, cones, or retinular cells are not transmitted to the brain in isolation from its neighbours. As already mentioned, the signals from neighbouring visual cells may interact with each other; they may be added together so that their sensitivity is the sum of their receptive areas or they may inhibit each other. Basic to the design of both

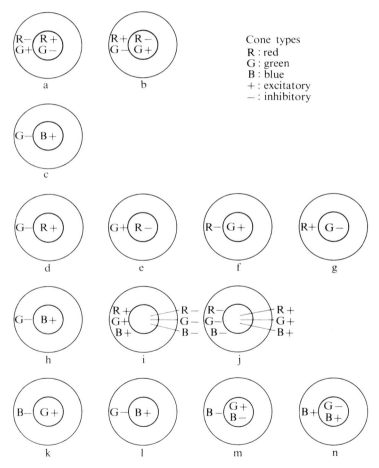

Fig. 2.33. Examples of the centre–surround organization in ganglion cell types in various animals: (a, b) goldfish; (c) macaque monkey retina; (d–j) macaque lateral geniculate nucleus; (k–n) ground-squirrel retina. (Data collected from various authors by Rodieck 1973.)

vertebrate and invertebrate retinas (see Wehner (1975) and Rodieck (1973), for reviews) is the phenomenon of lateral inhibition. The signal from a group of cells or facets may be inhibited when cells surrounding their receptive field receive the same kind of stimulus (Fig. 2.33). The signal produced by a patch of light falling on the central field will increase as the area of the patch increases until it exactly fills the receptive area. Henceforth, as the patch is further increased, the signal will actually decrease when the light begins to impinge on the inhibitory surround. The centre-surround organization is believed to enhance contrast perception, but to leave acuity unaffected.

Inherent in the transmission of information is that various salient features of the pattern are abstracted by the neural retina and transmitted inwards to the brain. Exactly how this is done is presently an active area of research and it is too early to make generalizations. Examples of the kind of information that is transmitted are the presence of moving edges, either dark or light, the presence of moving dark spots, characteristic spatial frequencies in the pattern, and edges or spots moving in particular directions. Some of these units are described in more detail when inherently conspicuous patterns are discussed later in this book (pp. 195–204).

Table 2.4 Rewards and penalties of various visual adaptations

Feature	Rewards	Penalties
Increase pupil area	Brighter image, better definition	Larger eye or reduced field of view
Increase depth of visual pigment	Better photon capture	Reduced colour discrimination
Yellow filters	Reduce scatter	Reduced sensitivity and spectral range
Little summation	Better acuity	Reduced sensitivity
Much summation	Better sensitivity	Reduced acuity
Long memory time	Greater sensitivity	Reduced movement perception
Short memory time	Improved motion perception	Reduced sensitivity
Different receptor types	Colour vision	Reduced sensitivity
Tapetum	Greater sensitivity	Reduced acuity
Screening pigments	Greater acuity	? reduced sensitivity

Colour information

A single receptor acts as a photon counter, but it captures more photons at some wavelengths than at others. The cell cannot distinguish between a dim light at a wavelength where it is sensitive and a bright light at a wavelength where it is less sensitive; thus at night, when only the rods are functional, we see the visual scene in terms of brightness and not colour. To see colour it is necessary to compare the signals from receptors of two types that differ in spectral sensitivity. In man there are in fact three classes of cone: one most sensitive to the 'blue' part of the spectrum, one to the 'green', and one to the 'yellow-green' (see Fig. 2.10, Plate 10, and Knowles and Dartnall 1977). It is noteworthy that there are no cones maximally sensitive to the red part of the spectrum. The sensation of red presumably comes by comparing the signal from the green-sensitive cones, which absorb very little red light, with the signal from the yellow-green sensitive cones that absorb more red light. The ecological value of such sensing mechanisms is discussed later in the book (pp. 143–5).

The interaction between the centre and surround of a receptive field is often an integral part of colour processing. The receptive field may receive the inputs from more than one cone type (Fig. 2.33) so that, for example, in the macaque monkey there are the blue-sensitive cones of the centre field which are inhibited by the green-sensitive cones of the surround. In goldfish, the central field contains both red- and green-sensitive cones, one

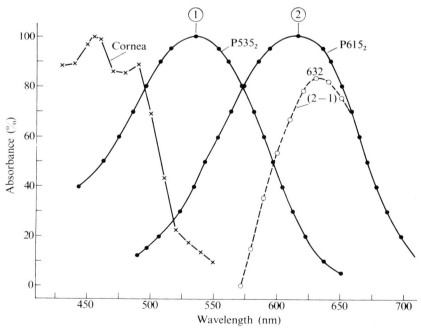

Fig. 2.34. Spectral absorbance curves of the two cone types in the perch retina and the spectral absorbance of the yellow cornea. If the signal from cone 1 inhibits the signal from cone 2, then the resulting spectral sensitivity maximum of the resulting 'ghost cone' is displaced to a longer wavelength and is considerably narrower. (Loew and Lythgoe, hitherto unpublished), see also p. 144.

excitatory and the other inhibitory; in the surround there is the same situation except that the cones respond in the opposite sense (Fig. 2.33 (a,b)) (see Rodieck (1973) for a review).

The inhibitory interaction between two cone types has important consequences for the colour vision of an animal, and also guides the interpretation of experimentally obtained spectral sensitivity curves (Fig. 2.34), (Sirovich and Abramov 1977). When two cones with different but overlapping action spectra inhibit each other, the extent of the inhibition depends upon the wavelength of the stimulating light. At wavelengths where the signal from both cones is equal, they will inhibit each other completely and no response from the ganglion cell serving the receptive area will be produced. At wavelengths where only one cone is excited, the response from that cone will not be reduced. The result is that the spectral sensitivity of the whole mechanism will be bimodal, with two sensitivity maxima displaced from the λ_{max} of the cones to shorter and longer wavelengths respectively, and both being narrower than the spectral sensitivity

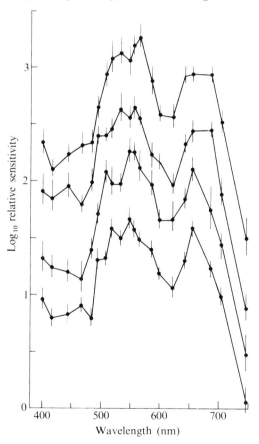

Fig. 2.35. Spectral sensitivity curves (photons incident on cornea) for four individual perch (*Perca fluviatilis*) obtained by a behavioural technique. The curves have been arbitrarily shifted on the *y*-axis for clarity. Note the bimodal shape of the curves. (From Cameron 1974.)

of the parent cone types (Fig. 2.34). The central dip falls midway between the λ_{max} of the two cone types (Fig. 2.35). Although the eye is less sensitive to light in this spectral band, we may anticipate that it has enhanced hue discrimination there.

Dark adaptation

The natural illumination falling upon the earth on a bright sunny day is about 10^8 times that on a moonless night. Even during the hours just before sunrise and just after sunset, the level of natural light changes by a factor of about 10^6. At night the eye is limited by the few photons available to it, whereas in very bright daylight bleaching of the visual pigment itself becomes a problem. During the change from day to night and during the much faster changes associated with movements between areas of different light intensities, the eye has to adapt to the prevailing light conditions for it is only then that it is functioning most efficiently. A useful and biological significant measure of efficiency is the brightness difference between an object and its background that the eye can just detect. Craik (1938) and Barlow (1962) have shown that contrast discrimination is at its most acute when the eye is adapted to the background intensity and a change in the adaptation state, either towards darker or lighter conditions, leads to a loss in discrimination. It is this loss in brightness discrimination that is the visually important factor, rather than the intensity of a light that can just be detected.

Mechanisms

Several different methods of dark and light adaptation are known; some methods are characteristic of particular animal groups, although a particular species normally possesses more than one method. Adaptation methods can be divided into three classes: (1) optical regulation of the light reaching the visual pigment; (2) absorption by the visual pigment; and (3) neural processing.

Optical

Change in pupil aperture is the most visibly apparent way that the eye can regulate the amount of light falling on the retina. Round pupils cannot close completely and the full excursion from closed to fully open adjusts the retinal illumination by only 1 log unit (Barlow 1972a; Gruber 1975). Although no data seem to be available, Walls (1942) believes that the slit pupil, common in non-basking nocturnal reptiles and mainly nocturnal mammals, can reduce its effective aperture almost to zero. In some shallow-living aquatic animals, particularly bottom-living species such as some flatfishes, rays, and cephalopods, the dorsal margin of the iris forms a flap or operculum that occludes all but the ventral rim of the pupil. In its most developed form, the operculum is elaborately sculpted so that the eye is left with a series of little pupils arranged in a semi-circle around the lower margin of the pupil.

In mammals the change in pupil aperture in response to changing illumination is temporary, giving other slower adaptation processes in the retina a chance to catch up with the change in illuminations. In birds, reptiles, and mammals that generally have very mobile pupils, dilation and contraction may be complete in a second or two. In fishes the movements are much slower and Walls reports that the elasmobranch pupil may take 2–3 minutes to close when the illumination is increased, and up to one hour to dilate in the dark. It is worth mentioning that in birds, which have the most mobile pupils of all, the size of the pupil seems scarcely to relate to changes in light intensity and has more to do with accommodation and emotional state.

Amongst invertebrates, the cephalopods regulate the pupil aperture by iris movements in much the same way as vertebrates. In arthropods, the aperture of each individual ommatidium is sometimes adjusted by the radial movement of pigment granules in the cells that surround the cone cells. Insects that are active at dusk and at night, such as the locust, *Locusta*, and the cockroach, *Periplaneta*, change the acceptance angle of each ommatidium; in the locust the acceptance of each ommatidium changes from $3.4°$ to $5.6°$, and in the cockroach from $2.4°$ to $6.7°$ (see Walcott (1975) for a review).

The pigment granules within the epithelial cells of the pigment epithelium and the rods and cones themselves frequently move in response to changes in light intensity in such a way that particular cell types are shielded from unwanted light. These changes are collectively known as retinomotor or photomechanical movements. Phylogenetically they appear to be older than the pupillary movements and usually one or the other mechanism is well-developed in a particular class of animal.

Retinomotor movements are best developed in birds, fishes, and frogs— indeed, the phenomenon was first studied in detail in the frog by Boll and Kühne who, by coincidence, both published their results in 1877. Since then there has been much work on the phenomenon, particularly in the early years, which has been reviewed on several occasions, most recently by Blaxter (1970), Ali (1971), and Ali (1975). Even though the underlying mechanisms are not understood, the natural history is comparatively well-known. Both the rods and cones and the pigment granules within the epithelial cells of the pigment epithelium may move in response to changing light intensity (Fig. 2.36). The illustration here is of retinomotor movements in the Caribbean French grunt (Fig. 2.37).

The nucleus of the rods and cones does not move, but the myoid, which

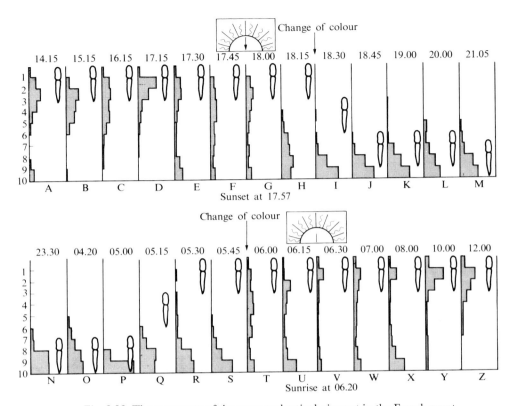

Fig. 2.36. The movement of the cones and retinal pigment in the French grunt, *Haemulon flavolineatum*, in one 24-hour period. The most rapid change in light intensity is in the hour immediately after sunset and in the hour that precedes dawn. During this time the light intensity (at the surface) changes from about 10^{13} photons cm^{-2} s^{-1} nm^{-1} at 550 nm to about 10 photons cm^{-2} s^{-1} nm^{-1}. In noon daylight the intensity is about 10^{14}–10^{15} photons cm^{-2} s^{-1} nm^{-1}. Change in colour is the time when the fishes blanched to their nocturnal colour form.

joins the nuclear portion and the ellipsoid, contracts or elongates in response to changes in light intensity. Approximately coincident with this movement is a migration of pigment granules within the cells of the pigment epithelium. In the light-adapted state the pigment granules are dispersed fairly evenly through the pigment epithelium; the rod myoids expand so that pigment granules surround the rod outer segment and ellipsoid. The cone myoids are contracted and the cones are pressed close to the external nuclear layer. In the dark-adapted state the cone myoids may elongate and the cones move in the direction of the pigment epithelium. At the same time, the rod myoids may contract and withdraw the rods away from the pigment epithelium.

The movements of the rods, cones, and pigment granules are not

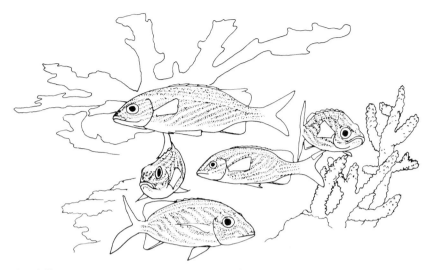

Fig. 2.37. French grunt, *Haemulon flavolineatum*, during the daytime in a loose, somewhat disorganized stationary school.

exactly synchronized and in some cases either pigment migration or rod and cone migration proceeds in the absence of the other. Within one species some types of rod or cone may move whilst others do not and there are topographical differences within the retina itself (see, for instance, Walls (1942) and Tansley (1965)).

Pigment movements that can possibly be compared to the retinal pigment movements in vertebrates have been observed in some arthropods (Kleinholz 1965; Walcott 1965), especially those with 'clear zone' superposition-type eyes. In bright light the pigment granules migrate longitudinally inwards from a position close to the cornea so as to clad the light-transmitting crystalline tract. Working on moths of the family Sphingidae, Höglund (1965) showed that this type of pigment migration was responsible for a reduction of 2–3 log units in the light intensity reaching the eye and required about 30 minutes for completion. As in vertebrates, pigment movements associated with dark adaptation are rather slow and require times of the order of an hour to complete (Walcott 1965).

Finally occlusible tapeta which are known in elasmobranchs and teleosts (Cyprinidae) should be mentioned. In the light-adapted state, pigment granules migrate from between the reflective cells to cover their surface, thereby screening out the reflections. In the spur dog (*Squalus acanthias*) (Fig. 2.38), Nicol (1965) has estimated that in the dark-adapted state the tapetum reflects 88 per cent of the incident light but after light-adaptation only $2\frac{1}{2}$ per cent of the incident light is reflected. Like the pigment migrations of the pigment epithelium, the process is slow and takes

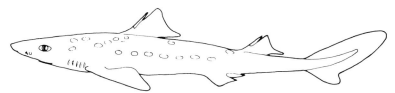

Fig. 2.38. The spur dog *Squalus acanthias*.

two hours to complete. In the spur dog there seems to be little difference in the rate of dark and light adaptation.

Visual pigment

The photochemical effects of light on the visual pigment molecule and subsequent chemical changes that do not require light have been described on pp. 48–9. For the present purposes it is sufficient to note that significant bleaching of visual pigment requires quite high light intensities but is roughly proportional to the number of quanta absorbed. Subsequent regeneration of rod visual pigment is usually complete after about 40 minutes in man, whilst cone pigments require only about 7 minutes to regenerate (see Rushton (1972) for a review).

That there is some relationship between the regeneration of rhodopsin and the progress of dark adaptation has been realized since Kühne showed in 1878 that strong lights bleached away frog rhodopsin and it required a period of hours to regenerate after darkness was restored. Dowling (1960) in a study on the electroretinogram showed that the logarithm of the rod threshold was rather accurately a linear function of the level of unbleached rhodopsin in the rods. In man, Rushton estimates that each 5 per cent of rhodopsin bleached raises the threshold by 1 log unit.

It is difficult to give reliable figures for the regeneration of visual pigment under natural conditions, principally because the previous light history is so important. For example, a day spent in bright sunlight on an exposed beach is sufficient to retard dark adaptation for a period of several hours (Hecht, Hendley, Ross, and Richmond 1948), whereas after exposure to comparatively dim light, adaptation was rapid. For the less extreme light doses, it is reasonable to estimate the visual pigment regeneration is completed after about 40 minutes in the rods and 10 minutes in the cones.

Receptor size

In at least two invertebrates, the net-casting spider and the Horseshoe crab (see p. 68), the actual size of the rhabdomes increases at night and reduces in the daytime. In vertebrates, the diameter of the rods and cones remains unchanged, but it seems that in the rods the severing of the apical portion of the outer segment, its phagocytosis in the pigment epithelium, and the replacement of new discs at the base of the outer segment, is initiated by the onset of light after a period of darkness; in nature, perhaps, the stimulus is the arrival of dawn (Besharse and Hollyfield 1977).

Neural processing

This is probably the most important and least understood mechanism involved in dark- and light-adaptation. During the full excursion from the fully light-adapted to the fully dark-adapted retina, the neural organization of the retina changes.

Dark-adapted	*Light-adapted*
Rods	Cones
No centre–surround	Centre–surround
Slow flicker fusion	Fast flicker fusion
No colour vision	Colour vision
Much summation	Little summation

The initial stages of adaptation are extremely rapid, completing about 2 log units in less than one fifth of a second, see below. The later stages of adaptation proceed more slowly. The change-over from a scotopic to photopic mechanism which is often marked by a shift in spectral sensitivity (pp. 81–2) and a kink in the dark-adaptation curve after pre-adaptation to bright light, is seen after about 10–15 minutes (Fig. 2.39). Perhaps the

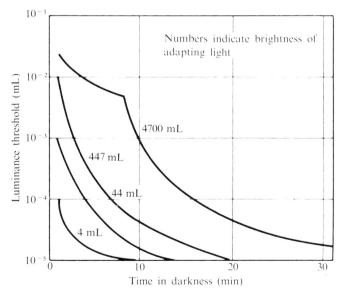

Fig. 2.39. The rate of dark adaptations in man after exposure to light of various brightnesses (shown by each curve). Bright daylight is about 1000 mL. (From White 1964 after Haig 1941.)

whole neural reorganization from bright light to dark takes place within about 30 minutes.

Rate and extent of adaptation

In most animals the progress of adaptation to increased light proceeds much faster than for a decrease. In humans, and perhaps most other animals, adaptation to increased illumination proceeds so rapidly that we are unaware of any inconvenience or disability except for the few seconds following a most brutal change from darkness to light.

The progress of dark adaptation is not so rapid and we know ourselves to be under severe disadvantage when, for instance, we enter a darkened theatre or drive at speed from a brightly lit road into an unlit tunnel. On the other hand, we are not aware of any shortfall of visual function when the intensity changes are smaller although equally sudden. When a cloud passes across the sun the ambient light intensity may be reduced by 50 per cent, and when we walk beneath trees on a sunlit day there are sudden and extremely rapid variations in light intensity.

In vertebrates, it is convenient to divide dark adaptation into three phases. There is an initial very fast neural adaptation (Barlow 1972*a*) that is complete in 0·1 or 0·2s in man and can respond to changes of as much as 1·7 log units. These fast changes have been reviewed by Baker (1963). The next phase in dark adaptation is typically completed within 15 minutes and marks the adaptation of the cones. The final phase is usually completed 30–60 mins after the onset of darkness.

Valid comparisons of the rates of dark adaptation in various animals are difficult, partly because the experiments are rarely designed to give ecological information and partly because a medley of electrophysiological, behavioural, and anatomical techniques have to be used. In general, however, it is clear that the rates of dark adaptation in man are comparable with other animals. Some that have been studied are the rat (Silver 1967; Dodt and Echte 1961); ground and tree squirrels (Dodt 1962; Dippner and Armington 1971; Lemon shark (Gruber 1975); the nocturnal gecko *Hemidactylus* (Dodt and Jessen 1961) and the diurnal gecko *Phelsuma* (Arden and Tansley 1962).

3 Intensity-limiting environments

Animals adapted for seeing in dim light are likely to be able to use vision at very low light intensities, but at the expense of acuity, perception of moving images, and colour vision. An animal adapted for bright light is likely to have good acuity, movement perception, and colour vision, but at the expense of sensitivity. Most of the time it is either day or night and it is often possible to classify an animal as either nocturnal or diurnal. Diurnal animals have to spend the period of darkness hidden or protected in some way from predators. Nocturnal animals, particularly those that live in deep water, may have an alternative strategy open to them, namely to move in synchrony with the natural luminance level so that they are always exposed to an optimal light intensity.

Visual pigments and sensitivity

The visual process in all animals seems to depend upon the absorption of photons by visual-pigment molecules. The absorption of a single photon may be enough to initiate a visual signal, but photons are more likely to be absorbed at some wavelengths than at others. There are some firm correlations between the spectral absorption of the visual pigments and the spectral quality of the light climate. There are also apparent correlations that a more careful examination show to be rather less convincing.

The Purkinje shift

The Czech physiologist, Purkinje (1819) noticed that in the twilight red objects, which appeared brighter than blue ones in the daytime, became darker as twilight got deeper. His conclusion that at low light intensities the human eye becomes relatively more sensitive to blue light than to red has been amply confirmed since and seems generally to be true of most vertebrates which have both scotopic and photopic visual systems (Fig. 3.1).

It is sometimes tacitly assumed that the shift in sensitivity to shorter wavelengths at low light intensities is an adaptation to the supposed increase in the relative amount of blue light at night compared to daytime. Perhaps this notion persists because the twilight sky viewed from a tungsten-lit room does appear blue compared to the scene inside the room. In fact, considered purely on sensitivity grounds, the shift towards shorter wavelengths at night appears to be maladaptive because starlight and

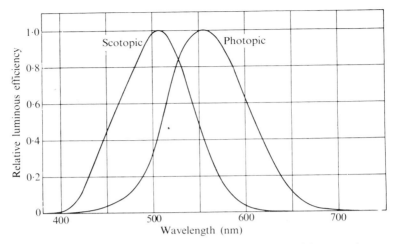

Fig. 3.1. The Purkinje shift in man. The spectral sensitivity of the eye at low light intensities (scotopic or night vision) and higher light intensities (photopic or day vision). (From Wyszecki and Stiles 1967.)

moonlight are significantly richer in the longer wavelengths than day-light (pp. 4–5). However, Munz and McFarland (1973, 1977) point out that one of the critical times for the survival of an animal may, in fact, be at twilight rather than the deepest part of the night. They consider that whereas a shift from the photopic sensitivity maximum at about 550 nm to a scotopic maximum of 500 nm in moonlight leads to a relative loss of sensitivity; during the twilight period the Purkinje shift results in an improvement. There is however no evidence that nocturnal animals are more sensitive to a long-wavelength light.

Spectral sensitivity under water

Fishes

The value of the aquatic environment as a natural laboratory for the study of visual problems of this nature was realized almost simultaneously by Clarke (1936) and Bayliss, Lythgoe, and Tansley (1936), the main point being that the spectral intensity maximum of downwelling daylight shifts sharply to shorter wavelengths at increasing depths in the clear open ocean. The possibility was considered that there might be a shift in the spectral sensitivity of deep-living fishes to render them more sensitive to the homo-chromatic blue light available to them. Owing to the intervention of the Second World War, the idea was not put to the test until Denton and Warren (1957) and Munz (1957, 1958), working independently, exam-ined the visual pigments in the retinas of deep-sea fishes. The results showed that not only were the visual pigments of the deep-sea fishes shifted in sensitivity to shorter wavelengths, but that the absorption maxima of the visual pigments coincided almost exactly with the wavelength of maximum water transparency.

The visual pigments were either characterized by measuring the spectral absorptance of the intact retina before and after bleaching by light (Denton and Warren 1957) or by first extracting the visual pigments from the retina with digitonin. Since deep-sea fishes have mostly rods in their retinas, it is reasonable to assume that it was overwhelmingly the rod pigments that were measured. Indeed, Dartnall (1960) believes that in extraction techniques it is chiefly the rod pigments that are obtained and only very searching investigations, such as those of Munz and McFarland (1975) may indicate the presence of cone pigments. The general conclusion that extraction techniques are mainly relevant to scotopic vision has lately been strengthened by a comparison of microspectrophotometric measurements of the pigment *in situ* in the visual cells and extraction measurements on the same species, where it is apparently the pigment in the rods that is overwhelmingly present in the extract.

The idea that the visual pigments of fishes were such as to confer the maximum sensitivity was soon extended to waters other than the clear blue oceans. It was noticed that fishes caught from the same body of water possessed very similar (rod) pigments and that the visual pigments absorbing at the longest wavelengths were found in water most transparent at the long wavelengths (see pp. 136–42).

The question of whether visual pigments are matched to the spectral quality of the light that reaches them can be formulated precisely enough to give a quantitative answer. The two foundations of such an analysis are the optical classification of ocean waters that we owe to Jerlov (pp. 21–3) and the similarity in the spectral absorption of the visual pigments. When such an analysis was performed (Lythgoe 1966, 1972), it became apparent that whereas most deep-sea fishes do possess the visual pigments that give maximum sensitivity, fishes that live in green coastal water and in most fresh water have visual pigments that are not sufficiently red-sensitive to give the maximum sensitivity. This conclusion has been further reinforced by a study by Loew and Lythgoe (1978) of rod and cone pigments in teleost fishes (pp. 140–2). This confirms the mismatch between rod visual pigments and water colour at long wavelengths. The rod mismatch is further highlighted by the situation in the double cones which seem to match the photic environment much more closely. A possible function of this offsetting in enhancing visual contrasts is discussed in Chapter 5 on colour-biased environments.

Reptiles

There is some evidence that similar adjustments in λ_{max} occur in vertebrates other than fishes, but the few species involved and the difficulty of obtaining them limits the amount that can be learnt. Amongst the reptiles, Liebman (1972) reports that the clear-water marine turtle, *Chelonia mydas*, has a rhodopsin of λ_{max} 502 whereas the freshwater turtles, *Pseudemys scripta* (Fig. 2.21), *Chrysemis picta* (Fig. 3.2), and *Chelydra serpentina* (Fig. 3.3), have porphyropsins of λ_{max} 518.

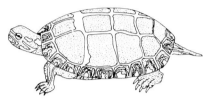

Fig. 3.2. The eastern painted turtle *Chrysemis picta picta*.

Fig. 3.3. The snapping turtle *Chelydra serpentina*.

Mammals

Amongst the seals the elephant seal, *Mirounga leonina* which spends much of its life in the open ocean, is judging by the well-developed sphincter on the posterior vena cava, capable of diving to great depths. Its teeth and stomach contents indicate that it feeds on squids and its 486_1 visual pigment is typical of mesopelagic fishes.

In contrast, the Weddell seal, *Leptonychotes weddelli* which does not seem to be particularly well adapted for deep diving and which feeds chiefly on (non-bioluminescent) fishes, has a 496_1 visual pigment that is typical of surface-living mammals (Lythgoe and Dartnall 1970).

McFarland (1971) has made a special study of the visual pigments of the other great group of aquatic mammals, the whales and dolphins. Eight dolphin species have been examined and these all have visual pigments of rather unvaried λ_{max} between 485_1 and 489_1. The dolphins are not normally considered deep divers and their visual pigments occupy a spectral region similar to that of at least some epipelagic fishes of the open ocean.

McFarland was also able to examine the visual pigments of two whale species, the grey whale, *Eschrichtius gibbosus* (Fig. 3.4) and the beaked whale, *Berardius bairdii* (Fig. 3.5). These two, together with Dartnall's earlier (1962) measurements from the humpback whale, *Megaptera nodosa* (Fig. 3.6) represent widely different ecological habits. The beaked whale

Fig. 3.4. The grey whale *Eschrichtius gibbosus*.

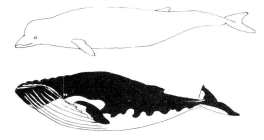

Fig. 3.5. The beaked whale *Berardius bairdii.*

Fig. 3.6. The humpback whale *Megaptera nodosa.*

belongs to a family Ziphiidae which is characteristically a deep-diving group. It is supposed to dive to 2400 m when harpooned and the specimen that McFarland used must have descended to at least 1000 m after it was hit. The absorption maximum of 481_1 nm for this specimen is typical of mesopelagic fishes and must surely be an adaptation to the mesopelagic environment which it visits on its feeding forays. The grey whale has a rhodopsin of λ_{max} 497 which is typical of coastal water fish and which correlates well with the non-oceanic habits of this whale. The grey whale adults spend the summer in the shallow waters of the Bering and Okhotsk seas; during the autumn and early winter, they migrate south either to Korea or Baja, California, where the young are born in shallow lagoons and bays, the family returning northward in spring. During this entire migration, the grey whales are thought to remain near the surface. The humpback whales spend their summers in high latitudes feeding near the surface, and their winters near the equator, where they do not feed but nevertheless descend to 1000 m or more where they vocalize vociferously. The humpback whale has a 491_1 visual pigment which is intermediate between the 497_1 of the shallow-living grey whale and the 481_1 of the deep-diving beaked whale.

Invertebrates

The general rule that the λ_{max} of the visual pigments are related to the spectral distribution of the ambient light appears to hold for invertebrates

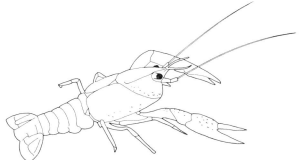

Fig. 3.7. The fresh-water crayfish *Procambarus* sp.

as well as vertebrates. In a review Goldsmith (1972) points out that deep-sea crustacea possess visual pigments of maximum absorbance between 462_1 and 480_1 nm whilst species living in shallower, more turbid water have pigments of maximum absorbance between 500_1 and 525_1 nm. Two freshwater crayfish, *Orconectes* and *Procambarus* (Fig. 3.7), each contain a 562_1-nm and a 510_1-nm pigment. The crabs do not fit the general scheme particularly well, but Goldsmith believes that the spectrum of crab rhodopsin is altered when the pigment molecules are extracted with detergent from the rhabdomeric membranes.

Offset visual pigments

Visual explanations

It was once thought that the typical rhodopsin wavelength of 500 nm was so located in the spectrum because 500 nm is near to the wavelength of maximum energy of sunlight. However, when the available data for sunlight and moonlight are presented in the correct photon units it is clear that a 500_1 rhodopsin does not absorb maximally at sufficiently long wavelengths for maximum sensitivity (see pp. 2–5).

It has been suggested (Lythgoe 1966, 1972) that a visual pigment of λ_{max} offset from the wavelength of maximum water transparency would have an advantage in the detection of bright objects against the water background. Although arguments of this sort appear to be correct in a formal sense (Munz and McFarland 1977; Easter 1975), their general application to scotopic vision is limited because they apply only to close objects somewhat brighter than the background. The present consensus of opinion appears to be that the theory of offset pigments is best applied to photopic vision (see pp. 136–9).

Visual noise from heat quanta

There is a possibility that at very long wavelengths heat quanta emitted by the animal's own body may sometimes trigger a visual signal. If this is so, an animal would see the infrared radiation produced by its own body and the meaningful images of the outside world would be degraded by heat noise. The effects of infrared noise would be worse at night since the infrared from a warm body would stay much the same when it gets dark but the amount of 'visible' light would decrease. There are fairly strong reasons to suspect that the need to avoid infrared visual noise is at least part of the reason why the visual pigments that mediate night vision absorb at shorter wavelengths than one might expect if sensitivity was the only criterion.

With present techniques it is impossible to find out by spectroscopic means whether the visual pigment molecule is more sensitive to longwave radiation when warm because at wavelengths beyond about 680 or 700 nm absorption of the pigment extract is so slight as to be unmeasurable. However, Stiles (1948) and Barlow (1957) have developed the view that thermal energy from molecular movements contributes some energy to the visual pigment molecule such that energy from this source combines with the energy provided by an infrared quantum to provide enough energy to initiate a visual signal.

Rhodopsins and porphyropsins

Distribution of porphyropsins

Porphyropsins have been found in the retinas of Agnatha, fishes, amphibia. and reptiles but not yet in mammals or birds, nor in any invertebrates. Where it occurs all the visual pigment may be porphyropsin, or it may be present in conjunction with rhodopsin. The possession of porphyropsin is closely linked with an aquatic mode of life and with a few exceptions it is confined to freshwater and brackish-water species (see Bridges 1972; Knowles and Dartnall 1977; Munz and McFarland 1977). The ready explanation for this is that porphyropsins absorb at longer wavelengths than their rhodopsin analogues and would thus be more sensitive in fresh water, which is normally somewhat redder than sea water. Whether or not the shift in spectral sensitivity of the rods that results from the rhodopsin–porphyropsin change actually enhances sensitivity is not certain. It seems more likely that if the change has a visual significance it is associated with the proportionally much greater shift in sensitivity of the red-sensitive cones (see pp. 51–2).

The correlation between the presence of porphyropsins and the fresh-water habit is well-illustrated in animals that spend only part of their life in fresh water. Adult terrestrial amphibians have rhodopsin with λ_{max} at 501–5 nm whereas their aquatic larvae have porphyropsins of λ_{max} near 522 nm (for a review see Bridges 1972). The change is not a necessary result of metamorphosis since in amphibia, which have an aquatic adult stage like *Xenopus* and *Necturus*, the larval porphyropsin is retained. An exception to this rule is found in the toads where in *Bufo halophilus* and *B. bufo* both the tadpoles and the adults have pure rhodopsin retinas.

Migratory fishes

Several species of fish move between fresh and salt water in the course of their breeding migrations. There is evidence that in several species the retina is porphyropsin-dominated in fresh water and rhodopsin-dominated in salt water. Of the several examples quoted by Munz and McFarland (1977) the most clear-cut are the coho salmon (*Oncorhyncus kisutch*), king salmon (*O. tsawytscha*), and the pink salmon (*O. gorbuscha*); which were studied in detail by Beatty (1966). These species have a 503-rhodopsin and its 527-porphyropsin analogue. During their non-breeding marine stage, the retinas are dominated by rhodopsin but as the fish move into tidewater at the start of their upstream breeding migration, there begins a gradual switch to a retina dominated by a porphyropsin that can account for over 90 per cent of the visual pigment. The adults apparently do not survive to return to the sea. Hatchery-reared king and coho salmon juveniles have a high proportion of porphyropsin in their retina, but whether the change-over to rhodopsin takes place before or after the fish return to the sea is not known. In the sockeye salmon (*O. nerka*) the position is not so clear-cut for these have a rhodopsin-dominated retina at all times with only a slight increase in porphyropsin at spawning time.

A shift in the balance between rhodopsin and porphyropsin can also be observed in land-locked and nonmigratory fishes and changes in daylength and hormonal balance can also produce such changes. In this chapter we have been considering only sensitivity changes that result from the rhodopsin–porphyropsin shift. However, it is clear that the effect of this shift gets greater as the λ_{max} of the pigment increases. The effect on scotopic vision may be small, but the effect on cone-mediated photopic vision, especially at longer wavelengths, may be profound and will be considered in Chapter 5.

The freshwater eels of Europe and North America (*Anguilla anguilla* (Fig. 3.8) and *A. rostrata* respectively) have a bizarre life history that

Fig. 3.8. The freshwater eel *Anguilla anguilla*. The main drawing is of the yellow (immature) form. The head is of the silver (mature) form which has larger eyes.

involves a journey of thousands of miles from their breeding grounds in the deep, blue waters of the Sargasso Sea to the freshwater rivers and ponds where they spend their immature adult life, and then back again to the Sargasso Sea. During their freshwater phase they have visual pigments typical of a freshwater fish, but in their deep-ocean phase, their visual pigments change to a set typical of a deep-sea fish. (See Bridges (1972), Crescitelli (1972), Beatty (1975), and Munz and McFarland (1977) for reviews.)

In the immature freshwater phase familiar to the angler, the body is yellow-brown, has a well-developed gut, a swim bladder, and small eyes from which a porphyropsin-523 and a rhodopsin-501 pair can be extracted. When the time comes for breeding, the eel begins a downstream migration during which time the eye and gonads get larger and the gut and swim bladder shrink. Within the eye the rhodopsin–porphyropsin balance swings entirely to rhodopsin and a second rhodopsin based on a different opsin makes its appearance (Wald 1958, 1960). For the American eel, the second rhodopsin has a λ_{max} of 482 nm (Beatty 1975). The overall sensitivity of the 501 and 482 pigments lies between the two values and is what one might expect in mesopelagic fishes.

Indeed, it is possible that the sexually mature silver eel is a truly mesopelagic fish. They are rarely caught in the ocean phase of their breeding migration and it is only by chance that they are found. The fate of the eels after spawning is unknown; but since they have no functional gut and do not re-appear on the mainland coasts as adults, it is presumed that they die.

There is evidence that spawning in both species occurs at depths of at least 400 m and the *Leptocephalus* larvae drift on the ocean currents to Europe and North America. The journey from the Sargasso Sea to the European coast takes some three years; the journey to America is much shorter. Near the coast the larvae metamorphose into the young adult elver form. A few of these remain in coastal water but the great majority migrate upstream and settle down for the 9–12 years of their mature adult life in freshwater rivers and lakes.

Luminance levels and lifestyle

Dim-light birds

The night-time is remarkable for the absence of birds. It is something of a puzzle why the amphibia and small mammals, for example, are so active at night when only a few birds such as the owls and nightjars are abroad. Flight poses difficult problems in dim light because images typically move fast across the retina and a high photon flux is needed to detect them (see

p. 68). However, bats also fly and the more relevant question may be why bats have developed an echo-location system, whereas birds, for all their acute hearing and variety of voice, have only rarely done so.

Martin (1977) has made a special study of the vision of the tawny owl, *Strix aluco* (Fig. 3.9). It shows various anatomical modifications to increase sensitivity including tubular eyes with a small f-number and very few coloured oil droplets in the retina. Nevertheless, using behavioural techniques, Martin has shown that the tawny owl is only about half a log unit more sensitive than man. The key to the owl's ability to catch small animals at night is as much to do with their exceptionally acute hearing, which allows them to pounce on their prey in total darkness, as it is due to superior visual performance (Payne 1962; Macdonald 1976). It is probably misleading to consider the senses of vision and hearing in isolation from each other. The information supplied by each must be integrated by the bird to give it enough information to locate and capture its prey.

Apart from the difficulties of flight, birds have an extra disadvantage in dim light, for their colour discrimination requires coloured oil droplets in the cones. These must necessarily reduce sensitivity which is likely to be especially disadvantageous at twilight, The proportion of orange and red coloured oil droplets is around 50 per cent for diurnal birds in general, but in nocturnal species the proportion is around 10 per cent (Table 3.1). The

Table 3.1 Proportion of oil droplets that are coloured in bird cones

Bird	Proportion (%)	Reference
(a) Nocturnal birds		
Caprimulgus europeaus Nightjar	10	Peiponen (1964)
Strix aluco Tawny owl	None[1]	Erhard (1924)
Tylo alba Barn owl	None	Erhard (1924)
(b) Swallows and swifts		
Apus apus Swift	6	Krause (1894)
	2–3	Peiponen (1964)
Hirundo rustica Swallow	10	Krause (1894)
	12	Peiponen (1964)
Riparia riparia Sand martin	9–10	Peiponen (1964)
Delichon urbica House martin	14–15	Peiponen (1964)

[1] Dr Bowmaker (private communication) tells me there are, in fact, a very few coloured oil droplets in the Tawny owl.

owls were once thought to have no coloured oil droplets at all (Erhard 1924) but Bowmaker has recently told me that the tawny owl has all the expected types of oil droplets although coloured ones are very sparse. The swallows and swifts are noteworthy because they too have few coloured oil

Fig. 3.9. The tawny owl *Strix aluco.*

droplets (Table 3.1). This could be to enable them to see their insect prey silhouetted against the sky (p. 133). It could also be that, like the European swift, *Apus apus*, which can remain on the wing throughout the night (Lack 1956), birds with few coloured oil droplets have a tendency to be more active than most in dim light.

There seem to be no truly cavernicolous birds. Probably the food available in caves is not sufficient to maintain their metabolism, but in any case they have not developed the echo-location sense to anything approaching the extent achieved by bats. The oil bird, *Steatornis caripensis* (Fig. 3.10), and various species of swiftlet of the genus *Collacalia* (Fig. 3.11)

Fig. 3.10. The oil bird *Steatornis caripensis.*

(whose nests go to make birds' nest soup), roost and fly in caverns so dark that the dark-adapted human eye can detect no light at all in them (Griffin 1958). Both the oil bird and the swiftlets have retained eyes of about normal size, presumably because they forage for food outside the

Fig. 3.11. The swiftlet *Collacalia* sp.

cave; the oil birds feeding at night on the hard fruit of the oil palm and the swiftlets feeding by day on insects.

The ability of the oil bird and some species of swiftlets, such as *Collacalia vanikosensis granti*, to fly in the dark is probably due to an echo-location sense (Griffin 1958; Griffin and Suthers 1970). The noise these birds use to generate echoes is a series of sharp clicks repeated several times a second. Griffin also mentions the possibility that the nighthawk, which is a close relative of the European nightjar, uses the echoes of its rasping voice as a method of locating its insect food.

Transition from day to night

Most animals are profoundly influenced by the huge changes in luminance that accompany the transition from day to night. Mostly they arrange their lives so that periods of greatest activity occur at particular periods in the 24 hours. Occasionally, even for the strictest time-keepers, the natural vagaries of life enforce activity outside these hours, often in conditions of great stress and danger. Other animals, particularly the larger mammals, fishes and amphibians, may be quite active at all times. These animals have both rods and cones in sufficiently large numbers to confer good, but not outstandingly good, vision by day and by night.

For maximum efficiency of vision, it is necessary for the eyes to be adapted to the illumination level that they are in fact experiencing at the time. Around dawn and dusk, the light level changes very rapidly, per-haps by a log unit every 10 minutes. Neural and pupillary adaptation mechanisms are sufficiently fast to keep the eye in the correct adaptation state, but they are not by themselves sufficient to cope with the large differ-ence between night and day. The slower changes associated with the regeneration of visual pigment in the rods and the migration of screening pigments lag behind the changes in the ambient daylight, which may mean that some animals are less efficient at dawn and dusk.

It is only rarely possible to give actual rates for dark adaptation that are relevant to ecological situations since the techniques for making such measurements are generally to isolate and describe particular physiological mechanisms rather than to study the ecology and behaviour of the animal in nature (p. 80). Also the brightness of the light used in pre-adaptation is of very great influence on the time course of subsequent dark adaptation. Barlow (1972a) has pointed out that the photopic and scotopic limits of the dark adaptation curve are normally demonstrated only after unnaturally bright pre-adaptation and indeed it is often to demonstrate the presence of these limits that the experiment was conducted. Nevertheless, in the cases where more or less 'natural' conditions of pre-adaptation were used, it seems as though the time course of adaptation for photopic to scotopic vision would approximately follow the natural fall in ambient light at dusk.

In general, therefore, it seems true to say that the rate of dark adaptation keeps pace with the decreasing daylight—but only just. An animal might well encounter difficulties in dark adaptation—and hence contrast dis-crimination—if a cloud obscured the sky or if the animal moved under-neath a leaf canopy at the critical time just before sunrise and just after sunset when the underlying changes in light intensity are most rapid. Light adaptation is much more rapid than dark adaptation and there can be little doubt that it is fast enough to keep pace with the transition from night to day.

Diving mammals

Diving animals have a special problem in dark adaptation because they may experience very rapid changes in light from bright sunlight at the surface to almost total darkness at depth. The elephant seal (*Mirounga angustirostris*) (Fig. 3.12) may dive to at least 100 fathoms (Scheffer 1964);

Fig. 3.12. The elephant seal *Mirounga augustirostris*.

the Weddell seal swims under ice 200 m thick and recording bathymeters attached to them have recorded depths of 350 m (de Vries and Wohlschlag 1964). The time course for such divers are uncertain, but Harrison and Tomlinson (1964) have shown that the common seal can be submerged to a depth of 30 fathoms for five minutes.

Whether or not most diving mammals dive faster into the water than they can adapt to the rapidly decreased light intensity, the newest recruit to their ranks, *Homo sapiens*, certainly has a problem (Hemmings and Lythgoe 1964). A scuba diver can easily swim downwards at around 30 m/min and usually does so in order to give himself the maximum time on the bottom. In coastal and fresh water, it is common for the water to be so

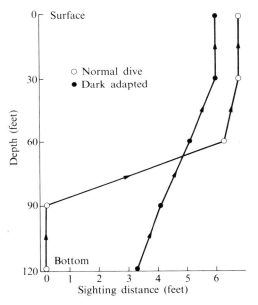

Fig. 3.13. The sighting distance of a black target, 6 × 6 in. viewed horizontally with and without dark adaptation at various depths in turbid water. The experiments were conducted at 11.00 a.m. on a cloudless day in March. The Scuba diver donned a red face plate and, after wearing it for 40 minutes, dived down a shot line to the bottom. On the bottom he changed the red face plate for a normal clear one and at intervals on the way up measured the sighting distance. At the surface he lingered for a few minutes to light-adapt and then dived to the bottom and repeated the measurements. Dark-adapted he could see the target at all depths and at 120 ft and 90 ft bioluminescence was very obvious. Light-adapted, it was subjectively dark with no bioluminescence at the 90 and 120 ft depths.

murky that it seems pitch dark at 30 m or less. After about 20 minutes on the bottom, the diver gets the strong subjective impression that visibility has improved and there is a just perceptible amount of light present. The improvement is, of course, due to the increased sensitivity of the eye through dark adaptation rather than any increased clarity of the water. If the diver pre-adapts by wearing a red faceplate and changes this for a clear one on the bottom, he is immediately aware that he can see, whereas without pre-adaptation it seems completely dark. The results of one such experiment are shown in Fig. 3.13. It was conducted at 11.00 a.m. on a cloudless day in April. The site was near-inshore off the south-west coast of Wales and the horizontal visibility about 6 ft. This is about average to bad visibility for that coast. Below about 80 ft a dark-adapted diver could see, but a light-adapted one could not. A striking observation on that occasion was that even at about 80 ft, in the middle of the day, bioluminescent plankters were abundant and were by far the most visible objects.

There is no doubt that a diving mammal can easily outswim a scuba diver, but has an even more limited time on the bottom. It would be interesting to know if they have any special adaptations, especially concerned with the rate of rhodopsin regeneration, to increase the rate of dark adaptation during a dive.

Diel activity on coral reefs

The coral reef provides a superb arena for observing fishes at different times of day and night (Hobson 1965, 1972; Stark and Davis 1966; Collette and Talbot 1972) because fishes often seem quite untroubled by a diver, provided he is a few metres away, and nowhere else can so many species be observed together at one time. Hobson observed that most reef fishes are either nocturnal or diurnal. During the active period their behaviour is dominated by feeding, and in the inactive period by the need to find security (Hobson 1972). It is a reasonable assumption that specialist nocturnal and diurnal species become less efficient visually when the light intensity gets brighter or darker than the range for which they are adapted. For their own security, both nocturnal and diurnal species need to remain in a place of safety during dawn and dusk. Predators have a different requirement for they need to encounter their prey at a time when it is visually disadvantaged relative to themselves. The periods of dawn and dusk are times of heavy predation (Fig. 3.14) (Hobson 1972; Collette and Talbot 1972; Ehrlich, Talbot, Russell, and Anderson 1977) and although we have little evidence, it seems reasonable that the visual systems of predators are tuned to function best at the intermediate intensities of dawn and dusk.

To the human observer, the change-over from the daytime population to the night-time one has an eerie quality but has a precisely timed

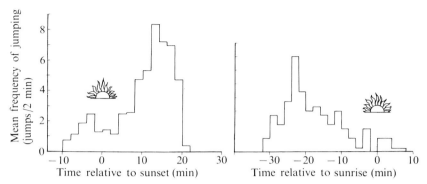

Fig. 3.14. Frequency of predation at dawn and dusk as measured by the frequency of jumping by the cabrilla *Mycteroperca rosacea* when preying on schooling *Harengula thrissina* in the Gulf of California. (From Hobson 1972.)

sequence of events (Fig. 3.15). Up until sunset the daytime populations of trigger fishes (Balistidae), surgeon fishes (Acanthuridae), parrot fishes (Scaridae), and wrasses (Labridae) are normally active in the water column although mid-water plankton-feeders like the damsel fishes (Pomacentridae) sink progressively lower in the water column as the light decreases. Some species show changes in behaviour, such as the aggrega-tion of normally solitary individuals and an increase in aggression near favoured night-time roosts (Hobson 1972; Ehrlich *et al.* 1977). A few minutes before sunset, the wrasse, which are amongst the first to take

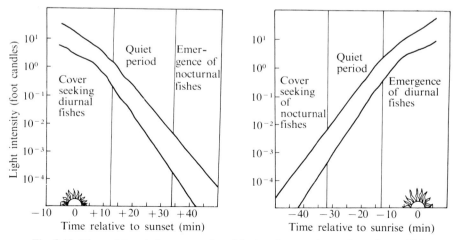

Fig. 3.15. The quiet periods on a coral reef during the morning and evening twilight periods relative to sunset (*left*) and sunrise (*right*). The diagonal band represents the normal variation in ambient light intensity. During the quiet periods the water column is substantially emptied of fishes except for predators. (Simplified from Hobson 1972.)

cover, occupy their roosts in crevices in the coral and by five minutes after sunset very few wrasse are to be seen at all. By 10–15 minutes after sunset, most of the diurnal species have taken cover and the evening quiet period has begun. It lasts for about 20 minutes until 30–5 minutes after sunset the observer suddenly realizes that, seen in the dim light, the water is once again filled with fishes, but this time it is the nocturnal squirrel and soldier fishes (Holocentridae), the cardinal fishes (Apogonidae), and several species of scorpaenid fishes that either remain hidden deep in the reef fissures in the daytime or keep close to the shelter of the reef.

Colonization of a shallower habitat

From our land-based perspective it seems natural that it is the deep-sea environment that is the difficult one to master, and that the drift of evolution has been to progressive adaptation to ever deeper habitats. Perhaps this is so, but in at least some instances representatives of taxonomic groups adapted to live in the deep oceans are gradually becoming re-adapted for life in shallower water.

The flashlight fish, *Photoblepharon pelabratus* (Fig. 3.16), is a bioluminess-

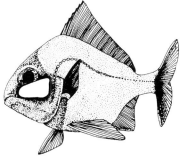

Fig. 3.16. The flashlight fish *Photoblepharon pelabratus.*

cent fish belonging to the order Beryciformes that has many deep water representatives. During the daylight hours it finds a dark refuge amongst the deep caves and fissures that honeycomb the coral reef. At night, if the moon is not too bright, it emerges to feed in schools along the reef front. It apparently uses its photophores in several different ways (Morin, Harrington, Nealson, Krieger, Baldwin, and Hastings 1975) such as to confuse predators and to illuminate and attract invertebrates on which it feeds. One very large family (Holocentridae) within the Beryciformes contains the squirrel and soldier fishes which are common on shallow tropical coral reefs. The soldier and squirrel fish retain several deep-water characteristics including large, rod-dominated eyes, red coloration, and a nocturnal habit. Many species do not, in fact, retire into the deep reef labyrinth but lurk in the entrance to their holes. Since they are often exposed to direct daylight, we must suppose that they are not damaged by it, but that they retain characteristics useful to a nocturnal predator.

The pearlfishes (Carapidae), which belong to the predominantly deep-water family Brotulidae, also manage to live in shallow water—not by inhabiting caves but by spending the daylight hours within the respiratory tree of sea cucumbers and less commonly in other echinoderms (Stark and Davis 1966). Pearlfishes are transparent with occasional pigment spots. Those organs that cannot be made transparent, such as gut and brain, are strongly silvered, presumably for camouflage. The eye has particular interest for that, too, has a silvered surface, including the iris which, according to Walls (1942), can be constricted to restrict the pupil aperture in bright light. Indeed, the pupil becomes so small that it requires a lens

Fig. 3.17. Norway lobsters, *Nephrops norvegicus*, at the mouth of their burrows in a muddy bottom. (From Chapman and Rice 1971; photograph by John Main, Crown copyright.)

to see it. The retina of one, *C. homei*, would give rise to no comment in a mesopelagic fish for it contains predominantly, perhaps entirely, rods that are stacked five or six deep to give an exceptionally deep photon-catching layer.

The Norway lobster, *Nephrops norvegicus*, (Fig. 3.17) is another good example of an animal that has extended its vertical range upwards by taking refuge from the brightest light (see p. 61). Most of its family (Nephropidae) are deep-water prawns, and only rarely, as in the case of lobster, *Homarus*, are there truly shallow-water representatives. The Norway lobster is an animal of considerable commercial importance because its tail provides scampi—a ubiquitous dish on restaurant menus. It is caught by trawling over soft muddy bottoms on the European continental shelf. Trawler skippers have long known that adequate catches can be obtained, even on fishing grounds of known productivity, only at particular times of day. The complication is that the best time for trawling varies from ground to ground and upon the degree of overcast of the sky.

Direct observations by divers (Chapman and Rice 1971; Chapman, Johnstone, and Rice 1975) show that *Nephrops* lives in deep and complex burrows, which it excavates itself in the firm, silty mud of the bottom

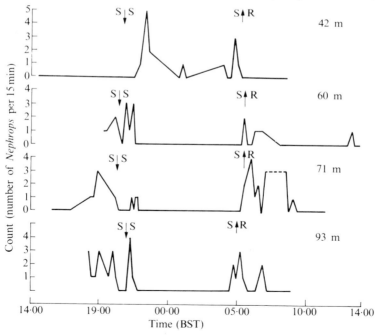

Fig. 3.18. Counts of the number of Norway lobster, *Nephrops norvegicus*, observed by underwater television in different Scottish lochs by day and night. (From Chapman, Johnstone, and Rice 1975.)

(Fig. 3.17). Trawling is effective only when the animals have left their burrows to feed—at all other times the trawl scrapes harmlessly across the mouth of the burrows. *Nephrops* appears to leave its burrows only when the light has fallen to a certain rather dim level and the times of emergence are related to the depth that it lives. In shallower water the animal is nocturnal; in deeper water it is more diurnal in its activity pattern (Fig. 3.18).

The shunning of bright light is not simply a device for avoiding visual predators, for as Loew (1976) has shown, the rhabdomes themselves degenerate irreversibly if exposed for less than an hour to light which to us is a comfortable intensity for reading.

The eye possesses features that one expects to find in crustaceans living in dimly lit places. There is no distal screening pigment migration in the light; the proximal screening pigment has a low mobility and is, in any case, present in low concentrations never actually screening the rhabdomes. Also, the well-developed tapetum is characteristic of nocturnal eyes. Because the need for rapid regeneration of photobleached visual pigment would be minimal, Loew proposes that the slow rate of regeneration of visual pigment in *Nephrops* eyes which would never naturally be exposed to bright light is responsible for the degeneration of the rhabdomes.

Vertical migration and the isolume

The open ocean can be divided into three horizontal zones according to whether there is enough light for both photosynthesis and vision, enough light for vision alone, or too little for either. The top zone is the euphotic or photosynthetic zone and contains the epipelagic fauna. The middle zone is the twilight zone and contains the mesopelagic fauna, and the deepest zone is the dark zone containing the bathypelagic fauna. The suffix pelagic refers to the free swimming or free-floating modes of life. Benthic refers to organisms closely associated with the bottom, and demersal animals tend to live in close association with the bottom but often swim above it. The actual depths of the three zones, of course, depend upon the clarity of the sea but it is conventional to consider that the epipelagic zone extends from the surface to 200 m, the mesopelagic zone from 200–1000 m and the bathypelagic zone deeper than 1000 m. In even the clearest waters Steeman Nielsen (1974) calculated that the theoretical lower limit of photosynthetic production is about 140 m, a figure that is approached in the exceptionally clear waters of the Sargasso Sea where photosynthetic production has been measured at 120 m.

Phytoplankton, which show little or no vertical migration, are thus concentrated in the upper 140 m of water and any animal that feeds directly upon them must also feed in this shallow surface layer. The light intensity required for photosynthesis is considerably greater than that needed for photopic vision (Clarke and Denton 1962) so that herbivorous zooplankton are exposed to efficient vision-aided predators.

Zooplankters such as the copepods and euphausiids that depend in large part for their food on phytoplankton (Makoto Omari 1974; Mauchline and Fisher 1969) ascend into the phytoplankton-rich zone during the night and sink to deeper water during the day, perhaps avoiding the worse of visual predation. Rising and falling in synchrony with the primary herbivores are many other species of zooplankton and fishes that feed on them. In addition, there are many species that undertake vertical migrations, but nevertheless never ascend into the euphotic zone (see, for instance, Foxton 1970a, b; Badcock 1970; Makoto Omari 1974; Mauchline and Fisher 1969).

Pelagic fishes (Blaxter 1976) and invertebrates (Waterman 1974) often keep within a preferred band of light intensity which effectively means that they move up in the water column as the surface light decreases and down as it increases. Although light-mediated, the response may not be visual. Indeed, Wales (1974) has shown that blinded herring larvae retain their ability to migrate up and down in a water column in the laboratory in response to changing light intensity.

The major influence of light on depth selection is shown by the reaction of vertical migrants to unusual changes in light intensity, such as solar eclipses, artificial light, and the full moon (see Blaxter (1976) for a review) Herring (Fig. 3.19) have been much studied because of their commercial

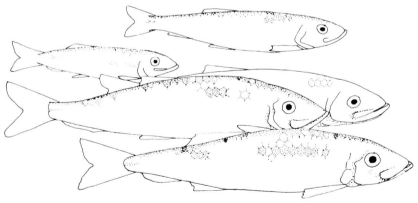

Fig. 3.19. Herring *Clupea harengus*.

importance. For centuries their schools have been caught at night in drift nets set at the surface of the North Sea (see Woodhead 1966), whilst in the daytime they sink deep into the sea, or if there is insufficient depth, the school hugs the bottom. In reasonably open water the herring move vertically so that they are always exposed to about the same light intensity;

and by knowing the depth of a particular school at a particular light intensity, it is possible to predict the depth that school will be hours in advance.

The value of correlated migration and light intensity studies, whilst consistent within themselves, is often weakened because both the spectral sensitivity of the animal and the spectral irradiance must be measured (see pp. 2–4). It is within this context that the work of Kampa and Boden (1957) and Kampa (1970) is of such value. During the SOND cruise undertaken in 1965 aboard the RRS *Discovery*, a sonic scattering layer was identified at all four stations. Although the midday depth of the layer varied from about 250 m in the Portugal station to about 600 m in the Tenerife station, the actual light intensity at the middle depth of the layer was between 1·5 and 3 $\times$ 10^{-5} μW cm^{-2} nm^{-1} at 470 (or 480) nm ($= 3\cdot6$–$7\cdot3$ $\times 10^7$ photons cm^{-2} s^{-1} nm^{-1}) for the three coastal stations (Portugal, Fuerteventura, and Tenerife). At the more oceanic Madeira station, the mid-layer irradiance level was somewhat greater, 8 $\times$ 10^{-5} μW cm^{-2} nm^{-1} at 480 nm ($=1\cdot9 \times 10^8$ photons cm^{-2} s^{-1} nm^{-1}).

The difference in preferred light intensity between different species and different stages in the life history of the same animal is to be expected since different animals migrate through different depth ranges. For the SOND cruise these have been described by Baker, A de C. (1970) for euphausiids, Thurston (1976a, b) for amphipods, Foxton (1970a, b) for decapods, and Badcock (1970) for fishes.

In the case of the sonic scattering layer on the SOND cruise, the animals were keeping to a light intensity not greatly different from the absolute limit of sensitivity that can be expected of any eye. Below this depth vertical migration is much less prevalent. There are also more or less non-migratory inhabitants of the euphotic zone (see, for instance, Thurston (1976) for amphipods). Most animals, however, are migratory and do remain fairly strictly within their preferred isolumes. It is likely that the eyes of these species are tuned to function at particular levels of light intensity and are able to dispense with the elaborate morphological and neural switching mechanisms associated with the changeover between photopic and scotopic vision. Specializations for vision near absolute threshold are generally easy to recognize, as are those for strictly diurnal vision. But it is in the mesopic range that marine creatures are often of most interest. Specialization for intermediate light intensities have scarcely been studied, even though they are likely to be of great ecological and evolutionary importance.

Other depth-controlling factors

Of all the depth-related environmental variables, hydrostatic pressure progresses most regularly with increasing depth. The pressure increase is about 1 atmosphere for each 10 m of depth, depending on salinity and temperature, therefore abyssal forms can tolerate at least 1000 atmospheres. Ekman (1953) gives instances of animals which can live from a few tens of metres of the surface down to abyssal depths; it is temperature that seems to be a more important factor than hydrostatic pressure. Vertically migrating animals suffer enormous pressure differences twice within the day; for instance, the myctophid fish, *Ceratoscopelus maderensis*, migrates through 650 m (Goodyear, Zahuranec, Pugh, and Gibbs 1972) and thus survives a pressure change of 65 atmospheres. The changes in the volume of closed gas-filled spaces in both vertebrates and invertebrates are used as pressure, and hence depth sensors, but because hydrostatic pressure does not show diel variation, it cannot by itself regulate diel vertical migration.

The temperature near the surface of the sea is generally greater than that near the bottom, but the temperature–depth profile varies greatly between different bodies of water. Whilst the effect of pressure on the physiology of an organism is uncertain, the effect of temperature is real and over-rides any effect of pressure (see, for instance, Marshall 1971).

The temperature does not decrease steadily with depth, but rather in a series of steps or thermoclines. These thermoclines can be very sharp and often mark the boundary between two water layers flowing in different directions so there is a current-sheer at the interface (Woods 1971). So sharp are these thermoclines, at least in shallow water, that they can actually be seen, betrayed in part by light-refractive effects at the interface between waters of different densities, and in part by small plankton and organic debris that sink in the less dense upper layer but float in the more dense lower layer.

These temperature discontinuities may have some influence on diel vertical migrations (see, for instance, Mauchline and Fisher (1969) and Marshall (1971)). In some instances, the deep permanent thermocline occurs at around 1000 m and it has been suggested that the 10 °C isotherm marks the boundary between the mesopelagic and bathypelagic faunas (Bruun 1957). However, Marshall's view is that the transition depth between the mesopelagic fauna correlates better with light than temperature (see p. 104).

Visual regression

Animals that habitually live in dim light adapt themselves to it in various ways such as by increasing the numerical aperture of the pupil, increasing the depth of the visual pigment layer, providing reflecting tapeta and so forth (pp. 104–5). If there is absolutely no light, as in deep caves, the eyes are useless and they regress to such an extent that in some animals, such as the adult cave salamander, *Proteus*, and the newly described Iranian cave fish, *Noemacheilus smithi*, the eyes are altogether absent (Greenwood 1976). It is more common, however, to find that when the conditions for vision have become so difficult that investment in bigger and more specialized eyes no longer results in a worth-while return in visual information, the eyes regress but do not entirely disappear. Apparently the small amount of information that the eyes can still give is worth having but they have been relegated in importance.

There comes a Quit point at which visual conditions are so difficult that the animal abandons vision as a prime sense. Several groups that have reached the Quit point are described below and also in Chapter 4. Frequently these have the ability to develop other senses, such as echo-location, the water displacement sense, and electroreception that can substitute for vision by giving some spatial information about the surroundings. Animals such as nocturnal cats and the deep-living cephalopods that have no suitable alternative senses continue to invest in their visual apparatus at a point when other animals like the bats and the fishes have developed other senses to substitute for vision.

The faunal break

Clarke and Denton (1962) consider that in the very clearest water fishes should be able to distinguish daylight down to about 1000 m; a figure that is accepted in the more precise calculations of Dartnall (1975). This figure of 1000 m is, of course, not a fixed quantity. Clarke and Kelly (1964) who measured light penetration in the Indian Ocean, conclude that the greatest depth for vision could vary between 700 m and 1300 m. Since the boundary between the twilight zone and dark zone is set by the lower limit of vision, it follows that in these waters the boundary between the meso-pelagic and bathypelagic fauna that respectively inhabit the two zones, is somewhere between 700 and 1300 m.

The mesopelagic and bathypelagic zones each have their characteristic assemblage of animals. Inhabitants of the bathypelagic zone do not, in general, migrate up into the mesopelagic zone. The mesopelagic animals, both fish and invertebrates, generally have large well-developed eyes, photophores and often silvery, transparent or countershaded bodies. The bathypelagic animals have poorly-developed or regressed eyes, poorly-developed photophores and non-reflecting bodies that look red or black or brown when brought to the surface.

Marshall (1971) considers that the faunal break comes at about 1000 m, which he points out is Clarke and Denton's (1962) estimate for the lower limit of daylight vision for deep-sea fishes. Marshall's view that the faunal break comes at the downward limit of daylight vision is supported by the results of the 1965 SOND cruise in slightly less clear ocean water. Here the faunal break in the clearest stations occurred around 650–700 m. For decapods (Foxton 1970), amphipods (Thurston 1976), fishes (Badcock 1970). At this depth the downwelling diffuse light energy is about $10^{-6}\,\mu\mathrm{W}$ cm^{-2} nm^{-1} at 480 nm (Kampa 1970). This corresponds to light intensity in photons of $2\cdot4 \times 10^6$ photons s^{-1} cm^{-2} nm^{-1}.

Although it is not invariably true that fishes living below about 1000 m have regressed eyes (Locket 1971), the trend is clear enough (Munk 1966; Marshall 1971). Parallel with the regression of the eye is the regression of the photophores and it must be assumed that the integrated system of bioluminescence and vision is not usually useful enough to justify its retention at depths where there is no sunlight. The common occurrence of bioluminescence and highly specialized eyes in the twilight mesopelagic zone suggests that the prime function of bioluminescence is for camouflage (see pp. 175–6) and not for other uses, such as the creation of visual displays.

The Quit point in bats

Bats are one of the most successful, if not the most successful, groups of tropical mammals. There are two main sub-orders of bats: the Mega-chiroptera, which have well-developed eyes, feed on fruit, and include the flying foxes; and the Microchiroptera (Fig. 3.20), which have small eyes, a well-developed acoustic sense (Griffin 1958; Henson 1970), and feed on a variety of food including fruit, fish, blood, and insects. The relationship between the visual and acoustic senses in the Microchiroptera of the Caribbean, principally Trinidad, has been the subject of a study by Julia Chase in a Ph.D. thesis for the University of Indiana (Chase 1972).

Fig. 3.20. The little brown bat *Myotis lucifugus*.

Chase divided the Microchiroptera into three groups: I, nocturnal insectivorous and piscivorous; II, nocturnal non-insectivorous; and III, partially diurnal insectivorous (Table 3.2). The capture of insects is a

Table 3.2 Eye size in Microchiroptera

	$\dfrac{\text{Eye wt}}{\text{Body wt}} \times 10^4$	Food
GROUP I: Nocturnal, insectivorous		
Phyllostomidae		
Chilonycteris rubiquiosa	0·5	Insects
Pteronotus daryi	1·7	Insects
Mormoops megalophylla	1·3	Insects
Natalidae		
Natalus tumidirostris	1·0	Insects
Vespertidionidae		
Myotis lucifugus	4·4	Insects
Eptesicus fuscus	4·3	Insects
Plecotus townsendi	3·0	Insects
Molossidae		
Molossus ater	1·3	Insects
GROUP II: Nocturnal, non-insectivorous		
Phyllostomidae		
Micronycteris megalotis	1·7	Fruit
Phyllostomus hastatus	5·2	Fruit/flesh
Glossophaga soricina	6·9	Nectar
Anoura geoffroyi	9·3	Nectar
Carollia perspicillata	5·3	Fruit
Sturnira lilium	6·5	Fruit
Vampyrops helleri	20·2	Fruit
Artibeus jamaicensis	7·2	Fruit
Artibeus lituratus	5·0	Fruit
Desmodontidae		
Desmodus rotundus	3·8	Blood
Diaemus youngi	3·5	Blood
GROUP III: Insectivorous, partially diurnal		
Emballonuridae		
Rhynchiscus naso	15·3	Insects
Saccopteryx bilineata	14·8	Insects
Saccopteryx leptura	18·3	Insects

Source: Chase (1972).

particularly difficult task because they are both small and fast-moving. In the daytime there is sufficient light for the task, but at night the long retinal integration time required to detect an object of their small size even if it is stationary is too long to detect the same object in motion (see pp. 68–70). Bats that roost in well-lit and exposed places in the daytime (Group III) and are partially diurnal in their activity patterns, have large eyes and are generally rather poorly endowed with acoustic senses. The strictly nocturnal insectivorous bats, however sensitive, cannot use their eyes for hunting insects because there are simply not enough photons to carry the information that is needed. In these bats the eye is near vestigial and is probably used only for such crude tasks as detecting the light at the mouth of their roosting cave and perhaps for setting their internal clock. Group II bats are nocturnal, but their visual task is less exacting than that of the nocturnal insectivores because they seek large, slow-moving or stationary objects, such as nectar-bearing flowers, blood-bearing vertebrates, and fruit.

The eyes of the nocturnal bats (Groups I and II) usually have retinas adapted for low light levels with dense receptor layers which are highly convergent. By contrast, the partially diurnal Group III bats have eyes more typical of diurnal animals with lower receptor densities and less convergence. By comparison to the other two groups, the eyes of the Group I nocturnal insectivorous bats are tiny (Table 3.2), and despite their retinal organization for nocturnal vision, have very poor vision both in bright and dim light.

Cave fauna

Most groups of animals have contributed members to the cavernicolous fauna of which the insects, arachnids, crustacea, fishes, and amphibia are prominent (Vandel 1964). Walls (1942) points out that normal surface dwelling animals that stray into the subterranean world do not contribute to a standing population of cavernicolous animals. Instead, the species that manage to establish themselves are 'pre-adapted' to the extent that they already possess well-developed senses other than vision, and it is these that allow them to get along in the dark.

A prolific source of recruits for the true cave fauna comes from various families of catfishes. These have long chemosensory barbels around the mouth which they use to locate food when grubbing in the bottom. Like so many fishes that live on, or partially buried in, soft mud, the eyes are very small. The brotulids are another example of Walls's 'pre-adaptation'. These are mostly deep-bottom-living fishes, varying in colour from dark blue to pinkish. The head is provided with minute sensory barbels and the eyes are regressed. Some species, two of which are blind, have secondarily come up to live in the surface waters, and two species in Cuba (*Stygicola* and *Lucifuga*) and *Typhlias* in Yucatan have apparently taken up permanent residence in caves. Cave salamanders (*Proteus* and *Typhlofoton*) have eyes in the larval stage, but at metamorphosis these regress under the normal dark conditions of the cave. However, if the salamanders are reared in the light, there is no regression and the salamander adult has normal eyes.

In at least one species of blind cave fish (*Astyanax mexicanus*) (Fig. 3.21)

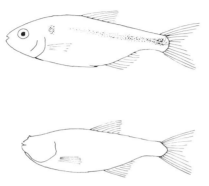

Fig. 3.21. Normally sighted and blind form of *Astyanax mexicanus.*

the larval fish have recognizable eyes but as the fish grows older these degenerate more and become covered with skin (Cahn 1958; Sadoglu 1957; Wilkins 1971). However, there is also a surface-living population of *Astyanax* that is normally sighted. By crossing the normal and blind varieties Sadoglu (1975) was able to show that in the blind population there are genes responsible for specific degenerative conditions in the eye.

Senses that substitute for vision

In deep caves where there is no light at all, the sense of vision is absolutely useless and an animal must rely on its other senses. In environments where there remains some residual light, some species may have hugely developed eyes in order to wrest the maximum possible information from what light there is, whereas others, although sharing the same light climate, may have regressed eyes but have developed alternative sensory systems. Which evolutionary path is taken seems to depend on whether the animal already has non-visual senses that can be developed. The deep-living cephalopods are an example. These have no lateral-line system like fishes and do not seem to have electric or complex auditory organs. Amongst the squids, vision remains a prime sense, at least judging by their eye size, at depths where many fishes have regressed eyes.

The senses that give the animal information about the spatial dis-
position of its surroundings are vision, hearing, the electrical sense, and
lateral-line sense. The senses of olfaction and taste are extremely sensitive
indicators of the chemical nature of the environment, but are not well
suited to tell much about the size, shape, and position of objects that the
animal is not actually touching. The chemical senses cannot substitute for
vision in the same way as hearing, the lateral-line, and electrical senses.

On the basis of embryology, morphology, and perhaps physiology as
well, these three senses plus the vestibular organs form a single organ
system collectively known as the acoustico lateralis (Russell and Sellick
1976). The environmental variables that are monitored by the various
subsystems of the acoustico lateralis and that give information about
spatial relationships are water displacement, compression waves in both
air and water, and the shape of electromagnetic fields. In the same way
that bioluminescence has been evolved to augment the sense of vision, so
techniques for producing sound and electric discharges to augment echo-
location and electroreception have been developed.

The sense of hearing monitors compression waves set up in the medium
by an oscillating body. Nocturnal animals often have particularly acute
hearing—the tawny owl (pp. 90–1) is an example—and one of the most
sensitive fishes to sound is the blind cave fish, *Astyanax jordani* (Popper
1970). However, it is when the animal uses the echoes from its own voice
that hearing becomes a real substitute for vision. The echo-location system
has reached its greatest refinement in the mammals. Bats are able to catch
flying insects by echo-location alone, and as a guide to their acuity, the little
brown bat, *Myotis lucifugus* (Fig. 3.20) is able to detect a wire 1 mm thick
between three and six feet away (Griffen 1958). Whales and dolphins
(Cetacea) are also able to detect objects by echolocation. The harbour
porpoise, *Phocaena phocaena*, and the Amazon river dolphin, *Inia geoffrensis*,
can avoid submerged wires about 1 mm in diameter; a level of performance comparable to that of bats. The Atlantic bottle-nosed porpoise,
Tursiops, is able to detect an air-filled cylinder 6 cm in diameter and 3 m
long at a range of 400 m (Evans 1973). The nearly blind Indian river
dolphin, *Platanista indi*, which lives in the silt-laden waters of the Ganges,
is known to be able to distinguish between whiting and mackerel (it prefers
whiting) when introduced to them in captivity (Pilleri 1974).

Water displacements are monitored by neuromast organs (Harris and
van Bergeijk, 1962) which are found in cyclostomes, fishes, and larval and
some adult aquatic amphibia. Neuromasts are generally arranged in lines
along the body, especially in the lateral line of fishes (Russell 1976). Each
neuromast organ is maximally sensitive to water displacements in a
particular direction so that an array of neuromasts can be used to distinguish the direction amplitude and wavelength of water displacement.
Almost any disturbance in the water, including movements of the animal

itself, will cause water displacements that will stimulate the neuromast organs. In particular useful information is likely to be gained from disturbances such as an insect floundering at the water surface (Schwartz 1971), the swimming movements of fishes (Pitcher, Partridge, and Wardle 1976), and nearby sound sources (Pumphrey 1950; Harris and van Bergeijk 1962). There must also be some information to be gained about fixed features, such as rocks, and sand ripples by the way that water flows around them.

The lateral-line system is particularly well developed in fishes living at low light levels. In species that live in the calm of very deep water or in caves, the neuromast organs are not protected in canals and grooves as they are in fishes living in more robust environments, but instead protrude directly into the water (Marshall 1971). Indeed, in some deep-living angler fishes, and in true cave fishes, the neuromast organs are actually stalked. There are few estimates on the useful range or resolution of the lateral line. Pumphrey (1950) estimates that a scabbard fish may be able to detect a mackerel-like fish at a range of 16–32 m and Schwartz (1974) estimates that some fishes may be able to detect a struggling insect trapped in the surface film 3–3·5 body lengths away.

Humans have nothing approaching an electric sense and it is hard to know how widespread it is in the animal kingdom. The electroreceptors are homologous to the neuromast organs that monitor water displacement, but instead monitor the strength and direction of voltage gradients in water. Often electrosensitive fishes live in silt-laden water and are nocturnal and have poorly developed eyes (Lissmann 1958). In extreme cases, like *Typhlonarke*, the animal is almost or entirely blind.

A body of different ionic composition to the surrounding water sets up an electric field around it. Fishes lying buried from sight in soft sand or mud set up electric fields, especially around the uninsulated respiratory and buccal membranes exposed during respiratory movements. Kalmijn (1974) has shown that dogfish (*Scyliorhinus* sp) and rays (*Raja* sp) are able to detect plaice at a range of 10 cm by electroreception.

Many species of fish possess electric organs that the pioneer work of Lissmann (1958) and Lissmann and Machin (1958) shows to be used both for communication and for getting spatial information about the near surroundings. The electric discharge sets up an electric field around the body. Objects that differ in electrical conductivity from the surrounding water alter the electric field in a way that the fish can interpret through the voltage changes monitored by the electroreceptors.

The weakly electric fishes may be divided into two groups, the 'hummers' and the 'buzzers'. The 'hummers' discharge a continuous sinusoidal wave of rather high frequency. This changes only at the approach of another fish that has a similar discharge frequency in order to prevent the two signals jamming each other. 'Buzzers' discharge at a lower variable frequency, the frequency increasing when something of interest is detected. The division between buzzers and hummers does not follow phyletic lines and one family may include species of both groups.

It is not yet certain what are the different capabilities of the wave species and the pulse species. Scheich and Bullock (1974) suggest that hummers are particularly suited for long distance social communication and have a good temporal acuity. Thus a fish that is moving rapidly in relation to its surroundings may use high frequency discharges. Buzzers may be better at assessing slow-moving or stationary objects, but are more easily jammed by other buzzing species and also by such natural events as lightning discharge. Scheich and Bullock remark that very little is known about the sensory capacity of electric fishes in nature, but it seems that electrolocation can be used for only a few centimetres around the fish.

Electroreception and the water displacement sense share a peculiar penalty that the senses of vision and hearing escape. The body must be elongate and held straight in the water, presumably so that the spatial relationship of the receptors, which extend along the length of the body, does not change. Lissmann (1958) has shown that electrically sensitive fishes tend to have a long dorsal fin that propels the animal by undulations along its length (Fig. 3.22). Many fishes that have a well-developed lateral

Fig. 3.22. The electric eel *Gymnarchus niloticus* showing undulations of the long dorsal fin typical of weakly electric species.

line and a good water displacement sense have two modes of swimming. In the slow mode, when the lateral line is most useful, the body is kept straight and is propelled by gentle undulations or sculling motions of the fins (Bone 1971; Marshall 1971). In the fast mode, the fish swims using violent undulations of the body which interferes with lateral line reception (Roberts and Russell 1972).

4 Vision through scattering media

Introduction

The light-scattering property of the atmosphere and water are amongst the most important and intractable factors that limit vision. On an even moderately misty day it is the scattered light in the atmosphere that obscures the distant landscape. Under water, scattering by suspended particles, such as sand and plankters, often reduces horizontal visibility from 50 m or so in clear water to small fractions of a metre when it is turbid.

The main problem is essentially one of visual noise for scattered light interposes a bright veil between the visual scene and the eye. It is not that the eye has inadequate sensitivity, but rather that it is sensitive to both the image-forming light that it requires to see and the non-image-forming scattered light that degrades brightness and colour contrasts.

Less important, perhaps, but nevertheless worth considering, is the problem of image-forming light that is deflected only slightly from the straight path between the object and the eye by large transparent plankters in the water, that have a similar, but not identical, refractive index to the water. Their effect is to spread the bright parts of an image into the darker parts, causing a blurring of the image.

The theory of contrast degradation

There are few options open to an animal that needs to see through scattering media. It may decrease its contrast-perception threshold to the physical and physiological limit, but there may be little scope for improvement in that direction. Alternatively, it may take advantage of any difference in the spectral distribution of the scattered and image-forming light and selectively reduce its sensitivity to the wavelengths in which scattered light is rich. For example, small particles scatter mostly short-wavelength light, so that a red-pass filter is useful for seeing distant landscapes on a hazy day. Large particles, such as water droplets in fog, scatter all wavelengths about equally so wavelength-selective filters are less valuable under these circumstances.

The problems of seeing through media that both absorb and scatter light were first worked out for the atmosphere by Koschmieder in 1924 and amplified by Middleton (1941, 1952). Duntley (1951, 1962, 1963) has extended these studies to the in-water situations which are mathematically similar to the atmosphere, although losses through absorption in water are significantly larger.

As the visual range (r) between the object and the observer increases, the radiance from the object itself decreases according to eqn (1.2) (p. 7). At the same time, the amount of diffuse light scattered in the direction of the eye from the intervening water or atmosphere increases. A point is eventually reached where the radiance of the diffuse light between eye and object becomes indistinguishable from that of the background light, $_bL$, and the radiance of image-forming light from the object ($_tL$) is reduced to insignificant levels (Fig. 4.1).

Fig. 4.1. A view on a misty day. The brightness contrast of the cows gets progressively less with distance due to the veiling effect of light scattered from droplets in the air.

By combining the effects of absorption and scatter, it can be shown that the apparent radiance of an object, $_tL_r$, varies with the sighting range:

$$_tL_r = {_tL_o}(\mathrm{e}^{-\pi}) + {_bL}\,(1 - \mathrm{e}^{-\pi}), \tag{4.1}$$

where the first term on the right describes the loss of image-forming light and the second term on the right describes the gain in non-image forming diffuse light (see also Fig. 4.2).

The difference in brightness between an object and its background can be expressed as a contrast, C:

$$C = \frac{{_tL} - {_bL}}{{_bL}}. \tag{4.2}$$

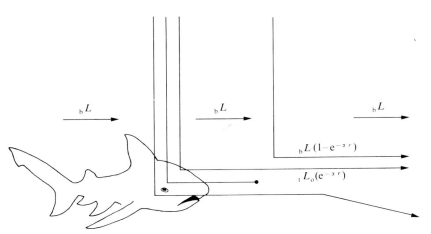

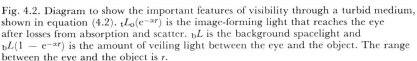

Fig. 4.2. Diagram to show the important features of visibility through a turbid medium, shown in equation (4.2). $_tL_0(e^{-\alpha r})$ is the image-forming light that reaches the eye after losses from absorption and scatter. $_bL$ is the background spacelight and $_bL(1 - e^{-\alpha r})$ is the amount of veiling light between the eye and the object. The range between the eye and the object is r.

For large objects in good light, the value of C that can ordinarily just be detected is constant (in man it is about 0·01). When C falls below this figure, the object can no longer be seen. It is evident that if an additional radiance $_vL$ is added to both $_tL$ and $_bL$ (eqn 4.2), then C is reduced:

$$C = \frac{(_tL + {_v}L) - (_bL + {_v}L)}{(_bL + {_v}L)} \tag{4·3}$$

or,

$$C = \frac{(_tL - {_b}L)}{(_bL + {_v}L)}. \tag{4·4}$$

In the particular case of contrast reduction in air or water, it can be shown by substituting eqn (4.1) into eqn (4.2) that C is reduced in the same way as a narrow beam of light (eqn 1.2):

$$C_r = C_0 e^{-\alpha r}, \tag{4·5}$$

where C_r is the apparent contrast at range r and C_0 is the inherent contrast.

The diffuse scattered light that is interposed between the object and the eye acts in the same way as a bridal veil or white net curtains at a window. For this reason, it is called veiling light. Another example of veiling light is considered later when the problems of sea birds looking down through the surface are described (pp. 134–5 and 180).

A useful measure of the visibility in media that both absorb and scatter light is the black-body distance (Le Grande 1939; Duntley 1960; Lythgoe

1971). A black body is a uniformly black target which has an area of not less than one-third of a square metre. The distance that the object just fades from sight is measured. The measurement is made horizontally, and if the sun is shining, cross-sun.

The physical basis for this particular measurement is that a black object has a radiance of zero. If the zero value is substituted into the equation defining contrast ($_tL = 0$), then contrast is always -1. A diver with normal vision using a face mask can perceive a brightness contrast of about 0·02. If in eqn (4.5) the value of 0·02 is substituted for C_r, -1 for C_o, and the measured visibility distance for r; the beam attenuation coefficient, a, for the water can be calculated.

a is the sum of the losses due to scatter and absorption and the black-body distance cannot distinguish the relative contributions of each. However, the black body distance is superior to the more common Secchi disc measurement because the latter cannot easily be interpreted in physical terms (Tyler 1968).

It follows from eqn (4.5) that contrast at a particular wavelength is reduced with viewing distance at the same rate irrespective of its value when viewed close to the eye. Thus the range that a target can be seen is greater for targets that have a large inherent contrast (C_o) against their background than those where the inherent contrast is small. The first conclusion from this is the obvious one that a target similar to the water background in colour, and only slightly different in brightness, will disappear from view at a closer range than targets considerably darker or lighter than the background (Fig. 4.3). In theory, there is no limit to the distance that a very bright target can be seen, but the visible range of dark targets is limited since it is evident from eqn (4.2) that no matter how bright the background light, the contrast is limited to -1

Contrast and the spectral quality of light

If it was possible to filter out the scattered non-image forming light and to retain only the light that does form an image, the problem of degraded contrasts would be solved. In some cases it is true that the non-image-forming light is richer in some wavelengths than others, and the use of the appropriate colour filter will improve image quality. Light scattered by particles of molecular size is also rich in plane-polarized light, and in clear water it is possible that some improvement in visibility could possibly be achieved by using the appropriate polarizing filter.

Rayleigh scattering

Where most of the scattering is from particles of molecular size, as in the clearest water and in the atmosphere, the spacelight and veiling light is

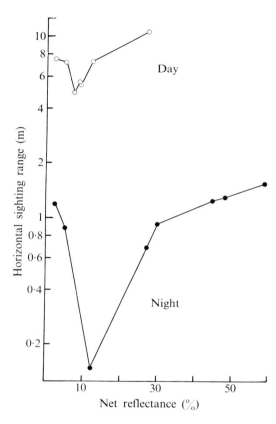

Fig. 4.3. Maximum visible distance of a series of blue fishing nets (reflectance maximum 480 nm) dyed to various degrees of darkness. The percentage reflectance of the bunched wet net is plotted against the maximum horizontal visible distance in clear Mediterranean water at 30 m depth. (From Hemmings and Lythgoe 1965.)

blue. An object such as a flying gull is mainly lit by light travelling the direct path from the sun, and the light reflected from the bird has a spectral distribution that is the product of the spectral irradiance of the sky-light (dominated by sunlight) and the spectral reflectance of its feathers. Provided the bird's reflectance is not strongly wavelength-selective, the spectral radiance distribution of the bird will be much broader than that of the blue sky behind it. The scene viewed through a minus-blue (i.e. yellow) filter will reduce the brightness of the sky more than that of the bird, which will then appear relatively much brighter against the sky than before. Markings on the bird itself will also be more visible because the piece of sky between the bird and the observer (i.e. the veiling light) will likewise be reduced in intensity and visual contrasts will improve (pp. 133–5).

Scattering within the eye

Light scattering in the outside environment causes severe problems, but there is also light scattering within the eye itself that is a source of visual noise.

Plate 1.

Snell's window photographed under water in a mangrove swamp.
The veiling light scattered from the sunbeams is clearly seen. The
blue sky can be seen through the window, but at more oblique
angles the light is reflected back from the surface and is the green
colour of the water spacelight. The water spacelight is, in fact,
unusually blue for mangrove water. On this day the water was
exceptionally calm.

Plate 2.
A rockpool photographed under water by natural light at Fort
Bovisand, Plymouth. In this shallow water the full spectrum of
colours is present.

Plate 3.

An underwater scene photographed on the seaward face of the
fringing reef of Aldabra Atoll. Note the blue colour of this ocean
water. There are two species of snapper *(Lutianus bohar* and *L.
gibbus)*, and one species of sweetlips *(Gaterin gaterinus)*. The tail of
L. gibbus, which looks dark in the photograph, appears red at the
surface. The yellow fins and lips of the sweetlips show up clearly
as yellow. The photograph was taken by natural light at about
30 m depth.

Plate 4.
A gurnard *(Trigla cuculus)* photographed in green coastal water.
The photograph was taken by natural light at about 10 m depth
in the English Channel near Brighton.

Plate 5.
A freshwater perch showing red fins in green fresh water.
Photographed by natural light at about 2 m depth, Santon
Downham, Suffolk, England.

Plate 6.
Coris formosa in the yellow-stained waters of the lagoon on Aldabra Atoll. The red–orange and cyan colours show up well in this kind of water. Photographed by natural light at a depth of about 2 m.

Plate 7.

Soldier fish (or squirrel fish), *Myripristis* species, photographed by flash in blue water at about 25 m depth. The fish near the camera look red, but the more distant fishes look grey–blue because the light from the camera flash loses its blue component in the longer path through the water.

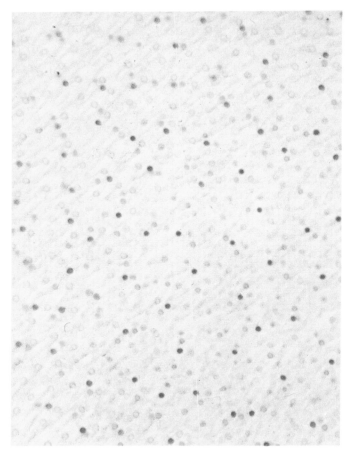

Plate 8.
Oil droplets in the house sparrow (*Passer domesticus*) retina.

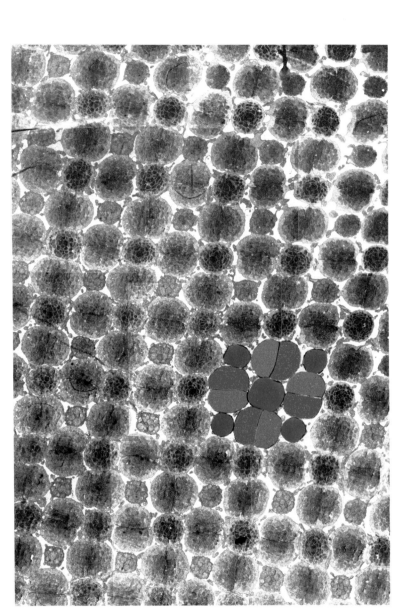

Plate 9.

Electron micrograph of the cone mosaic in the stickleback,
Gasterosteus aculeatus (Fig. 7.13); one mosaic is colour-coded. The
colours are those that light of the same wavelength as the
absorption maximum ($\lambda_{\max}$) of the visual pigment would appear.
The $\lambda_{\max}$s of the visual pigments are 452, 604, and 529 nm and
are probably a mixture of porphyropsin and rhodopsin.

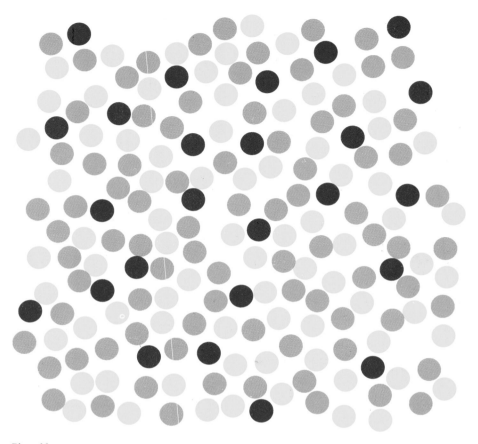

Plate 10.

Representation of the cone mosaic in the parafoveal region of the human retina. The colour code is explained in the underline to Plate 9. The visual pigments are those found in man (see p. 46). The arrangement of the cones is that found in the baboon by Marc and Sperling (1977). Note that the cone most sensitive to red is the one whose λ_{max} is situated in the yellow part of the spectrum.

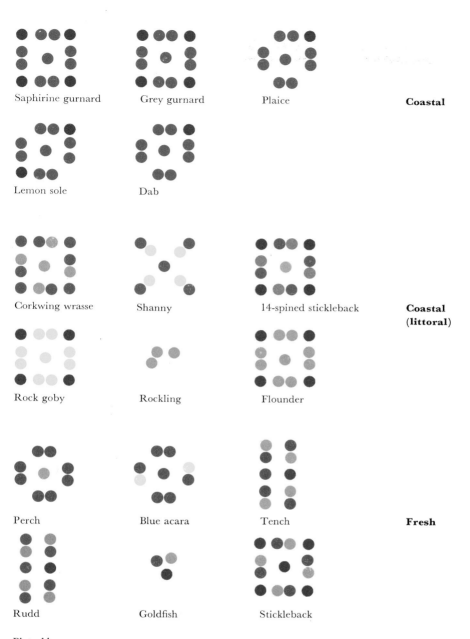

Saphirine gurnard Grey gurnard Plaice **Coastal**

Lemon sole Dab

Corkwing wrasse Shanny 14-spined stickleback **Coastal (littoral)**

Rock goby Rockling Flounder

Perch Blue acara Tench **Fresh**

Rudd Goldfish Stickleback

Plate 11.
Representation of the cone mosaics of fishes living in moderately
deep coastal water (Plate 4), very shallow (littoral) coastal
water (Plate 2), and fresh water (Plate 5). The colour code is
explained in the underline to Plate 9. The mosaic arrangements
have been determined by conventional histological techniques.
The visual pigments present in the various cone types were
measured by microspectrophotometry when dispersed on a
microscope slide. Thus the arrangement of cones may in reality
be quite variable. Note how red-sensitive cones are absent or
rare in coastal water where little red light is present. The data on
which this plate is based are set out in Fig. 5.8.

Plate 12.

Surgeon fish, *Acanthurus leucosternon*. Yellow and blue show up well in clear blue water. Black and white are also a conspicuous combination. The photograph was taken by bulb flash at about 10 m depth at Adabra Atoll.

Within the vertebrate eye, the cornea, lens, and retina all scatter light (see Rodiek (1973) for a review). The cornea is individually very significant, it scatters 25–30 per cent of the light scattered within the eye. The cornea owes its transparency to the precise spacing and arrangement of the collagen fibrils that make up its substance. Measurements of the wavelength-dependent scattering by the rabbit cornea indicate that the amount of scatter follows a $1/\lambda^3$ relationship (Farrel, McCalley, and Tatham 1973). There have been other analyses of the optics of vertebrate corneas, for example Benedek (1971), Goldman and Benedek (1967), and Feuk (1971) all have in common the probability that scattering is likely to increase at short wavelengths. However, Wyszecki and Stiles (1967) consider that in the visible part of the spectrum there is no evidence for the appreciable coloration of scattered light.

A minus-blue filter will effectively remove much of the scatter within the eye. It does not matter where within the eye the filter is situated since it makes no difference whether the light that is liable to be scattered first enters the eye, is scattered and is then removed; or whether it is prevented from entering the eye in the first place.

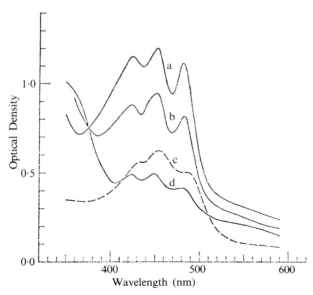

Fig. 4.4. Spectral absorption curves of the yellow corneas of (a) the green wrasse, *Labrus viridis*; (b) the rainbow wrasse, *Coris julis*; (c) the perch, *Perca fluviatilis*; and (d) the peacock wrasse, *Thalassoma (Julis) pavo*. (From Moreland and Lythgoe 1968.)

Chromatic aberration

Optical imperfections may also require wavelength selective filters to eliminate the non-image-forming light they produce. These imperfections come partly from scattering by the tissues of the eye itself, which is likely to be worst at short wavelengths. The eye may also be unable to bring the long and the short wavelengths into focus at the same place. If the visual cells are sensitive to unfocused light, the perception of contrast will be impaired.

Fluorescence

The mammalian lens fluoresces in ultraviolet light at wavelengths lower than about 400 nm (Le Grand 1948). The actual fluorescence is blue having a peak radiance near 425 nm. This fluorescence would add veiling light to all parts of the image on the retina and would reduce contrast sensitivity. Where the filtering effects of the various filter combinations within the eye are known, such as for man (Wyszecki and Stiles 1967) and for various fishes (Muntz 1975) and the grey squirrel (Cooper and Robson 1969), it seems that the filters would have the effect of removing half or more of the lens fluorescence.

Yellow filters and diurnal life

It is certain that yellow filters in the eye are associated with the diurnal mode of life; indeed, Tansley (1965) believes that they are universally present in terrestrial diurnal vertebrates and almost completely absent in nocturnal ones. Walls (1942) has reviewed the distribution of yellow filters in the eyes of vertebrates, a list that needs little revision or amplification except perhaps for the fishes where yellow filters are now known to be present in many diurnal species. Yellow lenses also occur occasionally in mesopelagic squids and fishes, but in this case their function is probably to 'break' the camouflage of other animals swimming above them (see pp. 175–6).

Shallow-living diurnal fishes in both freshwater and the sea often have yellow filters in the cornea or lens. Diurnal marine fishes living in blue coral reef water sometimes have yellow filters, especially the wrasse (*Labridae*), parrot fish (*Scaridae*), trigger fishes (*Balistidae*), and puffer fish (*Tetraodontidae*). In these clear blue waters short-wavelength scattered light is probably an important component in the ambient light and the yellow pre-retinal filters might have the same function under water as on land.

It is more difficult to explain the common occurrence of yellow filters in freshwater fishes (Muntz 1973, 1975) for here the yellow substances in the water themselves absorb blue light and at first sight it might seem that yellow intraocular filters would be redundant. A clue to the problem may

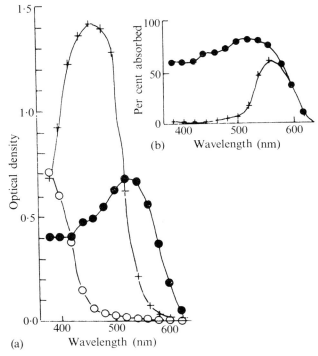

Fig. 4.5. (a) Spectral absorbance of the lens, retina and cornea of the Amazonian cichlid fish *Astronotus ocellatus*. (b) Percentage of light absorbed by the retina alone (filled circles) and by the retina *in vivo* with the lens and cornea in position (crosses). (From Muntz 1975.)

be that in most cases the yellow pigment is concentrated in the dorsal part (Walls and Judd 1933; Moreland and Lythgoe 1968; Muntz 1972, 1973, 1975) and will thus reduce the short-wave component of the downwelling light. A simple inspection of Plate 1 shows that for green (and certainly yellower waters also) there is more blue light coming from the direction of Snell's window than from other directions. In blue water this difference in spectral radiance will be less marked, and on overcast days Snell's window will have relatively less short-wavelength light. If an explanation of this kind has general validity one would expect that blue-water species would normally have pigment evenly distributed over the cornea, whilst in green and yellow waters it would be more often confined to the dorsal part. There are not yet enough data to show such a relationship but it cannot be universal as the one species where the dorsal concentration of pigment in the cornea has been measured (Fig. 4.6) is the rainbow wrasse, *Coris julis* (Fig. 4.7), found in the blue-water Mediterranean (Moreland and Lythgoe 1968). If the yellow pre-retinal pigments are to filter out light most scat-

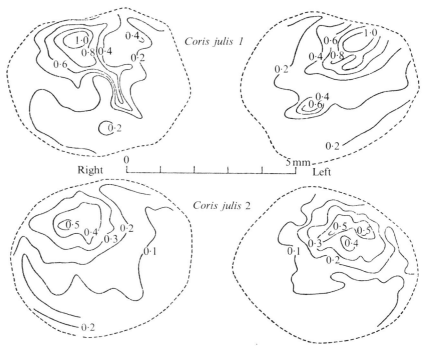

Fig. 4.6. The distribution of yellow pigment in the cornea of the rainbow wrasse, *Coris julis*. The lines are equal-density contours. (From Moreland and Lythgoe 1968.)

tered in the humors of the eye, or has already been scattered, the dorsal concentration of yellow pigment could simply be placed in the path of the brightest rays. The less bright light from other directions which contribute less to intraocular scattering would not be reduced in intensity.

One family of North Pacific teleosts (the Hexagrammidae) have solved the problem of low sensitivity that is normally inherent in eyes with pre-retinal filters (Orlov 1974). The cornea contains a layer of chromatophores extending right across the cornea. In darkness these cells are empty except for the crescent-shaped areas along the dorsal and ventral margins of the eye. In the daytime the pigment migrates across the pupil. In the partially light-adapted state a clear horizontal band extends across the cornea, but when light-adapted the whole area of the cornea is pigmented.

In *Pleurogrammus monopterigius* there is one yellow pigment that gives a corneal colour resembling that of many other fishes, such as pike or perch. However, in the masked greenling, *Hexagrammus octogrammus* (Fig. 4.8), and related species, there are two types of staining cell, one containing a yellow pigment, the other a red pigment. In the partially light-adapted state the yellow pigmented area extends further over the pupil than the red pigment. The optical density of the cornea exceeds 2·5 from 400 to 550 nm

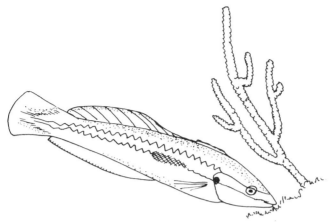

Fig. 4.7. The rainbow wrasse *Coris julis*.

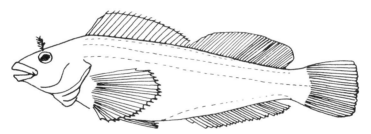

Fig. 4.8. The masked greenling *Hexagrammus octogrammus*.

for the mixed red and yellow corneas, which means that effective transmission is confined to the orange and red parts of the spectrum.

The ground and tree-dwelling squirrels seem to be the only large group
of mammals that are strongly and primarily diurnal. These all have yellow
lenses that are sometimes so deep in colour that they look orange. Our own
species, man, is a graphic example of the correlation between yellow filters
and daylight vision. Man and other primates possess a round fovea which
is used for all visual tasks needing accurate fixation and fine detail. It has
only cones and represents a small island of pure diurnal vision subtending
about 5° of visual field surrounded by a sea of rods (Rodiek (1973) for a
review). The fovea is screened by a patch of yellow pigment—the macula
lutea—that does not extend over the adjacent rod-containing region of the
retina. In the very centre of the fovea there is an area that subtends a mere
30′ angle containing only red- and green-sensitive cones. Indeed, the
minus-blue macula pigment would effectively obliterate the sensitivity
of the blue cones which would be occupying a light-absorbing area better

occupied by the red- and green-sensitive cones. In man the lens gets progressively yellower with age, beginning even before birth (Walls 1942; Wyszecki and Stiles 1967). It is not certain, however, whether this is a degenerative change, or is to limit the increased scattered light due to the degradation of optical quality in the ageing eye.

The most sophisticated colour filter devices are found in the coloured oil droplets situated in the inner segments of bird and reptile cones. Walls (1942) considers that these too are simple filters to exclude short-wavelength scattered light, and thus improve the visibility of distant objects through atmospheric haze. In the case of coloured corneas, lenses and macular pigment, the light reaching neighbouring rods and cones has all been filtered in the same way. In the case of the oil droplets, sometimes as many as five colour classes are present and they form specific partnerships with cones containing different visual pigments (see pp. 56–60). There is little doubt that these oil droplets are far more than a complicated haze-filter but are an integral part of a colour-coding system in the retina, perhaps analogous to the retinal neural interactions of the fish and mammalian eye.

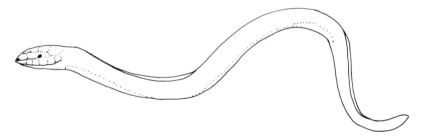

Fig. 4.9. The Californian legless lizard *Aniella* sp.

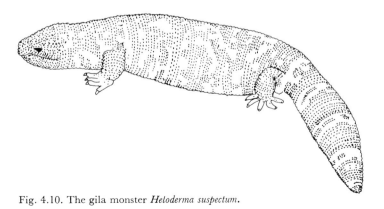

Fig. 4.10. The gila monster *Heloderma suspectum*.

Animals that have abandoned a diurnal life for a nocturnal one lose their colour filters in order to increase sensitivity. Walls (1934, 1942) thinks that once lost the coloured pigments in the oil droplets are never regained in the subsequent course of evolution although colourless oil droplets may remain. The snakes are almost certainly derived from lizard-like reptiles that became nocturnal and took up a fossorial way of life. In so doing, they lost their coloured oil droplets. Amongst lizards alive today, the fossorial *Anniella* (Fig. 4.9) and the nocturnal *Heloderma* (Fig. 4.10) have colourless oil droplets. In the course of time some snakes have become diurnal again; they have not regained their coloured oil droplets but, instead, have a yellow lens.

Possibly the best studied group are the geckoes (Underwood 1970; Crescitelli 1977). These lizards were originally diurnal with an all-cone retina. Their descendants then became nocturnal and their cones transmuted to a rod-like form sometimes retaining oil droplets that are never coloured. Some diurnal geckoes, such as the brilliant green gecko of the Indian Ocean Islands, *Phelsuma* (Fig. 4.11), have only a few oil droplets that are colourless. But as a substitute they have a yellow lens (Tansley 1964).

Fig. 4.11. A diurnal gecko *Phelsuma* sp.

Yellow filters are so universally present in the eyes of diurnal vertebrates and they occur in so many different anatomical structures that it seems likely that they play an important role in vision. By the same token, their absence in nocturnal vertebrates must mean that they become a real liability at night. With the exception of a few fishes (pp. 120–1) it seems that the yellow filters cannot be removed from the light path when it begins to get dark. Diurnal animals, therefore, have to find a place of safety sooner than they might otherwise need to.

It is possible that an important function of yellow filters is to protect the eyes from blue and ultraviolet which are known to cause photochemical damage to the retina (Ham *et al.* 1976). The undoubted optical advantages in possessing yellow filters may be incidental to this protective function. It has been calculated that 23 hours' continuous exposure to a landscape of fresh, sunlit snow would cause actual physical damage to the retina. Such prolonged exposures to such a brightly lit scene are unlikely in nature, but one has to remember that our eyes contain blue-absorbing filters in both the lens and the macula pigment in the retina. Sliney (1977) points out that people who have had their lenses removed in an operation for cataract are particularly prone to snow blindness. Their symptoms include impairment of night vision, a red cast to the visual scene, and, in bad cases, complete (but temporary) blindness.

Pattern and visibility

In addition to loss of image contrast due to veiling luminance and the absorption of image-forming light, there is also degradation of the image due to forward scatter of image-forming light at extremely narrow angles. There is both theoretical (Yura 1971) and observational evidence (Duntley 1974) for believing that it is large transparent zooplankters that are most significant in degrading the optical image through forward scatter.

A target bearing a grating-like pattern of alternating dark and light bars is useful for measuring image-transfer through turbid media. The intensity distribution of light across the grating should ideally form a sine wave since they are then easily accessible to Fourier analysis, but such gratings are difficult to construct and in practice square-wave gratings are often used (see pp. 202–4). Two relevant quantities of such gratings are the number of cycles of dark and light bars included per degree, and the difference in brightness between the dark and light bars. Such data are conventionally plotted as a modulation-transfer function where the contrast between the dark and light bars is plotted as a function of the number of cycles per degree across the pattern.

For most scattering water the sharp shoulders of a square-wave grating remain distinct even at long range when the difference between the dark and light bars is reduced almost to nothing (Duntley 1974). However, in water where there are many transparent zooplankters and scattering comes from refraction at the boundary between the animal's body and the surrounding water, the image of high-frequency gratings may be blurred or obliterated due to lightening of the dark areas by infilling from the light areas. Estimates of the range and frequency that this might occur are few and contradictory. Probably this is because the species composition and population density of the zooplankters concerned were not recorded.

Mertens (1970) considers that this blurring or 'roll-off' might occur at 1 cycle/radian, but Duntley (1974) later encountered waters where the roll-off was 17 cycles/radian. Duntley himself believes that for most ocean waters 20 cycles/radian or more are needed, except where there are large concentrations of transparent plankton.

For gratings, contrast perception is best in a particular frequency range and falls off at both higher and lower frequencies (Fig. 4.12). In man, the optimum frequency is about 4 cycles/degree, in the cat it is 0·3 cycles/degree (see Fig. 4.13) and in goldfish about the same as the cat. Apparently it is

Fig. 4.12. This is a photograph of a sine-wave grating. The spatial frequency of the grating increases from right to left. The contrast between the dark and light areas decreases from top to bottom. The grating is visible at lower contrasts at intermediate spatial frequencies. (Photograph by courtesy of Dr. F. W. Campbell.)

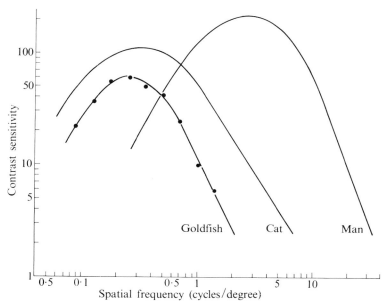

Fig. 4.13. The relationship between contrast sensitivity and the spatial frequency of a grid pattern for goldfish, the cat, and man. (From Northmore 1977.)

frequency of the grid rather than whether its profile is a square, sine wave, saw tooth, etc., that determines whether it will be visible or not. There appear to be a number of analysers that are sensitive to particular frequencies, whilst others respond optimally to edges, lines, or gratings (see for instance, Kulikowski and King-Smith 1973). Unordered patterns are also most easily recognized if their characteristic spatial frequency is about that to which the eye is tuned.

In a series of visibility tests conducted under water, Muntz, Baddeley, and Lythgoe (1974) showed that a grid consisting of black stripes on a transparent plexiglass board was visible at about 17 per cent greater distance than when the whole board was black. The frequency of the grid that was most visible corresponded to the grid frequency that could be best seen at low contrasts as measured in the laboratory.

The combined effects of light scatter and absorption in the atmosphere or in water will reduce the contrast of a grating but not its spatial frequency. Thus it may be that animals that habitually view the world through turbid media will be tuned to lower frequencies; partly because objects will be nearer before they can be seen and will thus form bigger images on the retina, and partly because forward scatter tends to obliterate high spatial frequencies more than low. Turbid water also tends to reduce illumination levels and it is likely that the visual system will be tuned to see larger objects because retinal summation will be greater (p. 65).

The most visible spatial frequencies have been measured in too few animals to know, for example, whether the low spatial frequency vision of goldfish is typical of fishes as a whole. Some fishes appear to use the great inherent visibility of a regular grating by having a pattern of vertical bars along their flanks (pp. 203–4).

Substitutes for vision in turbid media

The reduction of visual contrast caused by suspended particles poses an intractable problem for the visual system, particularly for aquatic animals. It is far more troublesome than low light intensities because the addition of self-generated light does little or nothing to help since it tends only to increase the amount of non image-forming light scattered back into the eye. Fishes that live in extremely turbid water tend to have rather small eyes and poor vision, and instead have developed other senses, such as chemoreception, water-displacement senses, and electroreception (pp. 108–11).

Suspended particles in the water absorb light as well as scatter it, so that turbid waters also tend to be dark water perhaps only a metre or so beneath the surface. It is difficult, therefore, to decide whether a catfish, for example, with small eyes and well-developed chemosensory barbels, has evolved to cope with the scattering nature of muddy water or the dim light at the bottom. Perhaps the distinction is meaningless because low light intensities make the perception of contrast more difficult and turbid water both reduces visual contrasts and the animal's ability to discriminate those contrasts that are present.

The senses that substitute for vision are surveyed in Chapter 3, but here it is worth mentioning the electroreception possessed by several fresh-water fishes. Lissmann (1958, 1963) pointed out that many of the weakly-electric fishes, particularly in the unrelated families Gymnotidae and Mormyridae, live in turbid water and are active mainly at night. Lissmann believes that by this strategy they are able to avoid the predators whose normally good vision would be virtually useless in dark, turbid water.

5 Colour-biased environments

Introduction

Taking the broad view of our planet, the most common colours are blues, browns, and greens. Most rocks and sand are some shade of brown; most vegetation is coloured green by chlorophyll; clear skies and distant landscapes are blue. Underwater, the dominant colour can be anything from an indigo blue to red–brown depending upon the relative importance of selective absorption and short-wavelength-selective scattering by the water itself, and the presence of chlorophyll and chlorophyll breakdown products.

Vision is such an important sense to man that an extremely rich language has grown up to describe its sensations. Science has further refined this language to describe with precision the various processes that are believed to be combined to give the total visual awareness in man. This poses a real problem because a language evolved to fit the human experience is likely to be misleading in the description of visual processes in other animals.

Many conceptual difficulties are avoided if the detection of an object of interest is considered as a separate problem to its recognition. For detection it is necessary only to be aware of some difference between the object and its background. Recognition implies that the object conforms to some pattern already known to the observer. The difference in radiance between a particular object and its background will only be at its maximum in one region of the spectrum, but since the wavelength of greatest difference varies with each visual display, more than one visual receptor, each most sensitive in a particular spectral region, will be helpful. The process of detection need not involve any colour awareness, but having receptors tuned to different wavelengths, it is possible to imagine how the strength of the signals from the different receptor types scanning the same scene might be compared to give the characteristic sensations of particular colours.

There are very few circumstances where we know enough about the photic environment and the colour vision of the animals that live there to come to any conclusions about specific adaptations of colour vision. There are, however, eco-visual systems where we may know enough to reach some conclusions. Two examples are the colour vision of birds in relation to green vegetation and the blue sky; and the colour vision of fishes in relation to the colour of the water. Our present concern is with the detection and recognition of objects not specially coloured in order to be particularly camouflaged or conspicuous. Nevertheless, the physical and physiological basis of visual display, which is discussed in Chapter 7, is an extension of some of the principles discussed in this chapter.

The green landscape

In lush and fertile landscapes the dominating colour is the green of chlorophyll, but owing to the inclusion of other colouring substances into the foliage and surface coverings, such as a waxy cuticle or fine hairs on the surface of the leaf, there is, at least to our eyes, an enormous variation in the shade of green in different plants.

Hue discrimination curves

The human eye has three cone pigments (p. 46, see also Plate 10) and, in the yellow–green and yellow regions of the spectrum is able to distinguish differences in the hue of monochromatic light closer in wavelength than in any other region except, perhaps, in the blue–green around 490 nm (see Wyszecki and Stiles (1967) for a review). In other words, we are able to distinguish more colours in the wavelength interval between about 560 nm and 610 nm than anywhere else in the spectrum, and at its best the human eye can distinguish pure spectral colours that are only 1–2 nm apart.

Hue-discrimination curves are useful tools in trying to understand the mechanism of vision by psychophysical techniques, but in real life the task is not to distinguish between monochromatic lights but between lights of much broader and more complex spectral distributions that may show greatest differences in radiant intensity at widely separated regions of the spectrum. But whatever the reason, it is intriguing that hue discrimination in man is greatest at around 590 nm which is near to the wavelength of maximum radiance beneath a forest canopy.

Hue-discrimination curves have been obtained for the pigeon, *Columba livia* (Fig. 5.1), which is the domesticated form of the rock dove, but which has diverged somewhat from the wild type over the years. The familiar town pigeons of European cities are domestic pigeons in the feral state. In the wild it feeds principally on green vegetation (Murton 1965) although in captivity it is fed mostly on grain and grain products. Hamilton and Coleman (1933) have found that hue discrimination in the pigeon is relatively good at 500, 540–50 nm and best at 600 nm where it can distinguish wavelengths separated by about 3 nm. At longer wavelengths hue discrimination is so bad as to be virtually non-existent. A broader view of their data shows that hue discrimination is generally best between 560 and 610 nm. In a later study, Wright (1972) derived curves that differ in

Fig. 5.1. The pigeon, a domestic form of the rock dove *Columba livia*.

detail from Hamilton and Coleman's but agree that discrimination is best around 600 nm.

Oil-droplet and visual-pigment combinations

Bowmaker (1977) has measured directly the pigments in the cones of the pigeon and related them to the colour of the oil droplets that each contain. There are at least six oil-droplet/visual-pigment combinations, each contributing a signal of characteristic spectral sensitivity into the neural net. As Bowmaker and Knowles (1977) point out, the action of the oil droplets in modifying the spectral sensitivity of individual cones is analagous to the neural interactions between the primary signals of different cone types that occur in the nerve network in the retina (pp. 71–3). The spectral sensitivity of the different oil-droplet and visual-pigment combinations in the pigeon are shown in Fig. 2.23 (p. 60). The two cone types that have narrow-band spectral sensitivity curves peaking at 613 and 567 nm are likely to be helpful to the pigeon in distinguishing between different types of foliage.

Discrimination of foliage types

The spectral reflectance curves of various green leaves are shown in Fig. 5.2. At wavelengths shorter than 500 nm the reflectance curves are flat. Between 510 and 580 nm there is a large reflectance peak due to the presence of chlorophyll and shows in physical terms the characteristic green component of all these leaves. At longer wavelengths there is considerable variation in reflection from different leaves, probably due to pigments such as anthocyanins; it is principally due to these long-wavelength reflectors that various leaves owe their subtly different colours.

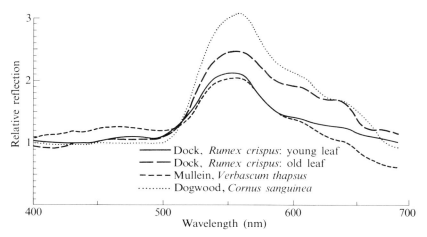

Fig. 5.2. The spectral reflectance of various green leaves. All the leaves show very similar reflectance at wavelengths lower than about 550 nm. At longer wavelengths, however, the influence of long-wave reflecting pigments, which are present in various amounts, becomes visible. All the leaves have broadly similar gloss characteristics except for the mullein which is covered by a woolly layer of colourless hair.

If it is part of the task of the pigeon retina to distinguish the spectral radiances of different plants, it needs to have cones whose responses, when compared to each other, show the greatest range of differences. Because the red-reflecting pigments are the most variable colour-selective reflectors in the leaves, it follows that one cone type should be most sensitive to them—these are the 613-nm cones. With these alone the pigeon could distinguish leaves only in monochrome. However, by relating the 613 cone to the 567 cone, it is able to derive information of the ratio of chlorophyll to red pigment. Finally, the blue-sensitive cones can function as a reference for either the 567 or 613 cone to give information about the amount of chlorophyll or red pigments present in a leaf.

The colours of the oil droplets—particularly the red and yellow ones—under the light microscope may allow preliminary conclusions about the dispositions of cones of different spectral sensitivity in the avian, and perhaps also the reptilian, retina. For instance, as long ago as 1883 Waelchli knew that the part of the retina that the pigeon uses for looking forward and downward contains more red oil droplets than elsewhere in the retina, and this is termed the 'red field'. The red oil droplet cuts out virtually all light at wavelengths shorter than 580 nm and it follows that sensitivity in cones with red oil droplets must be at longer wavelengths than that. Since no visual pigment has been measured in birds with an absorption above 575 nm (see p. 59) it is likely that the oil droplet that transmits light at wavelengths greater than 560 nm will combine with the pigment to give a sensitivity maximum between 560 and 580 nm. At shorter wavelengths, this type of argument becomes unreliable and we must await more data before useful conclusions can be drawn.

A red field is found in many other passerine birds although not always so well-developed as in the pigeon. In the pigeon the red field has about a quarter of the oil droplets which are red, another quarter are orange–yellow, and the rest look green, blue–green, or colourless (Waelchli 1883). This proportion seems to be typical of many other passerine birds that are

Table 5.1 The proportion of red and yellow–orange oil droplets in the central field of the retina of herbivorous birds

Bird	Red (%)		Yellow–orange (%)		Reference
Columba livia Pigeon	23	(12)	27	(12)	Waelchli (1883)
Amandava amandava Red avadavat	28·3	(22·0)	31·5	(23·3)	Ducker (1963)
Pyrrhula pyrrhula Bullfinch	22·9	(18·1)	26·7	(22·4)	Ducker (1963)
Carduelis carduelis Goldfinch	22·0	(18·5)	27·6	(23·3)	Ducker (1963)
Munia malacca Black-headed munia	27·5	(21·7)	21·6	(18·8)	Ducker (1963)
Ploceus abyssinicus Weaver	25·5	(20·3)	23·4	(22·9)	Ducker (1963)
Euplectes orix franciscanus Red bishop	23·1		27·5		Mayr (1972)
Amadina fasciata Cut-throat	20·5		22·7		Mayr (1972)
Uraeginthus angolensis Blue waxbill	23·7		24·4		Mayr (1972)
U. bengalus Red-cheeked blue waxbill	22·2		24·3		Mayr (1972)
U. cyanocephalus Blue-capped waxbill	21·0		27·5		Mayr (1972)
Chicken	19·0		19·0		Bowmaker and Knowles (1977)

Figures in parentheses refer to the yellow field when identified.
The values credited to Ducker have been calculated from his more detailed data.

closely associated with vegetation (Table 5.1). It is worth noticing in passing that most of the birds in this table have brightly coloured plumage, indeed we can guess that they were selected for study for that reason, yet they all have approximately similar proportions of the different coloured oil droplets. This lends some support to the view expressed in Chapter 7, that the visual mechanisms have evolved to serve the primary need to find food and to avoid enemies and the development of conspicuous and sexually attractive coloration takes advantage of visual mechanisms that already exist.

Sky and water

Photographers know that to give interest and drama to a skyscape a colour filter that cuts out the shorter wavelengths of the spectrum reduces the brightness of the blue sky and increases the relative brightness of the white clouds. Yellow, orange, and red cut-off filters all give this effect, but it is more pronounced for red than yellow filters. The cloudless sky owes its blueness to Rayleigh scatter (pp. 7–8) and so the sky becomes progressively less bright at longer wavelengths. The radiance from clouds and white birds that reflect light more or less equally through the visible spectrum is rich in light of all wavelengths. It follows that at long wavelengths the brightness contrast between the white object and the sky is at its greatest. However, dark objects displayed against the sky will be more difficult to detect if a red filter is used because the sky will itself become darker and contrast will be reduced. The strategy for seeing objects in silhouette is thus to be selectively most sensitive to the background light.

The use of cut-off filters reduces general sensitivity because only part of the spectrum is allowed to pass: red filters cut out much more light than yellow ones. Animals with cut-off filters necessarily sacrifice sensitivity and it is not surprising, therefore, that the nocturnal or crepuscular owls, nightjars, and European swifts have few coloured oil droplets in their retina (see pp. 90–1). The swift (*Apus apus*) holds particular interest because it feeds on flying insects which it takes on the wing. We may expect that insects show up as silhouettes when seen against the sky itself or the reflection of the sky from the water's surface. The swift is, therefore, adapted to both nocturnal vision and to catching insects on the wing. Swallows and martins (Hirundinae) are not closely related to the swifts (Apodidae) and do not fly late into the night. Like the swifts, however, they are modified by their fast and agile flight to catch insects on the wing. Also like the swifts, their retinas possess few coloured oil droplets, and are thus well suited for seeing silhouetted flying insects.

In Chapter 7 on display and camouflage, attention is drawn to the apparent correlation between dark coloration in birds, few coloured oil droplets, and a tendency to be active late in the evening. Amongst sea-birds, at any rate, one can imagine that there is a similar correlation between abundant coloured oil droplets, diurnal activity, and white or pale coloration.

Vision through the water surface

The water surface is an important obstacle to vision, both from below and from above. The most difficult direction is undoubtedly looking from the air into the water as a sea-bird must frequently need to do. First and most important, the reflections from the sky at the water surface interposes a disabling glare that reduces visual contrasts in much the same way as veiling light in air and water. Secondly, refractions at the water surface, which is seldom flat, continually distort the image. Thirdly, the magnifying effect of the air–water interface reduces the apparent brightness of sub-surface objects by a factor of $1/n^2$ or approximately 0·56, where n is the refractive index of water (Austin 1974).

The surface glare has the same spectral reflectance as the sky, but the upwelling light from the water itself has a spectral radiance dominated by the absorption and scatter of the water. Measurements made by earth satellites (Austin 1974) show that at wavelengths longer than about

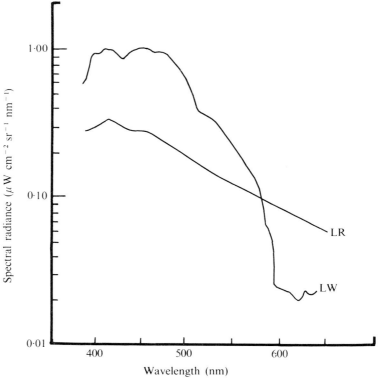

Fig. 5.3. Radiance reflected from the sky at the sea surface (LR) and upwelling light originating from the sea (LW) just above the surface. In this blue–green water surface reflection is greater than the upwelling light at wavelengths beyond about 575 nm. (After Austin 1974.)

575 nm, where water begins to absorb light strongly, the reflections from the sky are often brighter than the upwelling radiance of the water (Fig. 5.3). It follows that a visual mechanism most sensitive to wavelengths longer than 575 nm will be poorly adapted for seeing into deep water although very shallow objects might be well seen. Alternatively, a mechanism most sensitive to wavelengths in which the upwelling light is rich, and the sky reflections relatively poor, will be best suited for seeing through the surface. Using Austin's data, the best through-surface visibility would be at the following wavelengths:

Blue water	425–525 nm
Blue–green water	500–550 nm
Green water	520–570 nm

Muntz (1972) has shown that birds such as the razorbill, shag (Fig. 5.4),

Fig. 5.4. The shag *Phalacrocorax aristotelis*.

and shearwater that pursue fishes underwater have rather few red and orange oil droplets in their retina. It is likely that these birds are relatively more sensitive to shorter wavelengths; they would, therefore, be well adapted for seeing objects deep beneath the surface. By analogy with nocturnal birds, which also have few red and orange oil droplets, and coastal fishes that have few red-sensitive cones, they might also be well adapted for seeing in the dim green light under water. It is argued elsewhere (pp. 180–3) that the abundant red and orange oil droplets in the retinas of light-coloured sea-birds help them to detect other white sea-birds a long way off through atmospheric haze.

Through-water vision

Problems of scatter and absorption

An aquatic animal lives in a world where visual contrasts reduce very rapidly as the sighting distance increases, whilst at the same time the spectral bandwidth of light available to make the contrast discrimination is reduced by the wavelength-selective absorption of the water. The rapid reduction of visual contrast means that it is very unlikely that an object farther than some 40 m from the observer can be seen even in the clearest ocean water. Since fishes can cruise at about 4 body lengths a second, a 1-m fish will take 10 seconds to reach an object it can just detect in the

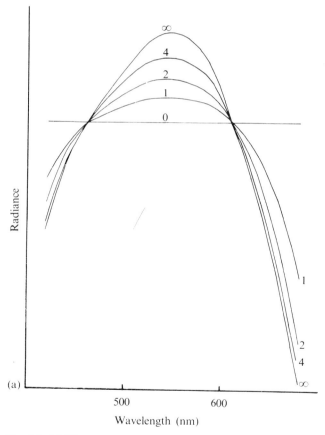

(a)

500   600

Wavelength (nm)

Fig. 5.5. (a) The spectral radiance of a grey target suspended in shallow water at zero range from the observer and at 1, 2, and 4 m. At range ∞ the target is so far distant that it is indistinguishable from the background spacelight. (b) As for (a) but this time it is the contrast between the object and the background space-distance. Most fishes are shaded to blend as much as possible into the water background, which probably at least halves the range at which they can be detected. Thus even in the clearest water a prey species might have only 5 seconds, and probably very much less, to respond to an approaching predator.

Matched and offset visual pigments

It is probably safe to assume that a common task of aquatic animals is to maximize the range that they can see through the water. Some techniques for doing this have already been discussed in Chapter 4, but in a selectively

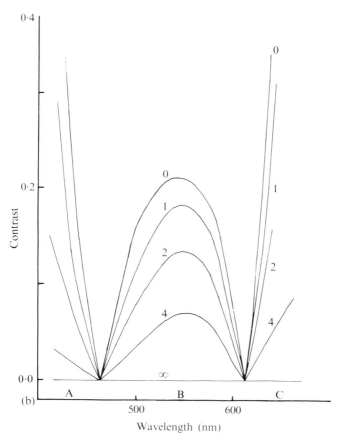

light that is measured. At a large visual range (∞) there is no contrast and the object is invisible. A, B, C are the positions of the λ_{max} of the hypothetical visual pigments mentioned in the text. A and C are offset; B is matched to the spectral radiance maximum of the water.

absorbing medium like water, the spectral sensitivity of the receptors and the radiance characteristics of the target become important and have to be taken into consideration.

If the spectral reflectance of all underwater objects could be averaged together, it is likely that the resulting spectral reflectance curve would be almost flat and the hypothetical object would look grey when viewed in white light. If such a grey object was submerged just beneath the surface and viewed at close range, it would still look grey because it would be chiefly illuminated by the white light from the sky, virtually unmodified by the selective absorption of the water. On the other hand, the water background spacelight against which the object is seen would possess the colour produced by the selective absorption and scatter of the water. The situation is summarized in Fig. 5.5. At wavelengths where the background spacelight is brightest, most grey objects will be darker than the background. Where absorption is greater and thus the spacelight is darker, the object is brighter than the background. At two wavelengths the object has exactly the same radiance as its background; an animal that is only sensitive at these two particular wavelengths will fail to detect anything in the water. However, it is possible to see how receptors most sensitive at points A, B, and C in the spectrum, where the difference in radiance between object and background is greatest, would be most efficient at detecting the grey object (Loew and Lythgoe 1978).

If the object retreats farther from the eye, the intervening volume of water begins to contribute its own spacelight. This becomes relatively greater as the distance between the object and observer increases until finally the radiance from the direction of the object can no longer be distinguished from that of the unobstructed water background. A mathematical description of this reduction in contrast is given on pp. 112–18, but the important point is that contrast reduction is greatest at wavelengths where absorption is greatest. At the limits of vision it is the visual receptor that is most sensitive to the wavelengths best transmitted by the water that is also the most efficient for detecting visual contrasts.

If the object and observer sinks deeper into the water, then the spectral distribution of the bright downwelling light becomes more and more like that of the water background, until the light illuminating the object has the same spectral distribution as the water background and at that depth the difference in radiance between the object and its background is the same at all wavelengths. In this case it is the receptor that has a spectral sensitivity that best matches the radiance of the water spacelight that will, in all cases, be the most efficient at detecting distant objects.

These arguments show that for deep water, for distant objects, and for objects darker than the background spacelight, a receptor having a sensitivity matched to the spectral radiance of the water background will be best. But in the important case of bright objects in moderate or shallow depths, a receptor most sensitive at wavelengths offset from the maximum transmission of the water will be the most efficient contrast detector.

A three-receptor system, one matched to the background spacelight, one offset to longer wavelengths, and one offset to shorter wavelengths, is likely to be the best detector system for the natural variety of visual tasks. A multi-receptor system does not necessarily mean that an animal has colour vision, but as Munz and McFarland (1977) have pointed out, it might be the base from which true colour vision has evolved.

Visual pigments and direction of sight

McFarland and Munz (1975b) have considered these ideas in relation to the hunting strategies of open water pelagic fishes. They considered two specific examples—the skipjack tuna, *Katsuwonus pelamis* (Fig. 5.6), and the mahi mahi, or dolphin fish, *Coryphaena hippurus* (Fig. 5.7). The mahi mahi

Fig. 5.6. The skipjack tuna strikes upwards.

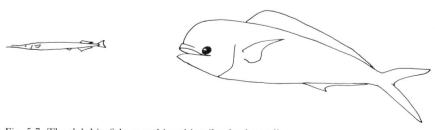

Fig. 5.7. The dolphin fish or mahi mahi strikes horizontally.

seldom ventures below 15 m and spends most of its time within 6 m of the surface. It chases flying fish, jack mackerel, sauries, and crustacea at the surface; its main visual axis is forward along the body axis and it has well-developed binocularity.

The skipjack swims deeper down to at least 70 m and it takes its prey by rushing up from beneath. Its visual axis is directed upwards and forwards. The skipjack thus sees its intended prey in dark silhouette against the brighter downwelling light, whilst the mahi mahi sees its prey mostly bright against the blue horizontal spacelight (see Chapter 6). When Munz and McFarland (1975) extracted the visual pigments of these two fishes they found that the skipjack has a single visual pigment of λ_{max} 483_1 nm. They believe that this pigment is contained in both the rods and in one class of cone and matches the spectral radiance of the water space-light for all directions, including straight up. The skipjack visual pigment is, therefore, well designed to see dark objects in silhouette.

The mahi mahi, on the other hand, has three extractable visual pigments (521_1, 499_1, and 469_1) and it is likely that these are all cone pigments, with the 499_1 pigment also being contained in the rods. The 521_1 pigment is clearly an offset pigment designed to detect bright objects near the surface. The 499_1 is probably a matched pigment designed to see dark objects and distant bright objects. The 469_1 pigment is more equivocal. It could act as either an offset pigment in blue–green water rich in phyto-plankton, or as a matched pigment in clear blue oceanic water. It should, however, be mentioned that the mahi mahi has a yellow lens and this will certainly reduce the photons available to the 469_1 cones relative to the other two and will also shift the effective spectral sensitivity to somewhat longer wavelengths.

Cone pigments and water colour

The spectral absorption of natural water is broadly characteristic of its geographical location. The open oceans are blue, and inshore and inland waters are green, yellow–green, or even orange–brown depending on how much chlorophyll and the yellow and brown products of vegetable decay they contain (pp. 19–20). In any particular place the water colour varies from hour to hour and from season to season, depending upon factors such as the state of the tide, rainfall, and plankton blooms. The visual system needs to be sensitive in the broad area of the spectrum where there is usually enough light to function, but it must also be capable of some flexibility to allow for the short-term variations in light transmission.

The λ_{max} of the visual pigments present in the cones of various fishes is shown in Fig. 5.8 and Plate 11. In Fig. 5.8 the fishes living in the relatively pure blue water (a–b) are placed at the top, fishes of green coastal water (c–m) in the middle, and fishes of green and yellow–green freshwater (n–r) at the bottom. It is at once evident that blue-water species have fewer

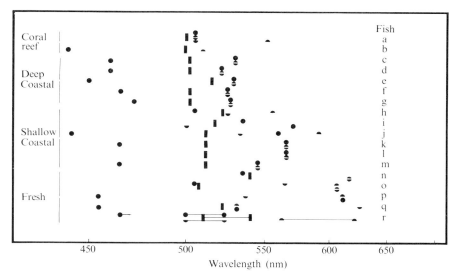

Fig. 5.8. The visual pigments in the rods and cones of various teleost fishes. Rods, rectangles; single cones, filled circle; single member of twin or double cone, half-circle. The lines joining the symbols in (r) (rudd) represent the possible rhodopsin–porphyropsin shift in λ_{max}. The fishes are: (a) damsel fish, *Pomacentrus melanochir*; (b) lion fish, *Dendrochirus zebra*; (c) saphirine gurnard, *Trigla lucerna*; (d) grey gurnard, *Eutrigla gurnardus*; (e) plaice, *Pleuronectes platessa*; (f) lemon sole, *Microstomus kitt*; (g) dab, *Limanda limanda*; (h) corkwing wrasse, *Crenilabrus melops*; (i) shanny, *Blennius pholis*; (j) 14-spined stickleback, *Spinachia spinachia*; (k) rock goby, *Gobius paganellus*; (l) shore rockling, *Gaidropsarus mediterraneus*; (m) flounder, *Platichthys flesus*; (n) perch, *Perca fluviatilis*; (o) blue acara, *Aequidens pulcher*; (p) tench, *Tinca tinca*; (q) goldfish, *Carassius auratus*; (r) rudd, *Scardinius erythrophthalmus*. (After Loew and Lythgoe 1978.)

red-sensitive receptors than freshwater species, but for some reason that is not explained, a corresponding variation in blue receptors in this sample is either slight or absent. Although the rods tend to absorb at longer wavelengths in yellow–green freshwater than in blue and green ocean water, the range is much less than for the cones.

It is unlikely that any rhodopsin has a λ_{max} greater than about 580 nm. Cones that are maximally sensitive to longer wavelengths almost certainly contain a substantial proportion of porphyropsin. The most readily available explanation for the presence of porphyropsin in freshwater fishes and not in marine, terrestrial and flying animals, may well be the apparent need to match the cone visual pigment to the often red-biased ambient light in fresh water (see pp. 21 and 52).

The paired cones are of particular interest because they seem to possess the visual pigment that gives good sensitivity to the normal range in the spectral distribution of the light they receive (Fig. 5.9). Several workers have suggested that the possession of double cones is related to sensitivity (Willmer 1953; Lyall 1957; Engström 1963) and is associated with vision

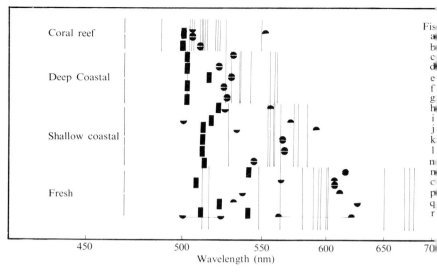

Fig. 5.9. The visual pigments in the rods and paired cones of teleost fishes compared according to habitat. The vertical lines represent the λ_{max} of the visual pigment that would have been most sensitive on particular occasions when spectral radiance measurements were made (see Loew and Lythgoe 1978 for details). The spectral bandwidth covered by the lines indicate the variation in the colour of water of each type that can be expected, otherwise details are as for Fig. 5.8. Note that the paired cones appear to have the visual pigments that make them most sensitive, whereas the rods are generally less sensitive to red light than might be expected on sensitivity grounds alone. (After Loew and Lythgoe 1978.)

in deep water, and, in Engström's view, are intermediate in sensitivity between rods and cones. This view that the double cones are approximately 'matched' in sensitivity to the ambient light and that they are associated with twilight conditions, is not well supported by the earlier work of Wunder (1925), quoted by Walls (1942), reporting that double cones are more common in shallow water teleosts. However, Engström casts some doubt on the reliability of Wunder's methods, and it seems likely that double cones are indeed associated with vision at the lowest light intensities attainable for photopic vision.

Bearing in mind that the combined sensitivity of the paired cones approximately matches the wavelength of greatest water transparency, it would seem likely that receptor B in Fig. 5.5(b) would be a double and receptors A and C would be singles. In fact, the shorter-wavelength receptor within a single cone is often present, but it is less easy to point to a single cone offset to longer wavelengths. It is in any case unlikely that a visual pigment of λ_{max} longer than about 625 nm will be found (pp. 63–5) so that offsetting to longer wavelengths using the unprocessed signal from a single cone type is unlikely.

Ghost cones

Simply by swimming up or down through the water column for a few metres a fish can experience enormous changes in daylight intensity, particularly at long and short wavelengths (see pp. 25–8). If we consider the red end of the spectrum, the human eye is amply able to see red colours in the first metre or so of water, but beneath about 25 m no red light is visible! An animal has two strategies open to it: either it can increase its sensitivity to red in an effort to compensate for the reduction in red light, or it can abandon the attempt to 'see' red as not worth the effort. It is fairly evident from a study of fish visual pigments that it is the latter course that is preferred (see pp. 140–2). Nevertheless, in shallow water where there is ample red light, it would be advantageous to see it. 'Ghost cones' may be a physiological device to see red as a distinct colour in shallow water, but not to be burdened with redundant red sensitivity in deep water where there is no red light.

On pp. 71–4, it is explained how inhibitory interactions between two cone types of different spectral sensitivity can produce a 'ghost receptor'. Such a ghost could have a spectral sensitivity that is narrower and located at longer wavelengths than either of the two parent receptors.

These ghost cones have a narrower spectral sensitivity curve and, except at extremely long wavelengths, are less sensitive than either parent. Although less sensitive, a long-wavelength ghost cone might be more suitable than an actual cone because they have a spectral sensitivity curve displaced to longer wavelengths than that allowed to visual pigments. Also, in a situation such as that envisaged in Fig. 5.5, it is nearly as important not to be sensitive to parts of the spectrum where the target has the same radiance as the background spacelight as it is to be sensitive to long wavelengths where the target is brighter than the background.

There is also the packing of cones in the retinal mosaic to be considered: in the light-adapted state the cones are withdrawn to rest directly on the external limiting membrane and in many species the inner segments of the cones are packed so tightly that there is no space for any more. In the surface waters all cones receive enough photons to function, but if the fish were to swim deeper into green or blue water, the red-sensitive cones would not receive enough light to function and would become passengers occupying valuable photon-catching area that could be used to good effect by the green- and blue-sensitive cones.

A ghost cone takes up no space in the mosaic, although the necessary circuitry presumably adds to the thickness of the retina. An example of how they might work is provided by the common European flatfish, the plaice, *Pleuronectes platessa* (Fig. 5.10). The plaice is most common in the green waters of the North Sea and English Channel, although it does find its way into the blue waters of the western Mediterranean. In northern Europe it lives in shallow water and down to depths of at least 100 m. The

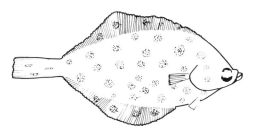

Fig. 5.10. The plaice *Pleuronectes platessa*.

first year of life is spent in very shallow inshore water but in the second year it begins to move deeper. Plaice become mature when they are 4–5 years old and are between 20 and 40 cm in length. The main spawning grounds are in deep water. After fertilization the eggs float to the surface, hatch after about three weeks, and the young metamorphose to the typical flatfish after a further three weeks. By this time the young fish have usually drifted close inshore where they sink to the bottom of the shallow nursery grounds (Wheeler 1969).

The cone mosaics in the plaice have the conventional square arrangement with a central single cone and identical doubles. Some of the corners of the mosaic square have additional single cones, but these are not seen in the retinas of adult fish (Engström and Ahlbert 1963). The central single and both members of the double cone contain a green-absorbing 530_1-nm pigment. The additional cones have a blue-absorbing 450_1 pigment (Loew and Lythgoe 1978). The rods have a 515_1-nm pigment. Purely on the basis of their photopigments one would expect the plaice to be most sensitive to wavelengths around 530 nm in the daytime in reasonably shallow North Sea water, and 515 nm in deep water and at night. The spectral sensitivity of the retinal ganglion cells tell a somewhat more complicated story (Hammond 1968): there are four distinct spectral classes falling in the region 440–60, 470–90, 510–40, and 560–90 nm. At lower stimulus intensity many of the same cells have a sensitivity between 510–30 nm which might indicate that the rods take over some of the cone signal pathways at low intensities. The 440–60-nm and 510–40-nm classes can be explained by the 450_1 and 530_1 cones. It is possible that the 470–90 and 560–90 nm peaks could be derived from inhibitory interaction between the 515_1 rod and the 530_1 cone.

The plaice lives in green water which will filter out both the short-wavelength blue light and long-wavelength red and orange light in deep water. The adult plaice, which live in deep water, lose the additional (blue-sensitive) cones (Engström and Ahlbert 1963) and the retina does not have to accommodate a 'passenger'. In the twilight conditions that prevail in moderate depths in the daytime, the plaice will have an orange–red sensitive channel derived from rod–cone interaction, but as the light decreases, the cones will no longer respond and the rod channel alone remains, giving straightforward scotopic vision.

Sensitivity, contrast, and colour vision

The proportional difference in radiance between different elements of the visual scene is likely to be greater at some wavelengths than at others. If there is sufficient light, the best tactic is for the visual receptor to be most sensitive to the wavelength where these contrasts are greatest. The greater the contrast, the fewer photons need be absorbed to detect it. However, contrasts are often large in regions of the spectrum where there are too few photons to register an image. The ecological problems of life in dim light and in environments where contrasts are poor are explored in the previous two chapters. In this chapter more attention has been given to the spectral quality of the environment, especially those which are simple enough for a rudimentary analysis to be possible given our present state of knowledge.

The roots of colour vision may lie in the fact that the region of the spectrum where contrasts are greatest depends upon the particular object and its particular background. For example, receptors of different spectral sensitivity are needed to detect a light grey fish and a dark grey one. The obvious solution is to have more than one receptor type of different spectral sensitivity. This does not, of itself, mean the animal has colour vision, simply that one set of receptors may record the presence of an object whereas another set does not. However, if the visual mechanism is able to compare the ratio of signals from the two sets scanning the same part of the image, then characteristic ratios may be coded as colour. This is the sort of mechanism required to distinguish ripe red fruit from unripe green ones no matter whether one of them is hanging in full sunlight and the other in deep shade.

6 Directional distribution of light

Air, land, and water

In almost all natural situations the angular distribution of light makes vision easier in some directions but difficult or impossible in others. In good light, visibility is usually best when the major source of light is shining from behind the observer onto the field of view. In deep twilight the reverse is true, for now only the brightest light is above the visual threshold and objects must be silhouetted against it to be seen at all.

The pattern of light distribution is significantly different on land and under water. On land there are relatively small differences in luminance between the landscape and the sky. On a cloudy day a photographer can use nearly the same exposure in whatever direction he points the camera; even on a sunny day it is only the 30′ arc subtended by the sun's disc that is too bright for the film and in the early morning and evening the sun can perfectly well be included in a landscape photograph. The underwater photographer does not have this licence. In open water with a lens having an acceptance angle of 70° or so, the lower part of the picture is likely to be under-exposed and the top part over-exposed. In shallow water this unequal light distribution is a result of the way that the 180° solid angle that includes the sky above water is compressed into the 98° solid angle of Snell's window under water (see pp. 13–14). In deeper water where Snell's window is no longer visible, downwelling light is still about 2 log units brighter than upwelling light; not because of light refraction at the surface, but because of the absorption of light by the water (see pp. 14–16).

The axis of best and worst vision usually lies along the direction of the main light flow and it is interesting to know how this influences the orientation and movement of animals. On land any such orientation tends to be over-ridden by the *force majeur* of gravity, and because most events of visual importance occur in a lateral band across the field of view. In deep water where there is neither surface nor bottom within reach, significant events are just as likely to take place above or below the observer. Another difference is that, for example, olfactory cues cannot be followed in the same way as they are on land because everything is suspended in the same water mass and moves along in company at the same speed, and there are no landmarks with which to judge the direction of the current and hence the direction from which the stimulus originates.

A good example of the influence of light direction on dynamic orientation is provided by the quite unnatural situation of aerial warfare. An aircraft attacking out of the sun is very difficult to see and scanning the sky for an attacker in the direction of the sun leaves a rich cluster of after-images that can take many minutes to clear. These dazzle effects make the silhouette of the aircraft difficult to see. In an effort to reduce the visibility of the aircraft still further by destroying the silhouette, attacking aircraft sometimes had brilliant searchlights mounted along the wings to match the luminance of the sun's disc. This camouflage device is now thought to be widespread among mesopelagic luminous fishes and is discussed in more detail on pp. 175–6.

Lifestyles and the direction of vision

A large predator armed in tooth and claw is unlikely to share the same visual preoccupations as a grazing rodent, and an animal of the open plains has to cope with a different kind of visual scene than one that lives in the middle layers of the forest. Hughes (1977) has exhaustively reviewed the known ways that the functional anatomy of the vertebrate eye (particularly the mammalian eye) serves various visual requirements. There appear to be three main features to be considered. First is the field that is monitored by the eyes, although not necessarily in a very detailed way. Secondly, there is usually an area that is scanned by both eyes at once. This is the binocular field in which stereoscopic vision is possible and visual thresholds are lower (pp. 148–9). Thirdly, parts of the retina are often designed for particularly acute vision in the most important directions (see pp. 149–51).

Total visual field (Table 6.1)

Predators have a rather narrow forward-directed field of view whilst prey species, liable to be pounced upon from behind, may often be able to monitor the scene through the full 360° without so much as turning their head. A wide field of view is likely to be had at the expense of binocularity, for as Walls (1942) points out, the field of view of a single eye is not usually more than about 170° so that if the eyes are to have overlapping fields, the eyes must face forward in the head.

Table 6·1 Fields of view

Animal	Total field scanned	Binocular field[1]
Rabbit	360°	24°
Rat	320°	80°
Grey squirrel	300°	60°
Cat	187°	99°
Man	208°	130°

Data from Hughes (1977)

Binocular vision

When the fields of view of each eye overlap, the same visual scene is seen from a slightly different angle in each eye. Some animals, like man, are able to integrate the two images and to get information about the distance of various objects from the eye. It is not clear how widespread is the use of binocularity for stereoscopic vision. Chameleons capture small insects by shooting out their long tongues. The length of tongue that is extended depends upon the chameleon's judgement of the range of insect. By fitting spectacles to a chameleon, Harkness (1977) was able to alter the apparent range of the insect to the chameleon and thus to cause it to overshoot or undershoot the target. She found that distance judgement was not affected by occluding one eye, but was affected if the power of the eyes' dioptric apparatus was changed by positive or negative lenses. This amounts to proof that in the chameleon it is not binocularity that is essential for distance judgement, but the focus of the eyes.

Binocular vision carries advantages that may become decisive at low luminances where it is a matter of chance whether an eye will capture enough quanta to produce a visual response. Two eyes have a better chance than one of seeing brief dim flashes of light, and Pirenne (1943) has shown that for man the binocular threshold is 0·1 log units better than the monocular threshold. Contrast detection is also better for binocular vision by a factor of $\sqrt{2}$ (1·41) (Campbell and Green 1965 *a, b*) but in this case it seems to be physiological summation from the two eyes that distinguishes the signal from spurious noise in the visual pathway.

Where the light is dim it is essential to capture as many photons as possible and this requires a large visual aperture, but the sheer size of spherical eyes means that an enlarged skull would be needed to house them. Instead, the large aperture is retained but the peripheral retina is discarded and the eyes become tubular in shape (Fig. 6.1). Tubular eyes

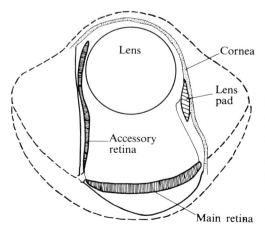

Fig. 6.1. The outline of a normal eye (broken line) superimposed on a tubular eye of a scopelarchid fish. The main retina receives a focused image of the visual scene above the fish. The accessory retina receives light from the ventral–lateral direction via the lens pad and is able to some degree to monitor events below the fish.

are particularly well developed in many mesopelagic fishes, but they are also found in animals such as owls and bush babies. Such eyes can be so crammed into the socket that they cannot track a moving object. Walls (1942) has made the memorable observation that the owl's eye cannot be moved within its socket even with a pair of pliers.

Frontally directed eyes carry the penalty of a poor field of view. This is compensated for to some extent by very mobile heads as in owls and primates. The mesopelagic fishes mitigate the problem in a different way; their eyes have an accessory retina which receives light directed onto it by a bundle of transparent fibres that act as light guides (the lens pad). The accessory retina and lens pad are so arranged that the fish has some peripheral awareness, thus the lens pad serves much the same function as the rear view mirror in a car (Locket 1977).

Areae and the direction of vision

The best indication of the most important directions for vision seems to be the position and shape of the areas specialized for acute vision in the retina and the smaller, even more specialized, foveae that sometimes occur within the area. In man the fovea is central and the surrounding area is circular in outline. However, this arrangement is by no means universal; a horizontal band-shaped area (the visual streak) seems to be more common.

In both mammals and birds a band-shaped area seems to be associated with an open-country habitat or, in the case of birds, large expanses of water (Luck 1965; Meyer 1977; Hughes 1977). They are not confined to lateral-eyed prey species that need to keep the whole visual hemisphere under surveillance; for example the cheetah (Fig. 6.2), which is beyond

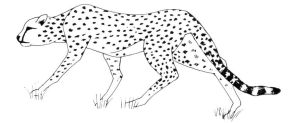

Fig. 6.2. The cheetah,
Acinonyx jubatus.

question a predator, has well-developed band-shaped areas (Fig 6.3). More arboreal species, such as the grey squirrel and cat, have disc-shaped areas more circular in outline, as do the small nocturnal scurrying creatures of the undergrowth, like the mouse and hedgehog. Hughes (1977) considers that for these animals the up and down directions are as likely to be important as the horizontal.

Birds are particularly interesting because 95 per cent of those exam-

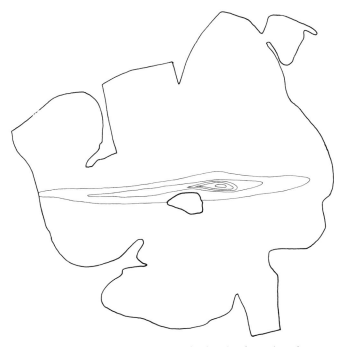

Fig. 6.3. Ganglion-cell density counts in the visual streak and area centralis of the cheetah left eye. The contours represent iso-density counts of 1000, 3000, 5000, 10 000, and 12 000 ganglion cells per mm². (After Hughes 1977.)

ined have foveae and only 54 per cent have only one fovea (Fig. 6.4(a)) (Meyer 1977). Many birds have two foveae, one which looks out laterally serves the monocular field of view, whilst the other, in the temporal part of the eye, serves the forward, binocular field of view. Bifoveate retinas seem to be characteristic of birds such as hawks and hummingbirds that obtain their food on the wing. Sea-birds and birds of the open country often have a horizontal visual streak (Fig. 6.4(c)) sometimes with a fovea. In birds of prey, which have the most excellent vision, there are two foveae plus a visual streak (Fig. 6.4(b)).

The precise function of the various retinal areas of acute vision in birds is not really understood. Birds are distinguished by their ability to fly and in my view, until we understand more about the visual problems specific to bird flight, the function of their retinal specializations is likely to remain obscure. Consider an every-day situation for a bird. It is approaching a tree with the intention of landing on a branch. First, it must discern the wind direction because, not being able to fly backwards, its landing speed will at least equal the wind speed if flying downwind. In making its landing approach, it may have to come in cross-wind. This means it is flying

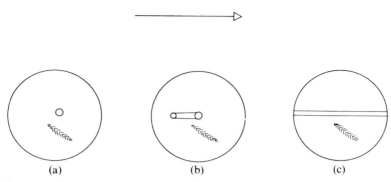

Fig. 6.4. Typical arrangement of areae and foveae in three representative types of bird. The position of the pecten is shaded. The arrow indicates the forward direction. (a) Single central fovea, perhaps the most common type. (b) A lateral and central fovea jointed by an elongate area, characteristic of birds of prey. (c) An elongate horizontal area characteristic of sea-birds. (After Meyer 1977.)

crabwise over the terrain. If it turns its head, the weight shift will tend to roll it in that direction and, as an involuntary consequence, to turn it also. In any wind at all, there will be turbulence thrown up by small rising and falling currents of air and by rotor-like movements set up by irregular features of the terrain. Indeed, the branch itself that it intends to land on may be moving and will also cause turbulence downwind. There are visual problems because the unpredictable air flow will constantly alter the actual direction and speed that the bird is flying relative to fixed objects on the ground and vision is needed to make the appropriate corrections. Compared to flight, the business of ground feeding must be simplicity itself. It seems possible that the bird's eye is primarily designed for the problems of flight. Such activities as feeding have to use the systems principally designed for flight.

Shallow water

The light climate

In shallow water the light climate is dominated by refraction at the water surface and by reflections from the bottom. In deeper water the combined effects of absorption and scatter cause about 98 per cent of the light to come from above and only about 2 per cent from below. Close to the bottom there will also be some effect from bottom reflections. In the surface zone the outline of Snell's window is clearly seen and, of course, the bright, broken image of the sun is located somewhere within it (p. 152; Plate 1). In clear water, Snell's window remains distinct down to a depth of some 30 m. Beneath that depth the radiant patch in the direction of the sun can be seen, but the margins of Snell's window cannot. At greater depths the direction of the sun is no longer significant and the light is distributed symmetrically about the vertical.

Snell's window

To the underwater swimmer, Snell's window intrudes very little into the visual scene; partly because of the restricted field of view of his facemask at normal horizontal viewing angles, and partly because if the diver does turn onto his back, his view is blocked by his exhaled bubbles. For aquatic creatures, with their often protruding eyes, Snell's window is probably an important and constant feature of the visual scene.

On a sunny day in shallow water, sunbeams are made clearly visible by the light scattered out of them, but unlike on land, in a forest for example, the sunbeams constantly change in direction as the water surface changes. The wavelets act as cylindrical lenses of constantly changing curvature and project a network of bright light onto the backs of shallow-living creatures and onto the sea bottom down to depths of around 5 m in clear water— much less in turbid water.

Dazzle

The very bright downwelling light from the sun seems to have resulted in a variety of anti-dazzle devices in shallow-living animals. The visual disability from bright, direct sunlight may result from internal scatter and reflections within the eye, and possibly by raising the adaptation state of the retina to luminance levels above those actually appropriate for that part of the visual display that is being watched.

Many shallow-living fishes—especially those that live in close association with the bottom—have a flap or operculum extending from the dorsal margin of the pupil (Walls 1942) and it is possible that one purpose of these is to exclude direct sunlight. Some shallow water cephalopods, such as the cuttlefish, *Sepia officionalis* (Fig. 6.5), also have a similarly shaped pupil which may have the same purpose.

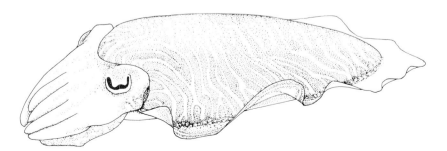

Fig. 6.5. The cuttlefish *Sepia officinale*.

The yellow pigment in the cornea of many diurnal teleosts is often concentrated in the dorsal part of the eye (Fig. 4.6, p. 120) (Walls 1942; Moreland and Lythgoe 1968; Muntz 1972) and may act as a partial screen against the sun. There seems to be no comparative study of the distribution of yellow pigment in the cornea and it is not known how many fishes have yellow pigment uniformly spread over the cornea and which have the yellow restricted to the dorsal part.

A more sophisticated sunshading device is found in the iridescence that is frequently present in corneas of marine teleosts (Lythgoe 1971, 1974a, 1976; Locket 1972). When the fish is illuminated from above, but viewed from the side, iridescent reflections are visible over the pupil aperture (Fig. 6.6). The typical colour is somewhere between yellow–green and

Fig. 6.6. Eye of the Nassau grouper, *Epinephelus striatus*. Note the pear-shaped pupil. Iridescent reflections are clearly seen over the pupil surface. (Photograph: Dick Clarke.)

blue–green, but some of the Epinephelidae (groupers or rock cods) have pinkish iridescence. In some fishes all belonging to the order Scleroparei (mail-cheeked fishes), the iridescence is broken up into one or two files of bright spots or into a series of bright lines.

As a general rule, however, corneal iridescence appears to the unaided eye very similar in different species and use of the optical microscope shows little difference between species. Under the electron microscope, however, the situation is dramatically different. At least six anatomically distinct structures that would produce iridescent reflections have been recognized (Fig. 6.7). The taxonomic distribution of the various types suggests that whatever it is that iridescence does, it is important and has been independently 'discovered' several times in the course of teleost evolution (Lythgoe 1974a, 1976).

The theory of iridescent reflections and their occurrence in animals has been reviewed by Land (1972). Whenever there is a boundary between two transparent materials of different refractive index, there will be some reflection at the interface (Fig. 1.19). If one or both the layers are of the

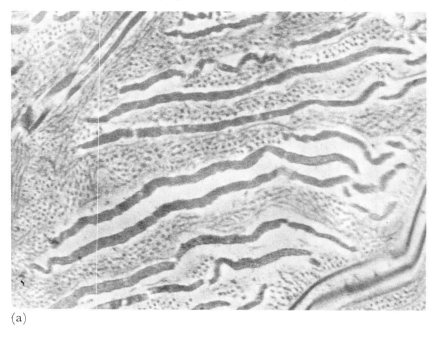

(a)

Fig. 6.7. Types of iridescent corneas in teleost fishes. The location of each type is shown in Fig. 6.8. (a) John Dory, *Zeus faber*. Iridescent layers in corneal stroma. Plates of electron-dense material are embedded in a clear matrix. Type 1a. (b) Lizard fish, *Synodus intermedius*. Iridescent layer corresponds in position to Descemets membrane. Electron-dense material is condensed into lamellae. Type 1b. (c) Saphirine gurnard, *Trigla lucerna*. Regularly arranged collagen fibrils in the corneal stroma are arranged into ranks. Type 1c. (d) Green spotted puffer fish, *Tetraodon samphongsi* Iridescent layer situated within corneal stroma. Adjacent to the iridescent layer is the yellow pigment layer. The parallel lamellae are rough endoplasmic reticulum. Type 2a. (e) Marine goldfish, *Anthias* sp. Iridescent layer is modified rough endoplasmic reticulum within the endothelium. Type 2b. (f) Sand goby, *Pomatoschistus minutus*. Iridescent layer between Descemets layer and stroma. Plates of cytoplasm embedded in non-staining matrix. Type 3.

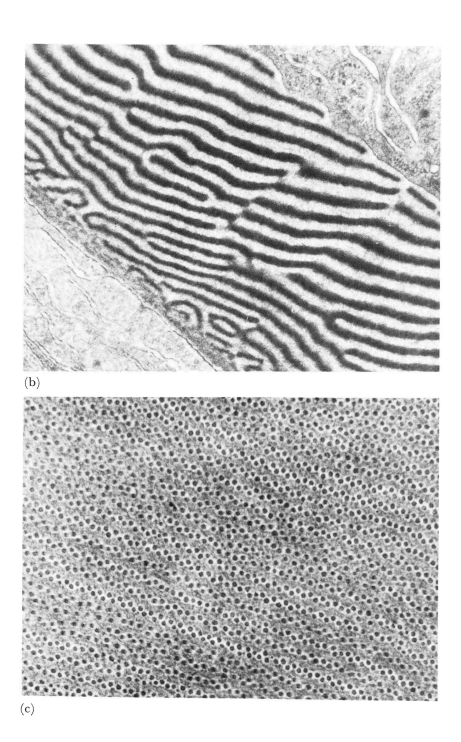

(b)

(c)

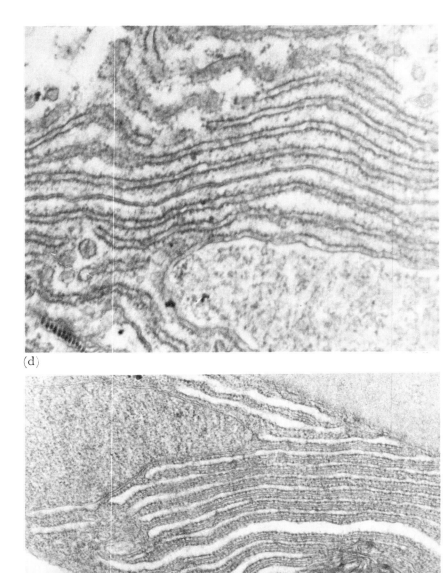

(d)

(e)

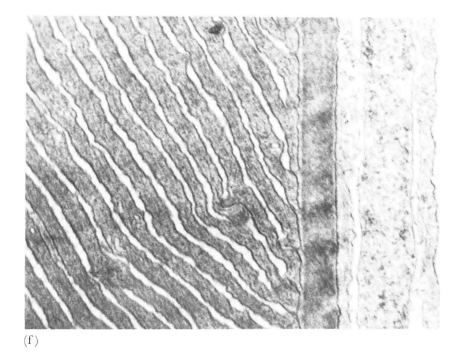

(f)

order of a wavelength of light in thickness, the light rays reflected from successive layer boundaries will mutually interfere. If the two waveforms are in phase, they will augment each other and reflection will be strong. This process is known as constructive interference. When the two waveforms are exactly out of phase, they will tend to cancel each other; reflection is suppressed and transmission maximized. This is known as destructive interference.

In the cornea the reflecting layers may be formed from connective tissue of various types, from modified endoplasmic reticulum, or from very thin plate-like cells separated by thin layers of connective tissue. So far no iridescent layer has been described in the epithelium, but iridescent layers have been seen in the remaining layers of stroma, Descemet's membrane, and endothelium (Fig. 6.8).

The iridescent layers are at their most simple in the modified endoplasmic reticulum of marine goldfish (Anthiidae) and hamlets (Hypoplectrodidae) and the dense layers in Descemet's membrane of the lizard fishes (Synodidae) and hawk fishes (Paracirrhitidae). The flat-cell type of iridescence which is among the types found in many of the perch-like fishes (Percomorphi) can be folded in a complicated way and are difficult to interpret, but in some gobies (Gobiidae) the lamellae are quite simple and their arrangement has been worked out (Fig. 6.9).

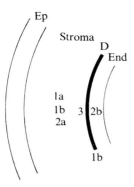

Fig. 6.8. The location of the various types of iridescent layer within the cornea: Ep, Epithelium; D, Descemet's membrane; End, Endothelium. The numbers refer to the tissue types illustrated in Fig. 6.7. (From Lythgoe 1974*b*.)

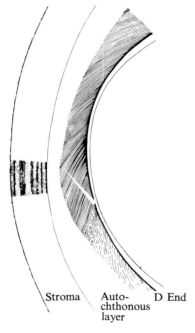

Fig. 6.9. Orientation of the reflecting plates in the cornea of the sand goby. *Pomatoschistus minutus*. The horizontal scale is exaggerated. The appearance of the reflecting plates under the electron microscope is shown in Fig. 6.7. (From Lythgoe 1974*b*).

The general resemblance to a venetian blind is striking, but since the lamellae are considerably less than a wavelength of light in thickness, our everyday expectations of the behaviour of light need to be modified. A venetian blind made of clear glass strips would still exclude much of the unwanted sunlight since it would be reflected away at the air–glass interfaces. But much of the light coming from the outside scene which the animal requires to see would also be lost by reflection. In the case of the goby, where there are about 18 layer-pairs, the losses by reflection of visually important light would be significant.

What seems to happen in the cornea is this. The direct rays from the sun strike the lamella at an oblique angle (Fig. 6.10). Most light is reflected by ordinary Fresnel reflection out of the eye again. There is also some light reflected out of the eye at a less oblique angle by the process of constructive interference. It is this light that gives an iridescent cornea its colour. Light from the outside visual scene passes into the eye at angles nearer to the normal and reaches the corneal lamellae at less oblique angles. At these angles reflection at each interface is suppressed by destructive interference and losses due to reflection are minimal. This is not to say that the cornea is more transparent with an iridescent layer than without it. For this to happen, the layer, like the anti-reflection coating on a camera lens, would need to be actually at the cornea surface as is the anti-reflection nipple array on the corneal surface of some insects (Miller, Møller, and Bernhard 1966).

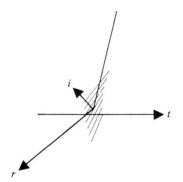

Fig. 6.10. Diagram of the reflection properties of the corneal iridescent layer such as that shown in Fig. 6.9. Bright light incident from above is reflected from the multilayer, partly by constructive interference (i) giving the coloured iridescence to the cornea, and partly by simple reflection (r). Light passing through the eye near the optic axis suffers little loss by reflection since at this angle of incidence there is destructive interference of the reflected rays. (From Lythgoe 1974b.)

The wavelength-selective nature of the corneal reflection does suggest the possibility that the cornea will be more transparent at some wavelengths than at others. In fact, it seems that the iridescent reflections are only an incidental result of the need to cancel reflection losses at the multilayer except at oblique incidence, and the colour-selective property of the multi-layer is so weak as to be insignificant. In some cases, particularly in species that lie flat on the bottom, or partly buried in the sand, corneal iridescence may relieve the blackness of the pupil and thus have a camouflaging function. In some of the groupers (Epinephelidae) that have a pinkish-bronze iridescence, the eye possesses a curiously dull appearance under water that may conceal it to some extent from prospective prey.

Feeding strategies and light distribution

Although the downthrust of gravity on an animal is the same whether the animal is in air or water, the upthrust of buoyancy which is equal to the weight of fluid displaced is much greater in water than in air. Terrestrial animals are constantly returned to earth by the force of gravity, whereas aquatic animals can arrange their bodies to sink or float by the inclusion of quite small volumes of gas or lipid. The freedom of three-dimensional movement combined with the more directional nature of underwater illumination means that the distribution of underwater light has a considerable influence on the mode of life of aquatic animals.

For our present purposes, shallow-water animals can be somewhat crudely divided into three classes according to the food they eat: (1) sessile animals and plants; (2) active, generally large, non-transparent animals; and (3) plankters that are small or transparent. Animals in each category tend to approach their prey from a characteristic direction which is determined by their own body form, the position of their prey, and by the direction from which the prey is most visible and the predator best hidden. The characteristic direction of attack and feeding can conveniently be called the 'feeding vector'.

The direction of the feeding vector can be judged by watching the animal in nature, but the necessary observations are often very difficult to make. Alternatively, the morphology of the eye and head can give strong presumptive information on the direction of most efficient vision. In most cases this will also correspond to the feeding vector, although in some unselective feeders that are themselves preyed upon, the information may apply less to the position of their food and more to the position of their predators.

Taking the head as a whole, it is evident that if some part of it obstructs the path of sight, then that direction is scarcely likely to be kept under visual surveillance by the animal. Conversely, the presence of 'sighting grooves', which are depressions in the skull usually along the snout forward of the eyes, suggests that the sight in the forward direction is often important. In fishes the lens is spherical or nearly so, but the pupil aperture is often pear-shaped (Fig. 6.6), which leaves a crescent-shaped aphakic space usually in the rostral part of the pupil that is not covered by the lens. The function of the aphakic space may be either to allow the forward accommodation movement of the lens (Sivak 1973) or to allow the greatest possible admissions of light coming from objects placed peripherally to the optic axis (Munk and Frederiksen 1974). Perhaps both functions are served together, but in any case the direction of the aphakic space indicates the direction of greatest visual interest.

Animals feeding on sessile organisms

In bottom-living, bottom-feeding teleosts, the area is in the dorsal, caudal part of the retina. This has been mapped in the plaice (*Pleuronectes platessa*) by Engström and Ahlbert (1963) but has also been noted in other bottom-living teleosts such as the dragonet, *Callionymus lyra* (Vilter 1947), the black-mouthed goby, *Gobius melanostomus* (Moskalkova 1971), and three eelpout, *Lycodes*, species (Anctil 1969).

Midwater predators

Most fishes are so constructed that their direction of maximum accelera-tion is in line with the body's axis. The direction of ambush and pursuit is, therefore, likely to be along this direction and it is scarcely surprising that some predacious fish have caudally placed foveae or areae that give them particularly acute vision in the forward direction, and a rostral aphakic space and sighting grooves along the snout (Walls, 1942).

In our present state of knowledge, however, it is unwise to generalize too much about the possession of high visual acuity in the forward direction. In a careful study of the density of cones in the retina of four, closely related fishes all belonging to the family Percidae, Ahlbert (1969) showed that in the most active predator, the perch, *Perca fluviatilis* (Fig. 6.11,

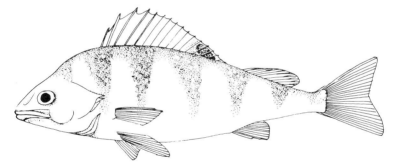

Fig. 6.11. The perch *Perca fluviatilis*.

Plate 5) which captures its prey by chasing (Neill and Cullen 1974) there was no well-marked fovea despite the presence of a rostral aphakic space, but there was a horizontal region of close-packed cones with the greatest concentration placed caudally (Fig. 6.12(a)). Ahlbert (1975) points out that a true area in Walls' sense also implies a greater complexity of the neural retina serving it. For practical reasons this was not investigated for the perch but, nevertheless, Ahlbert (1975) considere there is good reason to believe that areas of high cone density really do mark areas of particu-larly acute vision.

It is perhaps worth mentioning that a 'horizontal' band on the retina does not necessarily correspond to a horizontal band across the visual scene because fishes do not always arrange themselves horizontally in the water. In particular, many fishes swimming near large rocks align them-selves in the same plane as the rock face (Meyer, Heiligenberg, and Bullock

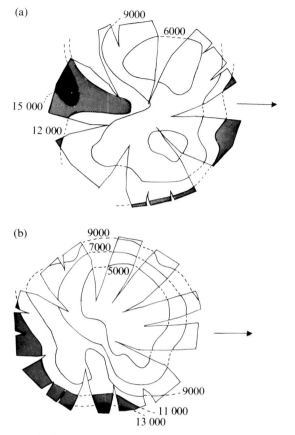

Fig. 6.12. The density distribution of double cones in
(a) the perch, *Perca fluviatilis*, and (b) the pollan,
Coregonus albula. The perch feeds by hunting, the pollan
feeds on plankton. The figures show the right eye;
arrows indicate forward direction. The values for density
are number of double cones/mm². (From Ahlbert 1969.)

1976). Indeed, it has been observed many times that fishes near the roofs
of caves may actually swim upside down.

Several species that feed on active prey do so by striking obliquely upwards from below. This has been observed in the field for saithe (*Pollarchius
virens*), cod (*Gadus morhua*, Fig. 6.13), and cuckoo wrasse (*Labrus ossifagus*)
by Larsson (ex Ahlbert 1976) and for cabrilla (*Mycteroperca*) by Hobson
(1965) and for adult salmon and trout feeding on fish by Nilsson (1963).
It has also been recorded for sea lions (Fig. 6.14) by Hobson (1966) down
to depths of almost 240 ft.

The upward-striking vector is probably due to the increased visibility of

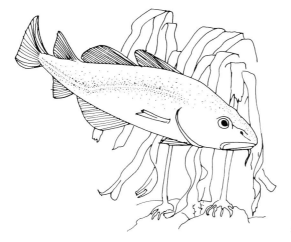

Fig. 6.13. The cod *Gadus morhua*.

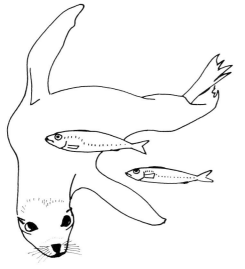

Fig. 6.14. Sea lions strike upwards at their prey.

fishes when seen from below silhouetted against bright downwelling light, whilst the predator is difficult to detect from above (see pp. 173–4 on camouflage). This mode of attack is likely to be especially effective under twilight conditions where it is only in the upward direction that there is sufficient light for vision (Hobson 1966). Indeed, in the aquarium at least, the Pacific salmon, *Oncorhyncus*, uses the silhouette feeding mode when scotopic, but reverts to a more horizontal attack when photopic conditions prevail (Ali 1959, 1976).

Plankton feeders

Most species of zooplankter are exceedingly difficult to see in mid-water and they achieve their remarkable camouflage by small size, transparency (Hamner, W. M. 1974; Hamner, W. M., Madin, Alldredge, Gilmer, and Hamner, P. P. 1975), and by matching the reflecting parts of their body to that of the background spacelight (see pp. 171–5). There is no way of camouflaging an opaque non-luminous body when it is seen in silhouette against the brightest part of the visual scene. Transparent bodies are, however, more difficult to detect since they provide a poor silhouette. However, the small differences in refractive index between planter and sea water are revealed when the planter lies across the boundary between a bright field and a dark field. On a reasonably calm day such a bright/dark boundary is provided by the edge of Snell's window at an angle between 47 ° and 48 ° from the vertical.

The natural forward motion of a fish coupled with the direction of maximum visibility of the zooplankters lead one to suppose that the visual axis of the fish would be in the upper forward direction. Various investigations on the density of cones in the retinas of plankton-feeding fishes support this view since areae of high cone density have regularly been recorded in the caudal ventral retina (Fig. 6.12(b)) (see Ahlbert 1975 for a review). Examples are chiefly found in the Salmonidae (for example the pollan, *Coregonus albula* (Fig. 6.15) and several clupeids. To a lesser extent

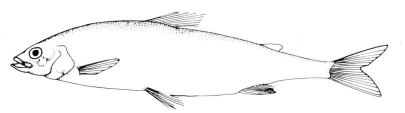

Fig. 6.15. The pollan *Coreganus albula*.

the ventral caudal area has been seen in the horse mackerel, *Trachurus symmetricus*, and the true Pacific mackerel, *Pneumotophorus diego* (=*Scomber japonicus*) (O'Connel 1963) (see Table 6.2).

Munk (1970) has described particularly good examples of high resolving power in the retina corresponding with the image of the light/dark bounddary at the edge of Snell's window. These are provided by *Aplocheilus lineatus* which is a freshwater fish from India and Ceylon, and the closely related *Epiplatys grahamis*, a freshwater fish from southern Nigeria and Cameroon. Both species swim in a slightly head-up position just beneath the surface and feed on small animals such as insects floating on the surface or just beneath it. Both have two parallel band-shaped areas in each eye

Table 6.2 Fishes with ventral-caudal area

Alosa rapidissima	American shad	O'Connel (1963)
Alosa kessleri kessleri		Baburina (1955*a*)
Clupeorella delicatula caspia		Baburina (1955*b*)
C. engrauliformes		Baburina and Kovaleva (1959)
C. grimmi		Baburina and Kovaleva (1959)
Clupea pilchardus	Sardine	Vilter (1950)
C. harengus	Herring	Engstrom (1963)
C. sprattus	Sprat	Engstrom (1963)
Anchoa compressa	Deep-bodied anchovy	O'Connel (1963)
Engraulis mordax	Northern anchovy	O'Connel (1963)
Coregonus albula	Cisco (pollan)	Ahlbert (1969)
Salmo salar	Salmon	Ahlbert (1975)
Salmo trutta trutta	Trout	Ahlbert (1975)

which are probably horizontal when the fish is in its normal swimming posture. One of the areas is positioned across the centre of the eye for horizontal vision, but the second area lies across the ventral retina in a way that it is looking upwards at an angle of 47° from the vertical in *A. lineatus* and 42–3° for *E. grahamis*. When it is recalled that the margin of Snell's window lies at an angle of 47° to the vertical, we may suppose that these two species are specially adapted to detect floating organisms at the boundary of Snell's window.

Deep water

Mesopelagic animals

The mesopelagic fauna occupies a zone that is conventionally considered to extend from a depth of around 200 m to about 1000 m, at which depth all daylight is exhausted (see p. 104). The visual world is relatively simple because the surface is too far above to impose its own discipline on the orientation of animals, and the position of the sun in the sky makes little difference to the directionality of underwater light. As daylight penetrates ever deeper into the sea, the angular distribution of the light settles down into a characteristic pattern with at least 98 per cent of the light coming from above and only about 2 per cent reflected upwards from below, a difference of nearly 3 log units (see pp. 14–16).

In the clear waters of the deep oceans, a 3-log-unit reduction in intensity is brought about by the absorption in a water column about 300 m deep. In the lower half, the mesopelagic range, only downwelling light will be perceptible even at high noon since the upwelling light is too dim to be seen.

The mesopelagic fauna contains many of the bizarre fishes that are classified in the popular mind as 'deep-sea fishes'. Some morphological features, such as the tubular eyes, ranks of light-emitting organs, and black or silver colouring, are direct adaptations to the dim and highly directional light in the middle sea. Other features attributable to the mesopelagic life have been described by Marshall (1954, 1971) and some of the adaptations are set out in Table 6.3. Although the morphology and anatomy of deep-living fishes is reasonably well-known, and we can have reasonable confidence that we understand the light climate in which they live, most of their behaviour and social organization is still unknown to us.

Table 6.3 Organization of mesopelagic and bathypelagic fishes

Features	Mesopelagic, plankton-consuming species	Bathypelagic species
Colour	Many with silvery sides	Black
Photophores	Numerous and well developed in most species	Small or regressed in gonostomatids; a single luminous lure on the females of most ceratioids
Jaws	Relatively short	Relatively long
Eyes	Fairly large to very large, with relatively large dioptric parts and sensitive pure-rod retinae	Small or regressed, except in the males of some anglerfishes
Olfactory organs	Moderately developed in both sexes of most species	Regressed in females but large in males of *Cyclothone* spp and ceratioids (most species)
Central nervous system	Well developed in all parts	Weakly developed, except for the acousticolateralis centres and the forebrain of macrosmatic males
Myotomes	Well developed	Weakly developed
Skeleton	Well ossified, including scales	Weakly ossified; scales usually absent
Swimbladder	Usually present, highly developed	Absent or regressed
Gill system	Gill filaments numerous, bearing very many lamellae	Gill filaments relatively few with a reduced lamellar surface
Kidneys	Relatively large with numerous tubules	Relatively small, with few tubules
Heart	Large	Small

Source: Marshall (1971).

Body orientation in life

We have no certain knowledge that deep-living fishes spend any significant fraction of time with their body arranged horizontally in the water. Indeed, in many cases we know that they do not (Bone 1973). If we cannot be sure of that, then we have difficulty in deciding if, for example, dorsally-directed eyes are, in fact, looking directly upwards in real life. Vertically migrating animals move through considerable vertical distances twice in each 24 hours and in the case of myctophid fishes, for example, direct observations from a deep submersible show that they swim upwards and downwards at angles near the vertical and only part of their life is spent with the body axis horizontal (Backus, Craddock, Haldrich, Shores, Teal, Wing, Mead, and Clarke 1968; Barham 1970).

The relationship between the direction of tubular eyes, depth, and the attitude of the body is well illustrated by the mesopelagic fish, *Benthalbella infans* (Fig. 6.16) (Merrett, Badcock, and Herring 1973). In common with many other ocean species, the young fish live in shallower water than the adult. Like other members of the Scopelarchidae, *Benthalbella* has tubular eyes. In the adult these look upward and slightly forward, but in the young, post-larval stages they are directed forward. According to Merrett *et al.*, the young fishes hang with the posterior part of their body vertical in the water and the eyes look upwards at an angle of about 30 ° to the vertical. At this stage the fish are living at 100–300 m and we may suppose that this attitude allows them to detect floating plankters most easily. For the young adults living at depths between 450 and 900 m only the downwelling light is bright enough for vision and in these fishes the body axis is horizontal and the eyes are directed nearly vertically upwards.

Mirror camouflage cannot work when the animal is silhouetted against the brightest area of the visual scene. In deep water this is vertically up-wards and any animal hunting by sight is most likely to find its prey by swimming below it and scanning upwards. The chief defensive strategy is to arrange downward pointing photophores along the belly and lower flanks so that the radiance of the animal is raised to equal that of the downwelling light (see pp. 175–6). The hunter's response is to arrange its visual axis so that it looks directly upwards whereupon it can see those animals that have not been able to assume perfect luminous camouflage.

Like silvery-sidedness, ventral photophores give a clue to the natural attitude of those that possess them. The hatchet fish as we shall see (p. 176) has downward-shining photophores, but so have the majority of light-bearing species. Indeed, it is interesting that very few species have photo-phores along their dorsal surface. One of the few that have are some male lantern fishes (Myctophidae) which have a large photophore on the dorsal part of the tail stalk.

What of the species with forward-looking tubular eyes; do they swim with their heads up and tails down? Perhaps some do, but it is hard to

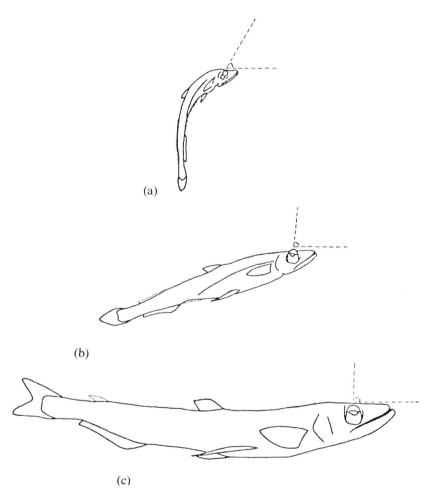

Fig. 6.16. Changes in the orientation of the eye and body of the pearleye, *Benthalbella infans*. The approximate depth ranges of capture in the daytime were: (a) in the region of 100–300 m for the post-larval stage; (b) 450–900 m for young adults; and (c) at least 1500 m for adults.

convince oneself that the peculiar little fish, the spookfish, *Winteria telescopa*, swims like that. It has forward and slightly upward directed eyes, but it also has an anal photophore whose light is channelled along the flat belly in a way that would obviously direct the light ventrally (Bertelsen and Munk 1964). We have to conclude that *Winteria* swims horizontally, is camouflaged for that orientation, and is able to detect its prey in the horizontal direction.

It is natural that these weird fishes should capture a large part of our attention, but it is less easy to assess how important they are in the meso-pelagic fauna as a whole. Marshall (1971) estimates that there are some 750 species of mesopelagic fishes of which it is possible to identify 30 (there are certainly more) that have tubular eyes. Marshall points out that 11 different families have members with tubular eyes, and this indicates that the eyes have evolved independently in different ancestral lines. Amongst the mesopelagic fishes as a whole, some 100 have silvery flanks (Marshall 1971) but amongst the tubular-eyed fishes at least half have a silvery sheen and some, such as the hatchet fishes (*Argyropelecus*) look as if they are made from polished silver. Of the 36 tubular-eyed fishes that provide the data for Fig. 6.17, 16 have downward directed photophores that are probably there principally for camouflage.

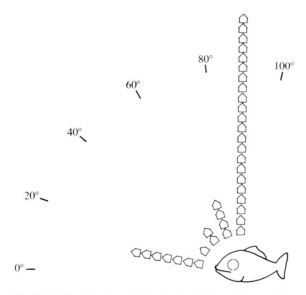

Fig. 6.17. The direction of the visual axis in tubular-eyed fishes. Most look directly upwards or directly forwards. (Data from: Brauer 1906, 1908; Hart 1973; Munk 1966; Bertelsen and Munk 1964; Merrett *et al.* 1973; Herring 1977*b*; Marshall 1971; Blache, Cadenat, and Stauch 1970.)

7 Camouflage and advertisement

Introduction

There is a large and growing body of knowledge about the uses of colours and patterns in nature and it comes as something of a surprise to find that as late as 1940 Cott had to devote a large part of his classic monograph on animal colorations to establish beyond doubt that the appearance of animals can indeed be a method of communication or of concealment. It would be redundant here to reiterate all the known uses of natural coloration which range from concealment and mimicry to sexual and agonistic display. Accounts of these are given by Cott (1940), Wickler (1968), and Hinton (1973). In this chapter displays are described that have clear visual significance; but it is well to remember that some natural colours such as the red of blood, the green of foliage, the red of precious coral, or the iridescence of mollusc shells have not arisen solely through visual factors in evolution. This is not to say that they have no visual significance; for example coral and sea shells are now collected to the point of extinction in some places because they look pretty, the red of blood near the surface of the skin is sometimes used as a visual display, and the green of fresh foliage is doubtless used by some animals as a guide to palatability. Other colorations like the dark colours of desert insects are more likely to play their main role in heat regulation (Schmidt Nielsen 1964) and their visual significance, although secondary, may be important and perhaps disadvantageous.

The general approach in this chapter is from an optical and physiological viewpoint. I have tried to show how the optical characteristics of particular environments, and the basic similarities in visual physiology between all animals, define rules that govern the visibility of animals and plants. If these rules are valid, then the biologist can make an educated guess whether an organism will appear conspicuous or be difficult to see in particular situations.

It is impossible to overstate the importance of considering the organism as it actually exists in nature. The pictures contained in the many beautifully illustrated books on natural history and in natural-history films on television are selected to be visually startling or attractive. Underwater photographs are almost always taken with the aid of artificial light to 'bring out' the red and orange colours that would normally not be there at all. Photographs of dull-coloured animals are either not published, or are posed against a colourful background to add interest to the scene.

It is generally easier to formulate answerable questions about camouflage than about conspicuousness. In camouflage it is necessary to consider whether small optical differences, including differences in movement, between object and background or between mimic and model, are large enough to be discriminated. If there is no optical difference, then detection is not possible by vision alone, no matter how sophisticated the eye or alert the brain. Any conspicuous object must necessarily differ optically from its background. But the magnitude of the difference is not by itself a reliable index of conspicuousness because the image must be one that attracts the attention of the brain.

Although there is some discussion here about the characteristics that make some colours and patterns inherently conspicuous, the ideas are far from established. One has more confidence in discussing conspicuousness in situations where the conditions for vision are so difficult, such as in turbid water or in dim light, that most objects cannot be seen at all and only the most conspicuous ones can be detected. In such situations it is sometimes possible to infer with reasonable confidence the types of display that are most easily seen.

Camouflage by radiance matching

It is in open water where there are no physical objects to offer refuge that the art of camouflage by radiance matching is most elegantly demonstrated. On land and very near the bottom under water, the complex patterns of the background must be accommodated in a camouflaged display. In mid-water these complex patterns are absent, but the angular distribution of underwater radiance varies through several orders of magnitude in different directions. An animal that is able to match its own radiance to that of the water background spacelight against which it is seen, is able to achieve a very fair degree of camouflage.

Countershading and silveryness

Thayer (Thayer and Thayer 1909) was perhaps the first to state clearly that the reason why so many animals are coloured dark above and light below is to counteract the bright reflections from their upper surface caused by the greater quantity of light that shines on them from above, compared to that from below. In Thayer's own words: 'The effect of obliterative gradation of light and shade is to render the creature's actual surface unrecognizable as the surface of any object or objects of the immediate foreground, causing it to pass for an empty space through which the background is seen.'

Cott (1940) showed how this countershading is particularly well displayed in fishes and further pointed out that the colour of the fishes, particularly on the dorsal parts, corresponded with the general colour of the water in which they swim. In rough-skinned fishes, such as sharks, it may be that countershading is the principal method of camouflage. But in many animals, such as cephalopods and teleost fishes, the body is silvery, especially on the flanks. These silvery sides have mirror-like properties that play an essential part in underwater camouflage (Fig. 7.1). Ward (1919) considered that the main advantage of silvery surfaces on fishes was to reflect the bottom, thus causing the fish to disappear. In a sophisticated study of the value of silvery-sidedness in camouflage, Denton and Nicol (1965*a*, *b*, 1966) showed how the orientation of the reflecting crystals in the scales of fishes is such as to hide the fish in mid-water (Fig. 7.2).

Fig. 7.1. The silvery sides of fishes (in this case the margate *Haemulon album*) can effectively camouflage them against the water background. Note also that when the water surface is not completely calm, the edge of Snell's window is broken up. (Photograph: Dick Clarke.)

On an overcast day and in turbid or deep water the angular distribution of light is symmetrical about the vertical. A flat surfaced mirror suspended vertically in the water will be hard to see because the light it reflects into the eye has the same intensity and colour as the observer would see

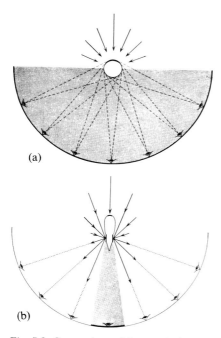

(a)

(b)

Fig. 7.2. Comparison of the properties a mirrored cylinder and a silvery fish under water. The cylinder appears darker than the background provided the angle of view is upwards. The reflecting crystals in the scales of the fish are so arranged that the whole flank reflects like a vertical mirror. Only from directly below the fish does it look darker than the background. (From Denton and Nicol 1966.)

behind it. Denton and Nicol have shown that although the scales follow the contour of the fish, the reflecting crystals embedded within the scales are orientated in such a way that the fish, when seen from the side, reflects light like a flat-surfaced mirror.

Mirror camouflage works well from all directions of view except looking vertically upwards from below. In this position, the bulk of the fish, which is silhouetted against the brightest part of the visual field, occludes the bright downwelling light required to match the radiance of the fish to its background. A partial solution apparently adopted by many species is to angle the reflecting crystals so that they reflect light displaced some degrees from the vertical but which is, nevertheless, nearly as bright as the light shining vertically downwards. Nevertheless, the difficulty of camouflaging a silhouette by reflecting light is a substantial problem. There are two alternative strategies that are employed. One is to make the body tissues as transparent as possible, the other is to use bioluminescence to match the bright downwelling light.

Some fishes, such as the Indian glass fish and the larvae of plaice and soles, are nearly transparent and, as such, will be difficult to detect in the diffuse light under water (Denton and Nicol 1966). However, there are always some tissues that cannot be disguised. Important amongst these are the eyes which can only form an image if the light reaches the retina through the pupil. The retina has to be screened from light coming from other directions and that means the eye will be opaque. The stomach contents cannot be made transparent, either because the prey is not transparent or camouflaged or, if it is, the camouflage will be destroyed as digeston proceeds. In cephalopods, the ink sac cannot be made transparent because the pigment it contains is designed to be visible. The problem of camouflaging opaque organs within a transparent or translucent body is solved by clothing the organ itself in a silvery argenteum, and the dorsal surface is darkly pigmented.

Logically we do not know if there are any perfectly camouflaged animals because we could not see them if there were. Amongst the vertebrates and terrestrial invertebrates this dictum is overstating the case. But amongst the zooplankton it is really true that in the open sea an alert and normally sighted diver simply does not see the plankters that surround him and may have difficulty in detecting one several centimetres in diameter at a comfortable reading distance even when its position is indicated by the pointed finger of his companion. In the case of zooplankters, it is the gonads and nerves that remain opaque, or at least translucent. But they tend to be more dispersed within the tissues than in the higher animals and thus defeat the resolution of the observer's eye. Extreme transparency is recorded in many unrelated groups including the Hydrozoa, siphonophores and true jelly fish, comb jellies, Heteropoda and Pterapoda, salps, larvaceans, and arrow worms. (Hammer *et al.* 1975.) Many of the zooplankton species that live very near to the surface in the blue water of the open ocean are themselves coloured a brilliant blue, especially the reproductive organs. Herring (1967), who has shown that these animals contain an extractable blue proteinated carotenoid, believes that this makes the animals less conspicuous to predatory birds that see them against the deep-water blue. The blueness must also help to camouflage the animals from fishes swimming at the same depth in the sea. If the opaque parts of the plankter were grey, i.e. they reflect all wavelengths equally, the light they reflect in shallow water from the downwelling sunlight would also be grey. In the open sea it will be viewed against the blue background spacelight and even if the brightness of the plankter and the background is nearly the same, the plankter will differ in colour and thus be seen. Blue coloration corrects the colour difference and the plankter is the more perfectly camouflaged.

Transparency as a camouflage technique is also used by an assemblage of Lepidoptera species that live within 2 m of the ground in the forests of tropical South America. These species are characterized by having extremely transparent wings with narrow dark margins, making the whole animal difficult to detect against the complex visual background of the forest floor (Papageorgis 1975).

Bioluminescence and camouflage

The difficulty of camouflaging an object that is seen in silhouette comes into prominence in deep water, where the only direction from which there is enough light to see by is directly from above (pp. 165–6). The silhouette cannot be disguised by reflection but Clarke (1963) has suggested that downward-directed photophores in both fishes and invertebrates are used to raise the radiance of the animal up to that of the downwelling daylight and also to match it in colour (Herring (1967) for a review). A similar technique has been tried in aerial warfare where bright lights are mounted along an aircraft's wings (Siegel and Fletcher 1969) in order to disguise its silhouette against the bright skylight when it is attacking out of the sun.

If it is indeed the function of ventral photophores to match the radiance of the downwelling light, then the match should be good for all upwardly directed angles of view. Denton, Gilpin-Brown, and Wright (1972) made careful studies of the radiance emitted downwards by the mesopelagic hatchet fish, *Argyropelecus affinis* (Fig. 7.3(a)) and the viper fish, *Chauliodus sloani*. *Argyropelecus* is silver but *Chauliodus* is black. Denton and his co-workers were able to show that the distribution of downward-directed radiance (Fig. 7.3(b)) from the fish closely matches the expected radiance distribution of the underwater spacelight. A similar light distribution has also been found by Herring (1976) for the decapod crustacea *Oplophorus spinosus* and *Systellaspis debilis*. Significantly Denton Gilpin-Brown and Wright (1970) have also shown that the light produced by the light-generating tissue in the ventral photophores of some fishes including *Argyropelecus* species has to pass through a colour filter which ensures that the colour of the emitted light matches that of the daylight at the depths where the animals live.

The problem still remained that the brightness required to match the downwelling light is different from depth to depth and from hour to hour

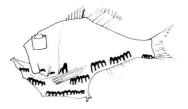

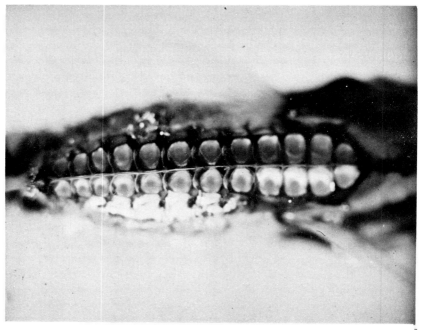

Fig. 7.3. (a) The hatchet fish *Argyropelecus affinis*. (b) The belly of a hatchet fish showing downward-directed photophores. (Photo by Peter David.)

according to the brightness of the daylight above the surface. However, evidence is now accumulating that several free-swimming squids and fishes alter the radiance of their photophores to tune with natural variations in ambient light (Herring (1977*a*) for a review). It is possible that an explanation for the photophores that are directed into the eye of some deep-living fishes is that they may be a device for matching directly the radiance of the ventral photophores to that of the daylight entering the eye (Nicol 1967).

Downward-directed photophores may also have a camouflaging function in some invertebrates. This has been suggested for pelagic cephalopods (Marshall 1971) and also in upper mesopelagic shrimps. In these the organ of Pesta is luminous and, at least in *Sergestes*, is rotated so that it always points downwards irrespective of the position of the body (Makoto Omari 1974).

Radiance mismatching and advertisement

Nocturnal

It is unlikely that many animals have colour vision at night. Thus to be camouflaged at night it is necessary only to match the background in brightness. However, there are probably exceptions to this generalization. The Amphibia have two classes of rod having different spectral sensitivities and some deep-sea fishes are known to have more than one visual pigment in their cone-free retina (see Lythgoe (1972) for a list), whilst the presence of coloured photophores in species such as *Pachystomias* and *Aristostomias* (Fig. 7.18) indicate the possibility of rod-mediated colour vision.

Visual displays at night

Camouflage is easier at night because the few photons available for vision make it more difficult to detect contrasts so that the match between the animal and its background needs to be less exact. It is also harder to detect fine detail, which means that fine patterns will not be resolved.

Conspicuous displays intended to be seen at night when it is too dark for colour vision usually involve the use of broad areas that are as different as possible in brightness from the background. Such displays are likely to be either black or silvery or white. White and silvery objects have the advantage that in very dark conditions the visual scene may be so dark as not to be seen at all, whereas the white and silver may remain visible.

Conspicuous white visual displays are found in the mature male nightjar (*Caprimulgus europeus europeus*). By day the nightjar crouches on the ground concealed by its brown mottled plumage, but during the active twilight and night period, conspicuous white patches on the outer wing primaries and outer tail feathers are visible. Nocturnal mammals such as the skunk and badger (Fig. 7.4) also possess conspicuous coloration where the contrast of the broad, white markings is augmented by black areas.

Fig. 7.4. The badger *Meles meles*.

In fact, nocturnal displays are rare; Cott (1940) noted that most nocturnal animals have concealing coloration whereas their diurnal relatives may be quite conspicuous. Cott's explanation for this is that for nocturnal animals the quiescent period is during the daytime when it is important to escape detection. As examples of groups where the nocturnal species are cryptic but several of their diurnal relatives are conspicuous, Cott (1940, p. 204) quotes frogs, newts and salamanders, day-flying moths, and homopterous birds. Amongst mosquitoes, diurnal species like *Haemogogus* and *Toxorhynchites* are often brilliantly coloured, or have striking adornments and conspicuous display behaviour, as does *Anopheles implexus*. Nocturnal mosquitoes, on the other hand, are usually drab in colour (Haddow and Corbet 1961).

Many nocturnal animals make use of non-visual displays to advertise their presence or their intentions. The porcupine rattles its black and white spines; mosquitoes come together in loud, humming swarms; foxes bark; snapping shrimps snap; and moths exude powerful pheromones. The emphasis on auditory and olfactory displays suggests that so far as vision is concerned the Quit point has been reached when the difficulty and danger in producing patterns that can be seen at night is no longer worth while and other means of advertisement are emphasized instead.

Diurnal

Animals that are active at night are limited by the fewness of photons available for vision and all must, therefore, share much the same physical constraints. Animals that achieve camouflage by matching exactly the radiance patterns of their background or mimicking some other object are undetectable by any visual method if they achieve an exact match. Our interest in dim-light displays and camouflage is, therefore, mainly centred on the nature of the display. Conspicuous displays in bright light are not limited by the light available. Fast movements and fine detail can be resolved and colour vision becomes possible. Any study of advertising displays in daylight have to take into account the visual system of the observer at least as much as the mechanism of the display.

The mechanisms of colour vision are presumably adjusted to serve their particular tasks of food finding and predator avoidance. To do this they possess cones of suitable spectral sensitivity whose signals are processed to facilitate the most searching analysis of the most pressing visual tasks. It seems reasonable to suppose that chromatic mechanisms tuned specifically to detect differences between closely similar hues can be superstimulated by radiances that are specifically designed to take advantage of their special characteristics.

Birds

Nearly all birds have coloured oil droplets in their cones that modify the spectral response of the visual pigments they contain (pp. 56–60). In the chicken and pigeon, which are the only birds that have been adequately examined, the combination results in narrow-band chromatic channels centred at around 530, 570, and 610 nm; that is in the green, yellow, and red parts of the spectrum. It is suggested on p. 131 that it is the 570–nm and 610–nm droplet/cone combinations that are most useful for distinguishing between different foliage colours on the basis of the relative amount of chlorophyll and red pigment they contain.

Naturally occurring reds, yellows, and oranges reflect the long wavelengths down to about 500 nm for yellow, 550 nm for orange and 600 nm for red (Fig. 1.18). Something yellow will stimulate both the 570 and 610 channels, whereas a red will stimulate only the 610 channel. It is to be expected that a red and yellow pattern will be particularly strongly differentiated by a bird, particularly those that have many red and orange oil droplets in the retina. The red and yellow bills of gulls that are an important feeding signal for their chicks (Hailman 1967) are a good example.

It has been known for some time that many flowers are specially adapted for pollination by birds. Werth (1915) found 159 ornithophilous species in Patagonia, Brazil, South Africa, and Western Australia and of these 84 per cent were predominantly red. Pickens (1930) studied 100 species of flowers visited by humming birds in eastern North America and of these 60 were red and orange. Similar colours have been noted in the bird-pollinated species of the phlox family (Grant and Grant 1965) whilst Proctor and Yeo (1976) show photographs of typical bird-pollinated flowers all patterned in the so-called 'parrot' colours of red, orange, and yellow.

Plants also signal to birds that their fruits are ripe (Rothschild 1975). Of 79 species of flowering plants in the British flora that carry succulent fruit, nearly all have conspicuously coloured seeds or berries. Of these 49 are red, 23 are dark blue or black, and the rest are orange, white, brown, and green. As usual in estimates of this kind, there are problems as to what constitutes a true species. (The blackberry, which has been variously estimated to be 1 or 300 species, is here taken to be the single species of Bentham and Hooker (1930).)

Colours that warn birds of disgusting taste or dangerous secretions are good indicators of the inherent conspicuousness of certain colours to birds. Of 9 noxious amphibia illustrated by Cott (1940) only one is not boldly coloured in red, yellow, or a combination of both. Warning colours in insects may also be tuned to the colour vision of birds that might prey on them. Jones (1932, 1934) found 31 species of insects belonging to 3 different orders that wild birds shunned when feeding. Of the 31 species, 19 were conspicuously marked in red, yellow, or orange. Four more exhibited the same colours but less conspicuously, whilst the remaining 8 had different types of coloration. By comparison, not one of 90 highly acceptable species showed red, orange, or yellow markings.

In considering the possibility that birds occupying particular ecological niches might possess their own characteristic assemblage of oil droplets, Muntz (1972) paid particular attention to nocturnal birds; the swallows, swifts, and birds that feed from the water. Using data supplied to him by Cullen, Muntz showed that sea-birds can be divided broadly into species that have only about 20 per cent red and orange oil droplets and those that have between 50 and 80 per cent. Birds that generally pursue fishes underwater, such as the shag (Fig. 5.4), razorbill, and shearwater, belong to the group with few red and orange droplets and those such as gulls (Fig. 7.5) and terns (Fig. 7.6) which, by and large, feed from the surface or just below it, have many red and orange droplets.

Fig. 7.5. Reflections from the sun and sky at the water surface make it more difficult for birds to see through it.

Muntz thought it possible that the many cones particularly sensitive to the longer wavelengths might help the gulls and terns to see through the water surface. Alternatively, it can be argued that red oil droplets, in fact, make the water surface even more difficult to look through because at long wavelengths the surface reflections are relatively bright compared to the sub-surface light. Rather, the explanation is to do with the feeding strategy of gulls and terns which makes it necessary to see for very long distances through atmospheric-hazes.

Although the surface of the sea may appear featureless and devoid of landmarks, it does not follow that the animals that live in the surface waters are evenly distributed across them. Plankton occurs in very large aggregations or blooms, and following these are schools of small fishes and cephalopods. In their turn, these are followed by the larger predacious

Fig. 7.6. The arctic tern *Sterna paradisaea*.

fishes, such as the tunas and sharks, whilst from the air, birds feed on the small fishes and the debris that remain after the larger species have fed.

An individual bird that discovers food and begins to wheel and dive above it will attract the notice of others—not necessarily of the same species—that will invite themselves to the feast. Charles Darwin (1889) and later Craik (1944) remarked that birds that roam over the ocean are made conspicuous by being either white or black. This conspicuous coloration has presumably been to serve the feeding strategy of sea-birds. Darwin (1889) and Armstrong (1944) mention the drab coloration of many juvenile sea-birds. These seem to be in a favoured position because they will see the distant feeding of conspicuous birds, whilst they themselves are less likely to be seen.

This discussion has been conducted with a strictly visual bias, but it should not be forgotten that the possession of highly reflective white plumage or highly absorbing black will materially affect the heat balance of an animal. A discussion of such effects will be found in Schmidt-Nielsen (1964).

At the root of these arguments is the assumption that black and white really are conspicuous colours. To the human eye and in the absence of hue differences, either black or white will be the most conspicuous coloration in any particular situation. Craik (1944) drawing an analogy with anti-submarine aircraft, which had white-painted bellies to camouflage them against the bright sky, suggested that white sea-birds were camouflaged to the fishes on which they prey. In the ensuing discussion, Pirenne and Crombie (1944) pointed out that the conspicuousness of a white bird depends upon the angle of view, the time of day and how overcast the sky.

This point has since been demonstrated by Cowan (1972); and Simmons (1972) has stressed the fact that white birds are indeed conspicuous when seen from a high vantage point and he strongly upholds the view that white birds are socially conspicuous.

It is likely that a white bird viewed against the sea will be even more conspicuous to gulls and terns than they are to man. As has already been mentioned, these birds are particularly well endowed with orange and red retinal oil droplets that will help them to see long distances through haze. This ability is particularly important for birds that use the scout-and-cluster feeding strategy. Red oil droplets will enhance the contrast between a white bird seen against the surface of the sea.

Black-coloured birds will be rendered less conspicuous against the sky or sea by the use of red-pass filters and it is interesting that some black sea birds do seem to have rather few red and orange oil droplets (Fig. 7.7). In

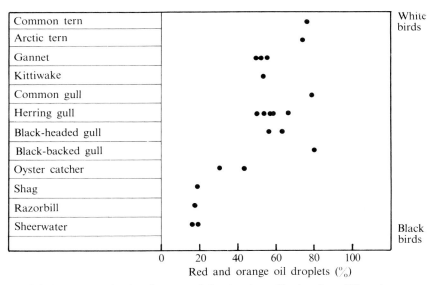

Fig. 7.7. Percentage of red and orange oil droplets (cut-off point above 521 nm) in a variety of sea-birds arranged in order of coloration from entirely white to entirely black. White birds have more red and orange oil droplets than black ones. (Data from Muntz 1972.)

their case a visual system that is maximally sensitive to the sea or sky radiance will be best. This may be an explanation for the paucity of red and orange oil droplets in the eyes of swallows (Fig. 7.8) and swifts which need to see their small insect prey darkly silhouetted against the sky or water surface. The fewness of red and orange droplets in the eyes of birds like the shag, shearwater, and razorbill that actually hunt underwater is

Fig. 7.8. The swallow *Hirundo rustica*.

most likely because the longer wavelength light is filtered out by the water, and red and orange oil droplets would seriously reduce sensitivity (p. 135).

The observation that nocturnal birds have few red oil droplets (pp. 89–92), presumably because their presence would sacrifice too much sensitivity, becomes particularly interesting in that Simmons (1972) thinks there might be a correlation between black plumage when seen from above and a preference for being abroad in twilight. Simmons points out that dark plumage is often associated with solitary skilled hunting and that a dark bird flying over the dark sea would be much harder to detect than a light coloured bird.

In surveying the colours of animals and plants that advertise to birds, it is remarkable how often black, either by itself or teamed with red, orange, or yellow, is used. Thus 29 per cent of all succulent fruit native to the British flora are dark blue or black, and there are black components to the patterns of all the noxious amphibia illustrated by Cott. To our eyes black is not particularly showy, but it would be interesting to know if there was any feature of avian vision that was particularly alerted to displays containing black.

Fish

Most colours are produced by the wavelength-selective reflection of daylight. When the spectral band of daylight reaching a surface is restricted, the range of colours that it can reflect are similarly restricted. Isaac Newton in his *Optiks* (1730) knew from the anecdotes of divers that certain colours are more visible than others under water, and nowadays one of the first items of diving lore acquired by the novice diver is that red objects no longer appear red even at moderate depths in the sea. This phenomenon is repeatedly observed by divers in the clear blue waters of the Mediterranean and tropical seas. In this water, yellow retains its 'colour' well and a yellow-painted object remains different in colour from the water background as deep as there is sufficient light for colour vision. The first systematic study of the relationship between water transmission and the visibility of colours was that of Kinney, Luria, and Weitzman (1967). Later Lythgoe (1971) and Lythgoe and Northmore (1973) concentrated on the red, orange, and yellow family of colours which lend themselves well to a study of advertising colours under water.

In each case, these colours absorb the short-wavelength end of the spectrum and reflect the long wavelengths. Whether the surface will look red, orange, or yellow depends upon the position of the cut-off between absorption and reflection (p. 32). If there is light only at the extreme short-wavelength end of the spectrum, the appearance of all these colours will resemble black; if there is light only at the extreme long wavelengths, all will resemble white or light grey. It is only when the location of the cut-off in the spectral reflectance curve coincides with the spectral band of available light (Fig. 7.9) that the surface will look coloured.

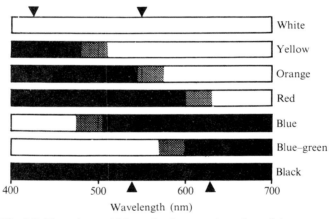

Fig. 7.9. The colours which result when certain regions of the spectrum are absorbed (black areas). The stippled areas are those where the absorption varies rapidly with wavelength. The triangular markers at the top and bottom of the diagram delimit the spectral region where 90 per cent of the daylight incident at the water's surface is absorbed, at 80 m in Jerlov type II oceanic water (top markers) and at 1 m in Jerlov type 9 coastal water (bottom markers). (From Lythgoe 1971.)

It follows from these arguments that yellow objects will remain different in colour from the water background at greater depths or distances than red ones will; but in green water it is the red objects that remain distinct (Fig. 7.10; Plate 5). By the same argument, a cut-off colour that reflects the short wavelengths and absorbs the long will also be visible if the spectral cut-off corresponds with the wavelength of maximum water transparency. Thus if red is visible so will the complementary blue–green; and if yellow is visible, so will the complementary indigo blue (Plate 12). The spectral

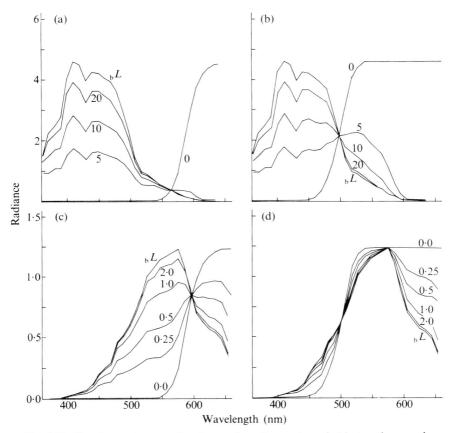

Fig. 7.10. The charges in spectral radiance of a yellow and a red object as they recede horizontally from the eye in blue (Gulf Stream) water and in green, fresh water. $_bL$ represents the spectral radiance of the water background. Distance in metres. (a) Red in blue water; (b) yellow in blue water; (c) red in green water; and (d) yellow in green water. Note that in (b) and (c) the object radiance and background radiance remains distinctly different in shape and will thus appear different in hue at a greater distance than (a) and (d). (From Lythgoe and Northmore 1973.)

reflectance of the red fin of the freshwater perch and the yellow fin of the marine whimple fish *Heniochus* (Fig. 7.11) are shown in Fig. 7.12.

These arguments are intuitively acceptable and find support in the colours of fishes that are used in display. Many inshore and freshwater fishes that live in green and yellow–green water possess brilliant red or orange patches of colour that have clear behavioural significance. Of these perhaps the best known is the red belly of the male stickleback, *Gasterosteus aculeatus* (Fig. 7.13). The red coloration of many European freshwater fishes such as the belly of the male char, *Salvelinus alpinus,* and the fins of the freshwater perch, *Perca fluviatilis* (Plate 5), intensify in the breeding

Fig. 7.11. The whimple fish *Heniochus acuminatus*.

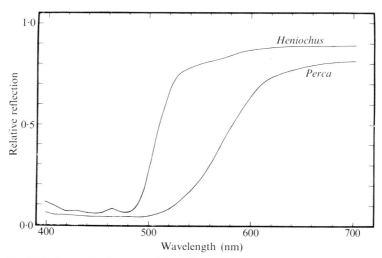

Fig. 7.12. Spectral reflectance of the yellow tail fin of the whimple fish, *Heniochus acuminatus*, and the red tail fin of the perch, *Perca fluviatilis*. (From Lythgoe 1971.)

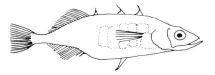

Fig. 7.13. The stickleback *Gasterosteus aculeatus*.

season and presumably form some kind of visual display. In the African lakes, the anal fin of the males of many species of *Tilapia* and *Haplochromis* bear egg-dummy markings that are often red or orange in colour (Fryer and Iles 1972) and many species also have iridescent blue markings.

In blue-water fishes the yellow markings of the coral fish, *Chaetodon lunula* (Fig. 7.14) intensify in agonistic display (Hamilton and Peterman

Fig. 7.14. The coral fish *Chaetodon lunula*. Like the majority of the Chaetodontidae, this species habitually swims in pairs.

1971). The yellow iris of the damsel fish, *Pomacentrus jenkinsi*, is also involved in display. Ehrlich, Talbot, Russell, and Anderson (1977) consider that in the chaetodontids which often swim in pairs, the yellow and white markings are important in allowing the individuals to find each other after a brief separation. The beaugregory, *Eupomocentrus leucostictus* (Fig. 7.15), of the Florida Keys and Caribbean is, except for the aggressive nest-

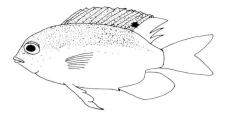

Fig. 7.15. The beaugregory *Eupomocentrus leucostictus*.

guarding males, coloured a brilliant blue above and yellow below. With the aid of models Brockman (1973) concluded that although movement was the most important feature of the model that provoked territorial attacks, blue and yellow coloration increased their probability and persistence.

Intuition and human observation of conspicuousness is not very reliable when extrapolated to other animals. It is safer to consider how deep, or at what range the difference between two spectral radiances will become indistinguishable. By comparing the light reflected from two surfaces, one yellow and one red, in deep water, it is possible to show that, save for trivial exceptions, the difference in radiance between a yellow object and its background will be greater at all wavelengths than a red object in blue water, but in green water, red will be more different from the water background than yellow. Lythgoe and Northmore (1973) attempted to relate this optical approach to the physiology of the eye by introducing the Stiles-Helmholz model of the (human) eye, but instead of incorporating the three fundamental human colour vision mechanisms into the Stiles–Helmholz model (Wyszecki and Stiles 1968), every possible trio of visual pigments ranged at equal frequency intervals between 435 and 667 nm were used instead. This computer-assisted analysis confirmed the view that red is inherently more visible than yellow in green water and yellow more visible than red in blue water almost irrespective of the eye observing them.

Slowly we are beginning to obtain an insight into how the information from the cones might be coded and analysed in the retina. On pp. 136–42 it is shown how it is possible that in its day-to-day life a fish might have one chromatic channel more or less matched to the wavelength of maximum water transparency, one or two offset to shorter wavelengths, and another offset to longer wavelengths. A retinal organization such as this would be well suited to detect the family of reds, oranges, and yellows in the appropriate water colour. A 'ghost cone' offset to long wavelengths occupying position C in Fig. 5.4 would be sensitive to the longwave reflections compared to the chromatic mechanism more closely matched to the spectral distribution of the underwater light.

Insects

Insects can see ultraviolet light whereas man cannot. On the other, hand man can probably see a little further into the red than most insects. It may be possible to discount our own awareness of red when trying to imagine the world as seen through an insect's eye, but it is scarcely possible to visualize ultraviolet patterns of which we can see nothing ourselves. By using suitable ultraviolet-pass filters with photographic film or video recording equipment, it is possible to demonstrate ultraviolet patterns and thus gain some insight into how particular visual displays appear to an insect.

Most insect receptors that have been investigated fall into two main groups (see Menzel (1975) for a review). One group has maximum sensitivity around 350 nm. The other has maximum sensitivity around 520 nm.

Blue receptors are less frequently found but are known to occur in the honey bee and have maximum sensitivity variously estimated between 420 and 460 nm.

Red sensitivity is more difficult to characterize but specific red-sensitive chromatic channels have been found in several species of butterfly including *Heliconius erato*, *Papilio troilus* (Swihart 1970; Swihart and Gordon 1971), and *Colias eurythemus* (Post and Goldsmith 1969). There is some argument about whether the red sensitivity is a result of red reflections from the tracheal tapeta present in many butterflies (Menzel 1975), or perhaps wavelength-selective optical filters in the eye. In fact, the only red receptor that has yet been measured intracellularly was found in the small larva of the dragonfly *Aeschna cyanea* by Autrum and Kolb (1968).

The colour vision of the honey bee, *Apis mellifera*, is probably better known than any other insect. It has trichromatic vision (Daumer 1956) not altogether unlike that of man (Le Grande 1964) except that it has sensitivity maxima at 345, 440, and 550 nm with best spectral hue discrimination at 400 nm (Helversen 1972). The ultraviolet mechanism is without parallel in vertebrates and it is here that insect colour vision is so different from our own.

Many insects, particularly the butterflies and bees, have mouthparts that are specifically designed to suck nectar from flowers, whilst many flowers rely upon their insect visitors for pollination. No one can seriously doubt that the colours of insect-pollinated flowers have evolved to advertise their presence to insects. Coincidentally, the overlap in spectral sensitivity of man and insects allows us to appreciate some of the visual displays not directed towards us. Very recently indeed on the evolutionary time-scale, man has selected and bred flowering plants specially to display to himself. These new varieties owe their existence to our aesthetic sense which is particularly gratified by bright, clear, primary (for humans) colours. In thinking about the natural evolution of flower colours, it is important to remember that the colour patterns of garden flowers may well be misleading in understanding the relationships between flower colours and the vision of their pollinators.

Wind and insects are the two most important pollination vectors of flowering plants; the presence of flowers cannot modify the wind but there is general agreement that the evolution of flowering plants and insects have been strongly influenced by their mutual interdependence (see Baker and Hurd (1968) for the review on which this section is based).

The flowering plants became prominent in the fossil record from the latter half of the Cretaceous and by the Tertiary had reached their present dominant position in the world's flora. Flying insects like dragonflies, which could not fold their wings, are known from the Carboniferous, long before flowering plants became numerous in the flora. By the Permian, four orders of insects, Coleoptera, Diptera, Mecoptera, and

Neuroptera, had appeared. These could fold their wings and must have had the necessary manoeuvrability to pollinate flowers. It was not until the beginning of the Eocene that Lepidoptera and Hymenoptera made their appearance. This is after the flowering plants (Angiosperms) were well established.

Present opinion is that the earliest flowering plants were pollinated by beetles. The main reason is that beetles were already well-established in the fossil record by the time the flowering plants first appeared. Modern flowers that show many primitive features, such as the water lilies (Nympheaceae), the magnolias (Magnoleaceae), the laurels (Lauraceae), and the buttercups (Ranunculaceae), which all belong to the order Ranales, are almost invariably visited by beetles attracted by the abundance of pollen.

The primitive flowers are generally shaped like flat bowls with the floral parts arranged in a spiral. The main thrust of evolution is for the floral parts, especially the petals and sepals, to be arranged in whorls rather than spirals and for the number of the floral parts to be reduced. The fewer stamens and less pollen was compensated for by increase in nectar. Later, the flower parts, particularly the petals, became fused together into a tube at the base of which the nectaries were situated. The nectar could then only be reached by the long-tongued insects such as butterflies and bees that must have co-evolved with the flowers. In the most advanced flowers the flower parts are not only fused and reduced in number, but the whole flower assumes a bilateral symmetry.

In some evolutionary lines there has been a tendency for particular flowers to have particular insect pollinators. A well-documented example is the yucca where the 30 species are exclusively pollinated by 5 species of the Moth genus, *Tegeticula* (Proctor and Yeo 1973). There are many species of orchid whose flowers mimic almost exactly a particular insect, and the pollen is transferred between flowers when the insect attempts to copulate with the flower (Van der Pijl and Dodson 1966). Interestingly, the lack of interest shown by other insect species except the specific vector is the only device the orchids use to prevent cross-pollination and this is the reason why such a huge variety of orchids can be bred by inter-specific cross-fertilization. Too rigid a dependence on a single insect pollinator restricts the potential range of a plant and it is noteworthy that most of the highly successful weeds that have spread world-wide lack specialized pollinators.

Plants often need animals to carry their pollen and their seeds. Seeds, being rather large, are typically carried by vertebrates which are rewarded by succulent fruit. Pollen, being rather small, is typically carried by insects which are rewarded by nectar and pollen. In both cases the plant advertises that it needs to trade and the advertising colours are designed to catch the notice of the appropriate carrier. All conclusions

Fig. 7.16. The celandine, *Ranunculus ficaria*, photographed (*top*) without a filter, and (*bottom*) with an ultraviolet-pass filter. The central part of the petals and the stamens do not reflect ultraviolet light and appear black. To our eyes the celandine is a uniform yellow colour.

about the attractiveness of different colours to insects—and they are many (see Proctor and Yeo (1973) for a review)—are extremely difficult to evaluate unless the ultraviolet reflections are taken into account. Daumer (1958) photographed 204 species of flower through an ultraviolet-, a blue-, and a green-pass filter that correspond to the three fundamental chromatic channels of the bee. From these photographs he estimated the relative reflection of the flower at each spectral location and made inferences about the appearance of the flower to the bee translated into human terms. A similar approach is the use of false-colour photography to actually construct colour photographs of the imagined appearance of a flower to a bee (Carricaburu 1974).

Many flowers have markings which guide the visiting insect towards the nectar or pollen (Daumer 1958). These may be visible to our eyes, or they may show up dark in ultraviolet photographs (Fig. 7.16). In the case of advanced bilaterally symmetrical flowers, there are banner petals that guide the insect in on the correct path (Faegri and Van der Pijl 1966; Jones, C. E., and Buchmann 1974). Daumer has shown how bees are attracted by the ultraviolet-dark centre of flowers and it is of interest that pollen seems not to reflect ultraviolet light, perhaps because of its high protein content. From the evolutionary point of view, it is plausible that the original motive of insects in visiting flowers was to eat the pollen and that sweet-smelling nectar came later as an added inducement to the insect. The original visual clue would have been the cluster of dark pollen-bearing anthers and we can speculate that honeyguides were, in fact, mimicking and reinforcing the appearance of pollen-rich anthers.

Flower colours and ecology

If colours of flowers have evolved to attract the animals that pollinate them, it follows that when a population of flowering plants is most likely to be pollinated by particular animals, the flowers will themselves tend to share similar colours. Thus most flowers that are pollinated by hawkmoths are white or pale in colour (Baker and Hurd 1968) and they report that many flowers in the Californian forests are pale because they are moth-pollinated. A flower that looks white to our eyes reflects all wavelengths of light between, say, 400 nm and 800 nm strongly and almost equally. Daylight is poor in ultraviolet light and starlight is even poorer. Thus even if white flowers reflect very poorly in the ultraviolet (and the indications are that this is usually so (Daumer 1958)), they will tend to appear bright to any animal that has reasonable sensitivity at wavelengths longer than the ultraviolet.

Flowers that open at night must be principally designed to attract night-flying animals such as moths and bats. At night the number of photons available for vision are so limited that colour vision is unlikely (pp. 37 and 71). It is more important to present as contrasting an image as possible. Bat-pollinated flowers are usually either white or dark purple. Often they smell strongly of fermentation and open only at night. Like bird-pollinated flowers, bat-pollinated flowers are often pendulous or present a large brush of stamens to the furry belly of the bat (A. Lack, personal communication). The white colour is explained because this will be most easy to see at night against a dark background. Dark colours would be best if the flowers were to be seen in silhouette, but at present we know little about how a bat actually approaches a flower.

Private wavelengths

Unfortunately for the animal designed to attract a mate or scare off an enemy the colours are also likely to attract a predator or frighten away the prey. Nevertheless, when the spectral sensitivity of the one animal differs from that of the other, it is possible to be at the same time cryptic to the one and conspicuous to the other.

Hinton (1976) has described the coloration of the female crab spider, *Misumenia vatia* (Fig. 7.17). These spiders live on flowers where they ambush visiting insects. They are able to change their body colour reversibly so they are yellow on yellow backgrounds and white on white backgrounds. But to our eyes the camouflage is wantonly destroyed by the red patches on each side of the abdomen. Hinton suggests that to another insect which is sensitive to ultraviolet but insensitive to red, the spider is cryptic against the flower, but to a bird, the red patches show up strongly, presumably warning of some noxious property. Photographs taken through an ultraviolet-pass filter support this conclusion for then the red patches on the spider disappear.

Fig. 7.17. The female crab spider *Misumenia vatia*.

In the mesopelagic zone of the sea, daylight is restricted to a narrow spectral band of blue or blue–green light and most of the bioluminescence is of the same colour, either to make the camouflage the more effective (pp. 175–6) or to give the maximum penetration through the water. Some mesopelagic fishes use quite another strategy for they have red and green photophores on the head behind and below the eye. In 1970 Denton *et al.* showed that one of these fishes, the loosejaw *Pachystomias*, has a retinal absorption curve with a maximum at 575 nm. The retina is, therefore, much more red sensitive than in most mesopelagic fishes that only have the usual blue or blue-green photophores. O'Day and Fernandez (1974) were able to extract the visual pigment of a related mesopelagic fish, *Aristostomias scintillans* (Fig. 7.18), which also has a red and a green suborbital

Fig. 7.18. *Aristostomias scintillans.*

photophore. Two pigments were characterized with λ_{max} at 526 and 551 nm. It is a reasonable hypothesis that both *Aristostomias* and *Pachystomias* are adapted to recognize the light emitted by their own species, but which is nevertheless of too long a wavelength to be seen by most other species of mesopelagic fishes.

Many crustacea that live in the deeper part of the mesopelagic zone and that are fed upon by fishes are bright red in colour. In ordinary blue-green bioluminescence or in the residual daylight that penetrates to these depths, a red animal will look little different from a black one. But a predator equipped with red bioluminescence and a red-sensitive eye would become a deadly hunter because the red prey would look bright, but lacking red sensitivity itself would not know it was under surveillance.

Two species of mesopelagic squid, *Histioteuthis meleagroteuthis* and *H. dofleini*, and four mesopelagic fishes, the greeneyes, *Chlorophthalmus agassizi* and *C. albatrossis* (Fig. 7.19), the hatchet fish, *Argyropelecus affinis*, and the pearleye, *Scopelarchus analis*, are known to have yellow lenses. The pearleye and hatchet fish have upward directed eyes, and the greeneye, *C. alba-*

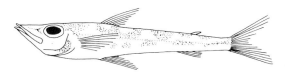

Fig. 7.19. The greeneye *Chlorophthalmus albatrossis.*

trossis, is not tubular but the optical axis is also directed upwards. In the squid, *Histioteuthis*, one eye is directed upwards, the other downwards, and it is the upward-directed eye that has a strong yellow colour. Muntz (1976), who has made a study of these animals, calculates that taking the spectral absorption of the visual pigments into account, the yellow filters will reduce the number of photons reaching the visual pigment by a third in the squid, *H. meleagroteuthis*, and by two-thirds in the pearleye.

Such a drastic reduction in sensitivity is not what one might reasonably expect at depths where the light is dim (see pp. 82–3 and 138). Muntz believes the explanation may be that the spectral radiance of biolumines-cent light is richer in longwave light than in downwelling daylight at these depths. Animals that camouflage their silhouette with ventral photophores must adjust their brightness to match the downwelling spacelight. A brightness match for the normal run of fishes which are most sensitive at around 470–80 nm will leave the photophores looking conspicuously brighter relative to the downwelling light for an animal that is most sensitive at somewhat longer wavelengths.

Patterns and display

Inherently conspicuous patterns

In the same way that most conspicuous colours are those that most strongly stimulate a visual apparatus already tuned to make the fine colour dis-criminations required to find food and avoid enemies, so conspicuous patterns may have evolved to stimulate most strongly visual mechanisms that already exist to interpret the spatial and temporal components of the outside world. Perhaps the best example is the way the centre–surround organization of the retina leads to the enhanced conspicuousness of disc-like patterns and to the enhancement of edges by the fine shading along the boundaries.

Boundaries

Boundaries between contrasting areas are often strong visual features used for display purposes, and paradoxically also to conceal the characteristic outline of an animal by drawing the attention to themselves and away from the actual contours of the body's form. This strategy of disruptive coloration has been fully described and illustrated by Cott (1940). Some of the main uses of disruptive colouring are to conceal characteristic out-lines, for example the concealment of the round black pupil in birds, fishes, and mammals by means of a highly conspicuous eye-stripe. Further examples of disruptive colouring include the concealment of characteristic limb patterns as with the leg bars of frogs; the breaking up of the whole body shape as with the reticulated pattern of snakes; and mimesis: the external resemblance of harmless insects to more dangerous ones such as wasps by superimposing the outline of the dangerous insect upon the body of the harmless one.

In the frog retina, Maturana, Lettvine, McCulloch, and Pitts (1960) described ganglion cells which responded most powerfully to the sustained edge of an object, either brighter or darker than the background which moved through the receptive field; for this type of cell a sharp edge is needed for the maximum response. Edge detectors have also been found in the rabbit retina (Levick 1967; Barlow 1972b); and the pigeon (Maturana and Frenk 1963). It is also probable that mechanisms exist to detect edges formed between areas of different colour. These may be derived from the inhibitory interaction of two types of visual cell containing different visual pigments. In the goldfish, the mechanism involves the opponency of the red and green-sensitive cones (Hemila, Reuter, and Virtanen 1976).

Enhanced edges

Physiologically, the result of the centre–surround organization of the retina can be monitored in a single retinal ganglion cell or ommatidium when the unsharp image of a dark edge is moved across a bright background. As the edge passes across the receptive field of the cell, the frequency of impulses shows first a sharp increase, then a fast decrease followed by a rapid return to the original frequency. The result of this rapid change in firing rate is seen in a display such as that in Fig. 7.20(b). The reader should see a lighter band on the light side and a darker band on the dark side. These are called Mach bands after Ernst Mach who first described them in 1865. In art, the visual contrast of an edge can be enhanced by painting a dark band on the dark side of an edge and a light band on the light side (Sutter 1880; Homer 1964). This technique was extensively used by artists such as Leonardo da Vinci and Paolo Veronese, who used it as a form of chiaroscuro to make the image stand out from the canvas. The pointillist school of French Impressionist painters also used the technique, particularly good examples being found in the works of Seurat (Homer 1964) and Signac (Ratliffe 1972).

A similar technique is extensively used in nature to enhance the visual contrast of displays (Figs 7.21, 7.22) is often exhibited by animals that have disruptive coloration of the kind that camouflages them against complex backgrounds such as rough bark or fallen leaves. Good examples are the wings of night-flying moths that must be camouflaged in the daytime, and the reticulated pattern of many snakes.

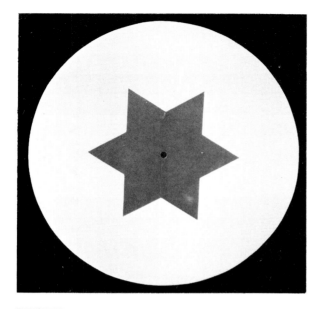

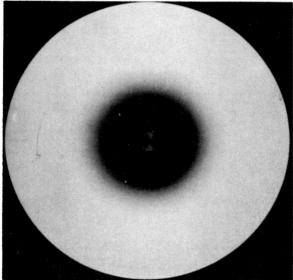

Fig. 7.20. Demonstration of Mach bands. (a) The display in (b) is generated by spinning a disc with a pattern such as that shown here. (b) Physically this results in a dark centre with an even gradation to a lighter surround. However, the viewer should get the sensation of a lighter ring in the light part of the display, and a darker ring in the dark part. Photographs by courtesy F. W. Campbell.

Discs

Cott (1940) noticed the similarity of many of these spots and discs to round-pupilled eyes (Fig. 7.21(a)) and somewhat forcefully argued that the common theme of such displays was to mimic eyes—either to terrify the intruder or to draw attention away from the often camouflaged true eye to a conspicuous false one on a relatively invulnerable part of the body that will not disable the animal if attacked. Such false eyes are particularly common amongst fishes amphibia and butterflies. Circular patterns are less common amongst birds, the peacock and some other pheasants are exceptions.

Visual displays, whether worn by vertebrates or invertebrates, are frequently directed towards vertebrates because these are often the major predators. The spatial organization of the retina of those vertebrates that have been studied (see Rodiek (1973) and Ripps and Weale (1976) for recent reviews) is fundamentally very similar. Each ganglion cell that forms part of the visual imagery pathway (as opposed to eye movement and pupillary reflexes) has an approximately circular visual field divided into a central and surrounding region. A stimulus on the central region causes an increase in nervous impulses from the ganglion cells, but the

Fig. 7.21. (a) The moth, *Telea polyphemus*, showing prominent 'eye' spots and enhanced edges running parallel to the wing margins. This specimen has a wing-span of 120 mm.

Fig. 7.21. (b) An enlargement showing the enhanced edge in detail.

same stimulus, falling on the surrounding region, will cause a decrease in the number of impulses.

Suppose a spot of light falls on the centre of the receptive area of a ganglion cell that increases its firing rate with that stimulus. If the spot is increased in area, the firing rate of the ganglion cell will increase until all the central area but not the surround is stimulated. As the area covered by

Fig. 7.22. The gerenuk, *Litocranius walleri*, showing an enhanced edge at the division between the dark and light areas of its flank.   Photo C. J. Pennycuick.

the spot continues to increase, the inhibiting surround will become activated and the firing rate of the ganglion cell will begin to decrease. Thus in the frog retina, Butenandt and Grüsser (1968) have shown that the optimum stimulus size is roughly proportional to the receptive field size.

The centre field in any particular area of retina is variable in diameter, but generally the more peripheral ganglia have the larger receptive fields (the ground squirrel is an exception). Receptive fields range in diameter from as little as 4′ in the spider monkey to at least 11 ° in the bullfrog (Table 7.2).

Table 7.2 Size of field in centre–surround cells

Animal	Size of field	Reference
Cat (X- and Y-cells)	0.1–1°	Stone and Fukada (1974)
Rana temporaria	3–9°	Barlow (1953)
Rana pipiens	1–8° (average 5°·22)	Glickman and Pomerance (1977)
Rana catesbeiana	5–11° (average 7°·77)	
Rat	3–10°	Brown and Rojas (1965) Partridge and Brown (1970)
Citellus mexicanus	0·5–5° (most no greater than 1·0–2°·5)	Michael (1968 *a*, *b*)
Spider monkey	4′	Hubel and Wiesel (1960)

There are other ganglion cells that fire when the illumination on the central field gets dimmer. This type of cell would be most sensitive to the appearance of a circular dark disc that exactly covers the central field. If that was surrounded by a light area, the response would be further enhanced.

Fig. 7.23. The John Dory, *Zeus faber*, showing dark spot with a light surround.

Many disc-like display motifs are surrounded by such a contrasting border (Fig. 7.23). In most cases the disc is dark and the surround is light, which is a pattern reminiscent of a dark pupil surrounded by the lighter iris. Such displays will strongly stimulate an off-centre ganglion cell of corresponding area since the dark disc covering the central area will result in an increase in firing rate, and the light area will illicit no inhibition from the surround.

Ganglion cells of this type have been implicated in the food search and capture behaviour in three species of frog: The common frog, *Rana temporaria*; the leopard frog, *Rana pipiens*; and the bullfrog, *Rana catesbeiana*. Barlow (1953) working on the common frog, found on–off units that had a central area of about 3 ° at the centre of the retina that responded strongly to sudden slight movements. Barlow remarks that a fly at the catching distance of about 2 inches from the frog would fill nicely a 3 ° receptive field and its motion is such as to stimulate the ganglion cell. It is possible that the on–off units act as 'fly detectors'.

There is some evidence that the area of the receptive field is matched to prey size; Glickman and Pomerance (1977) compared the receptive field size of these (Class II) ganglion cells in the leopard frog, which is about the same size as the common frog, to those of the bullfrog, which is about ten times heavier. The leopard frog eats insects, spiders, and small land snails, whereas the bullfrog eats insects, mice, crayfish, and even birds. The receptive field size of the leopard frog varies from 1–8° (average 5°·22) compared to 5–11° (average 7°·77) in the bullfrog.

Gratings and bars

Regularly spaced dark and light bars are very conspicuous to humans as witness their frequent use in traffic signs. There are good reasons for thinking that the conspicuousness of these gratings derives from a fundamental mechanism of image analysis in the visual pathway of vertebrates in general. It is possible in theory, although perhaps not in practice, to analyse even the most complex image in terms of a combination of sine waves of different frequency using Fourier analysis. At all levels in the visual pathway from the retinal ganglion cell to the cortex there are ganglion cells that are selectively sensitive to gratings of particular frequency. Robson (1975) in his review of spatial frequency analysers in the primate retina considers that although it is unlikely, bearing in mind the other neurological evidence, that spatial frequency analysis is the only analytical mechanism in the visual pathway, it may not be too fanciful to suppose that the visual system does perform some spatial frequency analysis.

Perhaps the most satisfactory way of describing the performance of an imaging system is to compare the spatial frequency of a grating with the least contrast between the dark and light bars required to visualize them. In Fig. 4.12 there is a grating pattern that gradually increases in spatial frequency from left to right. The contrast between the dark and light bars is graded from top to bottom and it is at once obvious that at a particular spatial frequency, which varies according to viewing distance and illumination, the bars can be detected at lower contrast than for higher and lower spatial frequencies (see Campbell and Maffei (1974) for a review).

Regularly spaced patterns of light and dark bars are common in fishes, but are also seen in mammals (e.g. opossum tails, zebras (Fig. 7.24),

Fig. 7.24. The zebra *Equus burchelli.*

Okapi), reptiles (banded snakes), and insects (wasps, bees). It may not be by chance that grating patterns are common in fishes (Fig. 7.25). The light-scattering nature of the water means that visual contrasts are rapidly reduced as the sighting range increases (see pp. 112–18) and under these conditions a grating of the right frequency for the particular viewing distance is more visible than a larger unpatterned target (see Chapter 4).

Gratings have a further important advantage for aquatic animals. Forward scattering by transparent zooplankters tend to degrade the boundaries of an image (pp. 124–5). Frequency detectors depend upon the spatial frequency of the display rather than the sharpness of the edges. Thus the visibility of gratings will be less reduced in plankton-rich water than some other displays.

Of all the animals, the zebra is one of the most strongly striped. As Cott (1940) points out, they are absurdly conspicuous in the open in bright sunlight. At twilight, however, they become one of the most cryptic of animals, even at 40–50 m, in the kind of thin cover they frequent. Galton (1851) had experienced this with zebras under South African starlight: a zebra was nearly invisible at distances so close that it could be heard breathing.

Fig. 7.25. Sergeant majors *Abudefduf sexfasciatus*.

If the underlying method of detecting zebra stripes is through spatial frequency analysis, then a ready explanation for the invisibility of zebras at night is at hand. Kelly (1961) has shown how the spatial frequency most easily detected at any particular contrast gets larger as the light level falls. At low light levels the spatial frequency of the zebra stripes is simply too low to be detectable until the animal is approached very closely.

End note

The main concern of this chapter is to explore the circumstances when one organism may be conspicuous or camouflaged from another. Conspicuousness in particular has many potential roles in the natural history of an animal and to recognize that an animal is conspicuous does not always help in understanding why it should be so. For example, we know from our own society that the colour red is judged to be conspicuous. It is used to colour all manner of articles that we need to notice, such as fire extinguishers, stop lights, crosses on ambulances, and hydrogen cylinders. It is also aesthetically pleasing to some and who is to say that other animals do not have an aesthetic sense? As one might expect, there are exceptions to the rule that red is conspicuous. The old style hospital blanket is dyed red, not, I am told, to be conspicuous, but rather to camouflage the blood stains. Sometimes it must be misleading to look for a visual function. Haemoglobin is red, but the fundamental reason is more likely to be a result of its chemical structure that is designed to serve the respiratory system. If blood were green, we would have learned to find green lips and green cheeks attractive.

The ways that the visual sense is concerned in broad problems of ecology and behaviour are far too complex to be explored by visual science alone. Conversely, the broadly based ecologist and naturalist must know what are the potential strengths and the certain limitations of the sense of vision. In this book I have tried to provide some of the ground rules for assessing the likely role of vision in the immensely complex problems of ecology.

References

Ahlbert, I. (1969). The organization of the cone cells in the retinae of four teleosts with different feeding habits (*Perca fluviatilis* L., *Lucioperca lucioperca* L., *Acerina cernua* L. and *Coregonus albula* L.) *Ark. Zool.* **22**, 445–81.

—— (1975). Organization of the cone cells in the retinae of some teleosts in relation to their feeding habits. University of Stockholm, Stockholm.

—— (1976). Organization of the cone cells in the retinae of salmon (*Salmo salar*) and trout (*Salmo trutta trutta*) in relation to their feeding habits. *Acta Zool. (Stockh.)* **57**, 13–35.

Ali, M.A. (1959). The ocular structure, retinomotor and photobehavioral responses of juvenile Pacific salmon. *Can. J. Zool.* **37**, 965–96.

—— (1964). Stretching of the retina during growth of Salmon (*Salmon salar*). *Growth* **28**, 83–9.

—— (1971). Les réponses retinomotrices: caractères et mécanisms. *Vision Res.* **11**, 1225–88.

—— (1975). Retinomotor responses. In *Vision in fishes* (ed. M. A. Ali,) pp. 313–55. Plenum, New York.

—— (1976). Retinal pigments, structure and function and behaviour. *Vision Res* **16**, 1197–8.

Anctil, M. (1969). Structure due rétine chez quelques téléosteens marin du plateau continental. *J. fish Res. Bd. Canada* **26**, 597–628.

Arden, G. B. (1976). The retina-neurophysiology. In *The Eye*, vol. 2A (ed. H. Davson), pp. 230–356. Pergamon, Oxford.

—— and Tansley, K. (1962). The electroretinogram of a diurnal gecko. *J. gen. Physiol.* **45**, 1145–61.

Armstrong, E. A. (1944). White plumage of sea birds. *Nature (Lond.)* **153**, 527.

Ashmore, J. F. and Falk, G. (1976). Absolute sensitivity of rod bipolar cells in a dark-adapted retina. *Nature (Lond.)* **263**, 248–9.

Austin, R. W. (1974). The remote sensing of spectral radiance from below the ocean surface. In *Optical aspects of oceanography* (ed. N. G. Jerlov and E. Steeman Nielson), 317–43. Academic Press, New York.

Autrum, H. (1948). Zur analyse des Zeitlichen Auflörsungsvermögen des lusektenanges. *Nach. Akad. Wiss Gottingen Math.–Phys. K1* **2**, 13–18.

—— and Stöcker, M. (1950). Die Verschemelzungsfrequenzen des Bienenanges. *Z. Naturforsch.* **5b**, 38–43.

—— and Kolb, G. (1968). Spektrale empfindlichkeit einzelner sehzellen der Aeschniden. *Z. vergl. Physiol.* **60**, 450.

Baker, A. de C. (1970). The vertical distribution of euphausiids near Fuertaventura, Canary Islands ('Discovery' SOND Cruise, 1965). *J. mar. biol. Assoc. U.K.* **50**, 301–42.

Baburina, E. A. (1955a). The eye and the retina in the Caspian shad. *Dokl. Akad. Nauk. SSSR* **100**, 1167–70.

—— (1955b). The structure of the eye and the retina in *Clupeonella delicatula caspia*. *Dokl. Akad. Nauk. SSSR* **102**, 625–8.

—— and Kovaleva, N. D. (1959). Retinal structure in the Caspian Clupeonellae. *Dokl. Akad. Nauk. SSSR* (N.S.) **125**, 1349–52.

Backus, R. H., Craddock, J. E.. Haedrich, R. L., Shores, D. L., Teal, J. M., Wing, A. S., Mead, G. W., and Clarke, W. D. (1968). *Ceratoscopelus maderensis*: peculiar sound-scattering layer identified with this myctophid fish. *Science* **160**, 991–3.

Badcock, J. (1970). The vertical distribution of mesopelagic fishes collected on the SOND Cruise. *J. mar. biol. Assoc. UK* **50**, 1001–44.

Baker, H. G. and Hurd, P. D. (1968). Intrafloral ecology. *A. Rev. Ent.* **13**, 385–414.

Baker, H. D. (1963). Initial stages of dark and light adaptation. *J. opt. Soc. Amer.* **53**, 98–103.

Barbier, D. (1955). Analyse du spectre du ciel nocturne. *Ann. géophys.* **11**, 181–208.

Barham, E. G. (1970). Deep-sea fishes: lethargy and vertical orientation. In *Proceedings of an International Symposium on biological sound scattering in the ocean* (ed. G. Brooke Farquhar), pp. 101–19. Ocean Science Program. Department of the Navy, Washington, D.C.

Barlow, H. B. (1953). Summation and inhibition in the frog's retina. *J. Physiol.* **119**, 69–88.

—— (1957). Purkinje shift and retinal noise. *Nature (Lond)*. **179**, 255–6.

—— (1962). Measurements of the quantum efficiency of discrimination in human scotopic vision. *J. Physiol.* **160**, 169–88.

—— (1972a). Dark and light adaptation: psychophysics. In *Handbook of sensory physiology*, Vol. VII/4 (ed. Jameson, D. and Hurvich, L. M.), pp. 1–28. Springer-Verlag, Berlin.

—— (1972b). Single units and sensation: a neural doctrine for perceptual psychology. *Perception* **1**, 371–94.

Barrett, R., Maderson, P. F. A., and Meszler, R. M. (1970). The pit organs of snakes. In *Biology of the Reptilia* (ed. C. Gans and T. S. Parsons), pp. 277–304. Academic Press, London.

Bayliss, L. E., Lythgoe, R. J., and Tansley, K. (1936). Some new forms of visual purple found in sea fishes, with a note on the visual cells of origin. *Proc. roy. Soc. B.* **816**, 95–113.

Beatty, D. D. (1966). A study of the succession of visual pigments in Pacific salmon (*Oncorhyncus*). *Can. J. Zool.* **44**, 429–55.

—— (1975). Visual pigments of the American eel, *Anguilla rostrata*. *Vision Res.* **15**, 771–6.

Behrens, M. and Krebs, W. (1976). The effect of light–dark adaptation on the ultrastructure of *Limulus* lateral eye retinular cells. *J. comp. Physiol. A.* **107**, 77–96.

Benedek, G. B. (1971). Theory of transparency of the eye. *Appl. Optics* **10**, 459–73.

Bentham, G. (revised by J. D. Hooker) (1930). *Handbook of the British flora* (7th edn). Reeve, Ashford.

Bertelsen, E. and Munk, O. (1964). Rectal light organs in the argentinoid fishes, *Opisthoproctus* and *Winteria*. *Dana Rep.*, **62**, 1–17.

Besharse, J. C. and Hollyfield, J. G. (1977). Ultrastructure changes during degeneration of photoreceptor and pigment epithelial cells in the Ozark Cave Salamander. *J. Ultrastruct. Res.* **59**, 31–43.

Blache, J., Cadenat, J., and Stauch, A. (1970). Clés de Détermination des poissons de mer signalés dans l'Atlantique Oriental. In *Faune Tropicale*, Vol. **18**, ORSTOM Paris.

Blatz, P. E. and Liebman, P. A. (1973). Wavelength regulation in visual pigments. *Exp. Eye. Res.* **17**, 573–80.

Blaxter, J. H. S. (1970). Light: Fishes. In *Marine ecology*, Vol 1, Part I (*Environmental factors*) (ed. O. Kinne), pp. 213–320 Wiley Interscience, London.

—— (1976). The role of light in the vertical migration of fish—a review. In *Light as an ecological factor* II, (ed. G. C. Evans, R. Bainbridge and O. Rackham), pp. 189–210. Blackwell Oxford.

Blest, A. D. and Land, M. F. (1977). The physiological optics of *Dinopis subrufus* L. Koch, a fish-lens in a spider. *Proc. roy. Soc. B.* **196**, 197–222.

Boll, F. (1877). Zur anatomie und physiologie der retina. *Arch. Anat. Physiol.* **4**, 783–7.

Bone, Q. (1971). On the scabbard fish *Acanopus carbo*. *J. mar. Biol. Assoc. U.K.* **51**, 219–26.

—— (1973). A note on the buoyancy of some lantern-fishes (Myctophoidea). *J. mar. biol. Assoc. U.K.* **53**, 619–33.

Born, M. and Wolf, E. (1970). *Principles of optics*. Pergamon Press, Oxford.

Bowmaker, J. K. (1977). The visual pigments, oil droplets and spectral sensitivity of the pigeon. *Vision Res.* **17**, 1129–38.

—— Dartnall, H. J. A., Lythgoe, J. N., and Mollon, J. D. (1978). The visual pigments of rods and cones in the rhesus monkey, *Macaca mulatta*. *J. Physiol.* **274**, 329–48.

—— and Knowles, A. (1977). The visual pigments and oil droplets of the chicken retina. *Vision Res.* **17**, 755–64.

Brauer, A. (1906). *Die Tiefsee-Fische*, **1**. *Systematischer Teil.-Wiss. Ergebn. dt. Tiefsee-Exped. 'Valdivia'* **15**, 432 pp. Vienna.

—— (1908). *Die Tiefsee-Fische*, **2**. *Anatomischer Teil. Wiss. Ergebn. dt. Tiefsee-Exped. 'Valdivia'* **15**, 266 pp., Vienna.

Bridges, C. D. B. (1964). Periodicity of absorption properties in pigments based on vitamin A₂ from fish retinae. *Nature (Lond.)* **203**, 303–4.

—— (1965). The grouping of fish visual pigments about preferred positions in the spectrum. Vision Res. **5**, 223–38.

—— (1967). Spectroscopic properties of porphyropsins. *Vision Res.* **7**, 349–69.

—— (1972). The rhodopsin-porphyropsin visual system. In *Handbook of sensory physiology*, Vol. VII/1 (ed. H. J. A. Dartnall), pp. 417–80. Springer-Verlag, New York.

Brockman, H. J. (1973). The function of poster coloration in the Beaugregory, *Eupomacentrus leucostictus* (Pomacentridae, Pisces). *Z. Tierpsychol.* **33**, 13–34.

Brown, J. E. and Rojas, J. A. (1965). Rat retinal ganglion cells: receptive field organization and maintained activity. *J. Neurophysiol.* **28**, 1073–90.

Bruno, M. S., Barnes, S. N., and Goldsmith, T. H. (1977). The visual pigment and visual cycle of the lobster, *Homarus*. *J. comp. Physiol.* **120**, 123–42.

Bruun, A. F. (1957). Deep sea and abyssal depths. *Mem. geol. Soc. Am.* 67 **1**, 641–72.

Buck, J. and Buck, E. (1976). Synchronous fireflies. *Sci. Am.* **234** (5), 75–85.

Butenandt, E. and Grüsser, O.-J. (1968). The effect of stimulus area on the response of movement detecting neurons in the frog's retina. *Pflugers Arch. ges. Physiol.* **298**, 283–93.

Cahn, P. H. (1958). Comparative optic development in *Astyanax mexicanus* and in two of its blind cave derivatives. *Bull. Am. Mus. Nat. Hist.* **93**, 501–31.

Cameron, N. (1974). Chromatic vision in a teleost fish: *Perca fluviatilis*. Ph.D. thesis. University of Sussex, U.K.

Campbell, F. W. and Green, D. G. (1965a). Monocular versus binocular visual acuity. *Nature (Lond.)* **208**, 191–2.

—— (1965b). Optical and retinal factors affecting visual resolution. J. Physiol. **181**, 576–93.

—— and Maffei, L. (1974). Contrast and spatial frequency. *Sci. Amer.* **231** (5), 106–14.

—— and Robson, J. G. (1968). Application of Fourier analysis to the visibility of gratings. *J. Physiol.* **197**, 551–66.

Carricaburu, P. (1974). Sous quel aspect les insectes voient-ils les objects colorés. *Vision Res.* **14**, 671–5.

Chamberlain, J. W. (1961). *Physics of the aurora and airglow*. Academic Press, New York.

Chapman, C. J., Johnstone, A. D. F. and Rice, A. L. (1975). The behaviour and ecology of the Norway lobster, *Nephrops norvegicus* (L). In *Proceedings of the ninth European marine biology symposium* (ed. H. Barnes), 59–74. Aberdeen University Press.

—— and Rice, A. L. (1971). Some direct observations on the ecology and behaviour of the Norway lobster, *Nephrops norvegicus*. *Mar. Biol.* **10**, 321–9.

Chase, J. (1972). The role of vision in echolocating bats. Ph.D Thesis, Indiana University.

Clarke, G. L. (1936). On the depth at which fishes can see. *Ecology* **17**, 452–6.

—— and Denton, E. J. (1962). Light and animal life. In *The sea*, Vol. I (ed. M. N. Hill), pp. 456–68. Interscience, London.

—— and James, H. R. (1939). Laboratory analysis of the absorption of light by sea water. *J. opt. Soc. Am.* **29**, 43–55.

—— and Kelly, M. G. (1964). Variation in transparency and in bioluminescence on longitudinal transects in the western Indian Ocean. *Bull. Inst. Oceanogr. Monaco,* **64**, 1–20.

Clarke, W. D. (1963). Function of bioluminescence in mesopelagic organisms. *Nature (Lond.)* **198**, 1244–6

Clayton, R. K. (1970). *Light and living matter: a guide to the study of photobiology.* Vol. 1, pp. 34–8. McGraw-Hill, New York.

Collette, B. B. and Talbot, F. H. (1972). Activity patterns of coral reef fishes with emphasis on nocturnal–diurnal changeover. *Bull. Nat. Hist. Mus. Los Angeles County* **14**, 98–124.

Collins, F. D., Love, R. M., and Morton, R. A. (1952). Studies in rhodopsin. 4. Preparation of rhodopsin. *Biochem. J.* **51**, 292–8.

Condit, H. R. and Grum, F. (1964). Spectral energy distribution of daylight. *J. opt. Soc. Am.* **54**, 937–43.

Cooper, G. F. and Robson, J. G. (1969). The yellow colour of the lens of the grey squirrel (*Sciurus carolinensis leucotis*). *J. Physiol.* **203**, 403–10.

Cornsweet, T. N. (1970). *Visual perception*. Academic Press, London.

Cott, H. B. (1940). *Adaptive coloration in animals*. Methuen, London.

Cowan, P. J. (1972). The contrast coloration of sea-birds: an experimental approach. *Ibis*, **114**, 390–3.

Cox, C. S. (1974). Refraction and reflection of light at the sea surface. In *Optical aspects of oceanography* (ed. N. G. Jerlov and E. Steeman Nielsen), pp. 51–75. Academic Press, London.

Craik, K. J. W. (1938). The effect of adaptation on differential brightness discrimination. *J. Physiol.* **92**, 406–21.

—— (1943). The nature of explanation. Cambridge Univ. Press.

—— (1944). White plumage of sea-birds. *Nature (Lond.)* **153**, 288.

—— (1966). The nature of psychology. In *A selection of papers, essays and other writings by the late K. J. W. Craik* (ed. S. L. Sherwood). Cambridge University Press.

Crescitelli, F. (1972). The visual cells and visual pigments of the vertebrate eye. In *Handbook of sensory physiology*, Vol. VII/1, (ed. H. J. A. Dartnall), pp. 245–363. Springer-Verlag, New York.

Dartnall, H. J. A. (1953). The interpretation of spectral sensitivity curves. *Br. Med. Bull.* **9**, 24–30.

—— (1957). *The visual pigments*. Methuen, London.

—— (1960). Visual pigments of colour vision. In *Mechanisms of colour discrimination*, (ed. Y. Galifret), pp. 147–61. Pergamon, Oxford.

—— (1962). The identity and distribution of visual pigments in the animal kingdom. In *The eye* (ed. H. Davson), pp. 367–426. Academic Press, London.

—— (1975). Assessing the fitness of visual pigments for their photic environment. In *Vision in fishes* (ed. M. A. Ali), pp. 543–63. Plenum Press, New York.

—— and Lythgoe, J. N. (1965a). The clustering of fish visual pigments around discrete spectral positions, and its bearing on chemical structure. In *Ciba foundation symposium on physiology and experimental psychology* (ed. G. E. W. Wolstenholme and J. Knight), pp. 3–21. J. & A. Churchill, London.

—— —— (1965b). The spectral clustering of visual pigments. *Vision Res.* **5**, 81–100.

Darwin, C. (1889). *The descent of man* (2nd edn, p. 493. John Murray, London.

Daumer, K. (1956). Reitzmetrische untersuchungen des Farbensehens der Bienen. *Z. vergl. Physiol.* **38**, 413–78.

—— (1958). Blumen, wie sie die Bienen sehen. *Z. vergl. Physiol.* **41**, 49–110.

Denton, E. J., Gilpin-Brown, J. B., and Wright, P. G. (1970). On the 'filters' in the photophores of mesopelagic fish and on a fish emitting red light and especially sensitive to red light. *J. Physiol.* **208**, 72P–73P.

—— —— —— (1972). The angular distribution of the light produced by some mesopelagic fish in relation to camouflage. *Proc. roy. Soc. B* **182**, 145–58.

—— and Nicol, J. A. C. (1965a). Studies on reflexions of light from silvery surfaces of fishes, with special reference to the bleak, *Alburnus alburnus*. *J. mar. biol. Assoc. UK* **45**, 683–703.

—— —— (1965b). Reflexion of light by external surfaces of herring, *Clupea harengus*. *J. mar. biol. Assoc. UK* **45**, 711–38.

—— —— (1966). A survey of reflectivity in silvery teleosts. *J. mar. biol. Assoc. UK* **46**, 685–722.

—— and Warren, F. J. (1957). The photosensitive pigments in the retinae of deep-sea fish. *J. mar. biol. Assoc. UK* **36**, 651–62.

Dippner, R. and Armington, J. (1971). A behavioral measure of dark adaptation in the American red squirrel. *Psychon. Sci.* **24**, 43–5.

Dodt, E. (1962). Vergleichende untersuchungen über das adaptiv Verhalten reiner Zapfennetzhäute *Citellus citellus, Sciurus vulgaris. Pflügers Archiv. ges. Physiol.* **275**, 561–73.

—— Echte, K. (1961). Dark and light adaptations in pigmented and white rat as measured by electroretinogram threshold. *J. Neurophysiol.* **24**, 427–45.

—— and Jessen, K. H. (1961). The duplex nature of the retina of the nocturnal gecko as reflected in the electroretinogram. *J. gen. Physiol.* **44**, 1143–58.

Dowling, J. E. (1960). The chemistry of visual adaptation in the rat. *Nature (Lond.)* **188**, 114–18

Ducker, G. (1963). Spontane Bevorzugung arteigener Farben bei Vögeln. *Z. Tierpsychol.* **20**, 43–65.

Duntley, S. Q. (1951). The visibility of submerged objects II. *Proc. Armed Forces–Nat. Res. Council Vision Comm.* **28**, 60.

—— (1960). Improved nomographs for calculating visibility by swimmers (natural light). *Bureau of Ships Contract NOBS-***72039** *Report* 5. 3 February.

—— (1962). Underwater visibility. In *The sea* (ed. M. N. Hill), pp. 452–5. Interscience, London.

—— (1963). Light in the sea. *J. opt. Soc. Am.* **53**, 214–33.

—— (1974). Underwater visibility and photography. In *Optical aspects of oceanography* (ed. N. G. Jerlov and E. Steeman Nielsen), pp. 135–49. Academic Press, London.

Easter, S. S. Jr (1975). Retinal specialisation for aquatic vision: theory and facts. In *Vision in fishes* (ed. M. A. Ali), pp. 609–17. Plenum, New York.

Ebrey, T. G. and Honig, B. (1977). New wavelength dependent visual pigment nomograms. *Vision Res.* **17**, 147–51.

Ehrlich, P. R., Talbot, F. H., Russell, B. C., and Anderson, G. R. V. (1977). The behaviour of Chaetodontid fishes with special reference to Lorenz's 'poster coloration' hypothesis. *J. Zool.* **183**, 213–28.

Ekman, S. (1953). *Zoogeography of the sea.* Sidgwick & Jackson, London.

Engström, K. (1963). Cone types and cone arrangements in teleost retinae. *Acta Zool.* **44**, 179–243.

—— and Ahlbert, I. (1963). Cone types and cone arrangement in the retina of some flatfishes. *Acta Zool.* **44**, 119–29.

Erhard, H. (1924). Messende untersuchungen über den Farbensinn der Vögel. *Zool. Jahrb., Allg. Zool. Physiol.* **41**, 489–552.

Evans, W. E. (1973). The echolocation by marine delphinids and one species of fresh water dolphin. *J. acoust. Soc. Amer.* **54**, 191–204.

Faegri, K. and Pijl, L. van der (1966). *The principles of pollination ecology.* Pergamon, Oxford.

Farrel, R. A., McCally, R. L., and Tatham, P. E. R. (1973). Wavelength dependencies of light scattering in normal and cold swollen rabbit corneas and their structural implications. *J. Physiol.* **233**, 589–612.

Feuk, T. (1970). On the transparency of the stroma of the mammalian cornea. *IEEE Trans. bio-med. Engng.* **17**, 186–90.

—— (1971). The wave-length dependence of scattered light intensity in rabbit corneas. *IEEE trans. bio. med. Engng.* **18**, 92–6.

Fingerman, M. (1965). Chromatophores. *Physiol. Rev.* **45**, 296–339.

Fox, D. L. (1976). *Animal biochromes and structural colours.* University of California Press, Berkeley.

Fox, H. M. and Vevers, G. (1960). *The nature of animal colours.* Sidgwick & Jackson, London.

Foxton, P. (1970a). The vertical distribution of pelagic decapods (Crustacea: Natantia) collected on the SOND Cruise (1965). I. The Caridea. *J. mar. biol. Assoc. UK* **50**, 939–60.

—— (1970b). The vertical distribution of pelagic decapods (Crustacea: Natantia) collected on the SOND Cruise (1965). II. The Penaeidea and general discussion. *J. mar. biol. Assoc. UK* **50**, 961–1000.

Fryer, G. and Iles, T. D. (1972). *The Cichlid fishes of the great lakes of Africa.* Oliver & Boyd, Edinburgh.

Galton, F. (1851). *South Africa*, p. 187. Minerva Library.

Glickman, R. D. and Pomerance, B. (1977). Frog retinal ganglion cells showing species differences in their optimal stimulus size. *Nature (Lond.)* **265**, 51–3.

Goldman, J. N. and Benedek, G. B. (1967). The relationship between morphology and transparency in the non-swelling corneal stroma of the shark. *Invest. Ophth.* **6**, 574–600.

Goldsmith, T. H. (1972). The natural history of invertebrate visual pigments. In *Handbook of sensory physiology* (ed. H. J. A. Dartnall), pp. 685–719. Springer-Verlag, Berlin.

—— (1975). The polarization sensitivity–Dichroic absorption paradox in Arthropod photoreceptors. In *Photoreceptor optics* (ed. A. W. Snyder, and R. Menzel), pp. 392–409, Springer-Verlag, Berlin.

Goodyear, R. H., Zahuranec, B. J., Pugh, W. L., and Gibbs, R. H., (1972). Ecology and vertical distribution of Mediterranean midwater fishes. *Mediterranean biological Studies final report* **1**, (3), 91–229.

Gorn, R. A. and Kuwabara, T. (1967). Retinal damage by visible light. A physiological study. *Arch. Ophthalmol.* **77**, 115–18.

Govardovskii, V. I. (1972). On the possible adaptive significance of the position of visual pigment absorption maxima. *Zh. evol. biochim. fiziol.* **8**, 8–17.

—— (1976). Comments on the sensitivity hypothesis. *Vision Res.* **16**, 1363–4.

—— and Zueva, L. V. (1974). Spectral sensitivity of the frog eye in the ultraviolet and visible region. *Vision Res.* **14**, 1317–22.

Grant, V. and Grant, K. A. (1965). *Flower pollination in the phlox family.* Columbia University Press, New York.

Green, D. G. (1970). Regional variation in the acuity for interference fringes on the retina. *J. Physiol.* **207**, 351–6.

Greenwood, P. H. (1976). A new and eyeless cobitid fish (Pisces, Cypriniformes) from the Zagros Mountains, Iran. *J. Zool. Soc. Lond.* **180**, 129–37.

Griffin, D. R. (1958). *Listening in the dark.* Yale University Press, New Haven, Conn.

—— and Suthers, R. A. (1970). Sensitivity of echolocation in cave swiftlets. *Bio. Bull.* **139**, 495–501.

Gruber, S. H. (1975). Duplex vision in the elasmobranchs: histological, electrophysiological and psychophysical evidence. In *Vision in fishes* (ed. M. A. Ali), pp. 525–40. Plenum, New York.

Haddow, A. J. and Corbet, P. S. (1961). Entomological studies from a high tower in Mpanga Forest, Uganda. V. Swarming activity above the forest. *Trans. R. ent. Soc. Lond.* **113**, 284–300.

Haig, C. (1941). The course of dark adaptation as influenced by intensity and duration of pre-adapting light. *J. gen. Physiol.* **24**, 735–51.

Hailman J. P. (1967). The ontogeny of an instinct. *Behav. Suppl.* **15**, 1–196.

Ham, W. T., Mueller, H. A., and Sliney, D. H. (1976). Retinal sensitivity to damage from short wavelength light. *Nature (Lond.)* **260**, 153–4.

Hamilton, W. F. and Coleman, T. E. (1933). Trichromatic vision in the pigeon, all illustrated by the spectral discrimination curve. *J. comp. Psychol.* **15**, 183–91.

Hamilton, W. J. and Peterman, R. M. (1971). Countershading in the colourful reef fish *Chaetodon lunula*: concealment, communication or both. *Anim. Behav.* **19**, 357–64.

Hammond, P. (1968). Spectral properties of dark-adapted retinal ganglion cells in the plaice (*Pleuronectes platessa*, L). *J. Physiol.* **195**, 535–56.

Hamner, W. M. (1974). Blue-water plankton. *Nat. geogr. Mag.,* October.

—— Madin, L. P., Alldredge, A. L., Gilmer, R. W., and Hamner, P. P. (1975). Underwater observations of gelatinous zooplankton; sampling problems, feeding biology and behaviour. *Limnol. Oceanogr.* **20**, 907–17.

Harkness, L. (1977). Chameleons use accommodation cues to judge distance. *Nature (Lond.)* **267**, 346–9.

Hárosi, F. (1975). Absorption spectra and linear dichroism of some amphibian photoreceptors. *J. gen. Physiol.* **66**, 357–82.

—— (1976). Spectral relations of cone pigments in goldfish. *J. gen. Physiol.* **68**, 65–80.

—— and MacNichol, E. F., Jr. (1974). Visual pigments of goldfish cones. *J. gen. Physiol.* **63**, 279–304.

Harris, G. G. and Bergeijk, W. A. van (1962). Evidence that the lateral line organ responds to water displacements. *J. acoust. Soc. Amer.* **34**, 1831–41.

Harrison, R. J. and Tomlinson, J. D. W. (1964). Observations on diving seals and certain mammals. *Symp. Zool. Soc. Lond.* No. 13, pp. 59–69.

Hart, J. L. (1973). *Pacific fishes of Canada.* Fisheries Research Board of Canada, Ottawa.

Harvey, E. N. (1952). *Bioluminescence.* Academic Press, New York.

—— (1955). Survey of luminous organisms. In *Luminescence of biological systems* (ed. F. H. Johnson), pp. 1–24. American Association for the Advancement of Science, Washington, D.C.

Hays, D. and Goldsmith, T. H. (1969). Microspectrophotometry of the visual pigment of the spider crab *Libinia emarginata. Z. Vergl. Physiol.* **65**, 218–32.

Heath, A. R. (1977). Normal and pathological changes in a fish retina resulting from manipulated light and dark regimes. D. Phil. Thesis, University of Sussex.

Hecht, S. and Verrijp, C. D. (1933). Intermittent stimulation by light. *J. gen. Physiol.* **17**, 237–82.

——, Hendley, C. D., Ross, S., and Richmond, P. M. (1948). The effect of exposure to sunlight on dark adaptation. *Am. J. Ophthalmol.* **31**, 1573–80.

—— Shlaer, S., and Pirenne, M. H. (1942). Energy, quanta and vision. *J. gen. Physiol.* **25**, 819–40.

Helversen, O. von (1972). Zur spektralen unterschied-sempfindlichkeit der Honigbiene. *J. comp. Physiol.* **80**, 439–72.

Hemilä, S., Reuter, T., and Virtanen, K. (1976). The evolution of colour-opponent neurones in colour vision. *Vision Res.* **16**, 1359–62.

Hemmings, C. C. and Lythgoe, J. N. (1964). Better visibility for divers in dark water. *Triton* **9**, (4), 28–31.

—— (1965). The visibility of underwater objects. In *Symposium of the Underwater Association for Malta (1965)* (ed. J. N. Lythgoe and J. D. Woods), pp. 23–30. The Underwater Association, London.

Henson, O. W. (1970). The ear and audition. In *Biology of bats*, Vol. II (ed. W. A. Wimsatt), pp. 181–263. Academic Press, London.

Herring, P. J. (1967). The pigments of plankton at the sea surface. *Symp. zool. Soc. Lond.* **19**, 215–35.

—— (1976). Bioluminescence in decapod crustacea. *J. mar. biol. Assoc. UK* **56**, 1029–47.

—— (1977a). Bioluminescence of marine organisms. *Nature (Lond.)* **267**, 788–93.

—— (1977b). Bioluminescence in an evermannellid fish. *J. Zool. Lond.* **181**, 297–307.

Hinton, H. E. (1973). Natural deception. In *Illusion in nature and art* (ed. R. L. Gregory and E. H. Gombrich), pp. 96–159. Duckworth, London.

—— (1976). Possible significance of the red patches of the female crab-spider, *Misumenia vatia. J. Zool. Lond.* **180**, 35–9.

Hobson, E. S. (1965). Nocturnal–diurnal activity of some inshore fishes in the Gulf of California, *Copeia* (3), 291–302.

—— (1966). Visual orientation and feeding in sea lions. *Nature (Lond.)* **210**, 326–7.

—— (1972). Activity of Hawaiian reef fishes during the evening and morning transitions between daylight and darkness. *Fish. Bull. Nat. Mar. Fish. Ser.* **70**, 715–40.

Höglund, G. (1965). Pigment migration and retinular sensitivity. In *The functional organization of the compound eye.* (Ed. C. G. Bernhard), pp. 77–88. Pergamon, Oxford.

Homer, W. I. (1964). *Seurat and the science of painting.* M.I.T. Press, Cambridge, Mass.

Hubel, D. H. and Wiesel, T. N. (1960). Receptive fields of optic nerve fibres in the spider monkey. *J. Physiol.* **154**, 572–80.

Hughes, A. (1977). The topography of vision in mammals. In *Handbook of sensory physiology*, Vol. VII/5. (ed. F. Crescitelli), pp. 613–756. Springer-Verlag, Berlin.

Ivanoff, A. (1974). Polarization measurements in the sea. In *Optical aspects of oceanography* (ed. N. G. Jerlov and E. Steeman Nielsen), pp. 152–75. Academic Press, London.

—— and Waterman, T. H. (1958). Factors, mainly depth and wavelength, affecting the degree of underwater light polarization. *J. mar. Res.* **16**, 283–307.

Jerlov, N. G. (1951). Optical studies of ocean water. *Rep. Swed. deep sea Exped.* **3**, 1–59.

—— (1968). *Optical oceanography*. Elsevier, London.

—— (1976). *Marine optics*. Elsevier, Amsterdam.

—— (Johnson and Liljequist, G. (1938). On the angular distribution of submarine daylight and the total submarine illumination. *Sven. Hydrogr. Biol. Komm. Skr., Ny Ser. Hydrogr.* **14**, 1–15.

—— and Nygård, K. (1968). Inherent optical properties from radiance measurements in the Baltic. *Univ. Copenhagen. Inst. Physic. Oceanogr. Rep.* **1**, 1–7.

Jones, C. E. and Buchmann, S. L. (1974). Ultraviolet floral patterns as functional orientation cues in hymenopterous pollination systems. *Anim. Behav.* **22**, 481–5.

Jones, F. M. (1932). Insect coloration and the relative acceptability of insects to birds. *Trans. Ent. Soc. Lond.* **80**, 345–85.

—— (1934). Further experiments on coloration and relative acceptability of insects to birds. *Trans. Roy. Ent. Soc. Lond.* **82**, 443–53.

Kalle, K. (1937). Meereskundliche Chemische Untersuchungen mit Hilfe des Zeitzschen Pulfrich-Photometers. *Annln. Hydrogr. Berl.* **65**, 276–82.

—— (1938). Zum problem der meereswasserfarbe. *Ann. Hydrol. Marine Mitt.* **66**, 1–13.

—— (1966). The problem of Gelbstoffe in the sea. *Oceanog. Marine Biol. Ann. Rev.* **4**, 91–104.

Kalmijn, A. J. (1974). The detection of electric fields from inanimate and animate sources other than electric organs. In *Handbook of sensory physiology*, Vol. III/3, pp. 147–200 (ed. A. Fessard). Springer-Verlag, Berlin.

Kampa, E. M. (1961). Daylight penetration measurements in three oceans. *Union. Geold. Geophys. Intern. Monographie* **10**, 91–6.

—— (1970). Underwater daylight and moonlight measurements in the eastern North Atlantic. *J. mar. biol. Assoc. UK* **50**, 391–420.

—— and Boden, B. P. (1957). Light generation in a sonic scattering layer. *Deep Sea Res.* **4**, 73–92.

Kelly, D. H. (1961). Visual responses to time-dependent stimuli. I. Amplitude sensitivity measurement. *J. opt. Soc. Amer.* **51**, 422–9.

King-Smith, P. (1969). Absorption spectra and function of the coloured oil drops in the pigeon retina. *Vision Res.* **9**, 1391–9.

Kinney, J. S., Luria, S. M., and Weitzman, D. O. (1967). Visibility of colours underwater. *J. opt. Soc. Am.* **57**, 802–9.

Kleinholz, L. H. (1965). Hormonal regulation of retinal pigment migration in crustaceans. In *The functional organization of the compound eye* (ed. C. G. Bernhard), pp. 89–101. Pergamon, Oxford.

Kirschfeld, K. (1969). Absorption properties of photopigments in single rods, cones and rhabdomeres. In *Processing of optical data by organisms and machines* (ed. W. Reichardt), pp. 116–43. Academic Press, London.

—— (1974). The absolute sensitivity of lens and compound eyes. *Z. Naturforsch.* **29c**, 592–6.

—— (1976). The resolution of lens and compound eyes. In *Neural principles of vision* (ed. F. Zettler and R. Weiler), pp. 354–69. Springer-Verlag, Berlin.

—— Franceschini, N., and Minke, B. (1977). Evidence for a sensitising pigment in fly photoreceptors. *Nature (Lond.)* **269**, 386–90.

Knowles, A. and Dartnall, H. J. A. (1977). Photobiology of vision. In *The eye*, Vol. IIB (ed. H. Davson), pp. 1–689. Academic Press, London.

Koschmieder, H. (1924). Theorie der horizontalen Sichtweite. *Beitre. Phys. freien Atm.* **12**, 33–5 and 171–81.

Krause, W. (1863). Uber die endigung der Muskelnernen. *Zeits. f. rat. Med.* **20**, 1–18.

Kropf, A. (1967). Intramolecular energy transfer in rhodopsin. *Vision Res.* **7**, 811–18.

Kühne, W. (1877). Uber den Sehpurpur. *Untersuch. Physiol. Inst. Univ. Heidelberg* **1**, 235–337.

Kulikowski, J. J. and King Smith, P. E. (1973). Spatial arrangement of line, edge and grating detectors revealed by subthreshold phenomena. *Vision Res.* **13**, 1455–78.

Lack, D. (1956). *Swifts in a tower*. Methuen, London.

Land, M. F. (1972). The physics and biology of animal reflectors. *Prog. Biophys. Mol. Biol.* **24**, 75–106.

Laughlin, S. B., Menzel, R., and Snyder, A. W. (1975). Membranes, dichroism and receptor sensitivity. In *Photoreceptor optics* (ed. A. W. Snyder and R. Menzel), pp. 237–59. Springer-Verlag, Berlin.

Le Grand, Y. (1939). La pénétration de la lumière dans la mer. *Ann. Inst. Océanogr.* **19**, 343–436.

—— (1948). Recherches sur la fluorescence des mieuxil oculaires. Publ. Inst. Biofisica. Univ. de Brasil, Rio de Janeiro.

—— (1964). Colorimétrie de l'Abeille *Apis mellifera*. *Vision Res.* **4**, 59–62.

Levick, W. R. (1967). Receptive fields and trigger features of ganglion cells in the visual streak of the rabbit's retina. *J. Physiol.* **188**, 285–307.

Liebman, P. A. (1972). Microspectrophotometry of photoreceptors. In *Handbook of sensory physiology*, Vol. VII/1 (ed. H. J. A. Dartnall), pp. 481–528. Springer-Verlag, Berlin.

—— and Granda, A. M. (1971). Microspectrophotometric measurements of visual pigments in two species of turtle, *Pseudemys scripta* and *Chelonia midas*. *Vision Res.* **11**, 105–14.

Limbaugh, C. and North, W. J. (1956). Fluorescent benthic Pacific coast coelenterates. *Nature (Lond.)* **178**, 497–8.

Lissmann, H. W. (1958). On the function and evolution of electric organs in fish. *J. exp. Biol.* **35**, 156–91.

—— (1963). Electric location by fishes. *Sci. Am.* **208**(3), 50–9.

—— and Machin, K. E. (1958) The mechanism of object location in *Gymnarchus niloticus* and similar fish. *J. exp. Biol.* **35**, 451–86.

Lloyd, J. E. (1975). Aggressive mimicry in Photuris fireflies: signal repertoires by femmes fatales. *Science* **187**, 452–3.

Locket, N. A. (1971). Retinal structure in *Platytroctes apus*, a deep-sea fish with a pure rod fovea. *J. mar. biol. Assoc. UK* **51**, 79–91.

—— (1972). The reflecting structure in the iridescent cornea of the serranid teleost *Nemanthias carberryi*. *Proc. roy. Soc. B.* **182**, 249–54.

—— (1977). Adaptations to the deep-sea environment. In *Handbook of sensory physiology*, Vol. VII/5 (ed. F. Crescitelli), pp. 67–192. Springer-Verlag, Berlin.

Loew, E. R. (1976). Light and photoreceptor degeneration in the Norway lobster, *Nephrops norvegicus* (L). *Proc. r. Soc. Lond. B.* **193**, 31–44.

—— and Dartnall, H. J. A. (1976). Vitamin A_1/A_2-based visual pigment mixtures in cones of the rudd. Vision Res. **16**, 891–6.

—— and Lythgoe, J. N. (1978). The ecology of cone pigments in teleost fishes. *Vision Res.* **18,** 715–22.

Luck, C. P. (1965). The comparative morphology of the eyes of certain African Suiformes. *Vision Res.* **5**, 283–97.

Lundgren, B. and Højerslev, N. K. (1971). Daylight measurements in the Sargasso Sea. Results from the 'Dana' expedition January–April, 1966. *Univ. Copenhagen, Inst. Phys. Oceanogr. Rep.* **14**, 1–44.

Lyall, A. H. (1957). Cone arrangements in teleost retinae. *Q. J. microsc. Sci.* **98**, 189–201.

Lythgoe, J. N. (1966). Underwater vision. In *British Sub-Aqua Club diving manual* (2nd ed). Eaton Publications, London.

—— (1968). Visual pigments and visual range underwater. *Vision Res.* **8**, 997–1012.

—— (1971). Iridescent corneas in fishes. *Nature (Lond.)* **233**, 205–7.

—— (1971). Vision. In *Underwater science* (ed. J. D. Woods and J. N. Lythgoe), pp. 103–39. Oxford University Press.

—— (1972). The adaptation of visual pigments to their photic environment. In *Handbook of sensory physiology*, Vol. VII/1 (ed. H. J. A. Dartnall). Springer-Verlag, Berlin.

—— (1974a). The structure and phylogeny of iridescent corneas in fishes. In *Vision in fishes* (ed. M. A. Ali), pp. 253–62. Plenum Press, New York.

—— (1974b). The iridescent cornea of the sand goby, *Pomatoschistus minutus* (Pallas). In *Vision in fishes* (ed. M. A. Ali), pp. 263–78. Plenum Press, New York.

—— (1976). The ecology function and phylogeny of iridescent multilayers in fish cones. In *Light as an ecological factor*, Vol. II (ed. G. C. Evans, R. Bainbridge, and O. Rackham), pp. 211–47. Blackwell, Oxford.

—— and Dartnall, H. J. A. (1970). A 'deep sea' rhodopsin in a mammal. *Nature (Lond.)* **227**, 955–6.

—— and Northmore, D. P. M. (1973). Colours underwater. In *Colour '73*, pp. 77–98. Adam Hilger, London.

Macdonald, D. W. (1976). Nocturnal observations of tawny owls preying upon earth worms. *Ibis* **118**, 579–80.

McFarland, W. N. (1971). Cetacean visual pigments. *Vision Res.* **11**, 1065–76.

—— and Munz, F. W. (1975a). The photic environment of clear tropical seas during the day. *Vision Res.* **15**, 1063–70.

—— —— (1975b). The evolution of photopic visual pigments in fishes. *Vision Res.* **15**, 1071–80.

Mach, E. (1865). Uber die Wirkung der räumlichen Vertheilung des Lichtreizes auf die Netzhaut, I. ber. *K. Akad. Wiss. Wien. Mathematisch-naturwissenschaftlichen Klasse.* **52**, 303–22.

Makoto Omari (1974). The biology of pelagic shrimps in the ocean. *Adv. mar. Biol.* **12**, 233–324.

Marc, R. E. and Sperling, H. G. (1977). Chromatic organization in primate cones. *Science* **196**, 454–6.

Marshall, J., Mellerio, J., and Palmer, D. A. (1972). Damage to pigeon retinae by moderate illumination from fluorescent lamps. *Exp. Eye Res.* **14**, 164–9.

—— —— —— (1973). A schematic eye for the pigeon. *Vision Res.* **13**, 2449–53.

Marshall, N. B. (1954). *Aspects of deep sea biology.* Hutchinson, London.

—— (1971). *Explorations in the life of fishes*, Harvard University Press, Cambridge, Mass.

Martin, G. R. (1977). Absolute visual threshold and scotopic spectral sensitivity in the tawny owl, *Strix aluco. Nature (Lond.)* **268**, 636–8.

—— and Muntz, W. R. A. (1978). Retinal oil droplets and vision in the pigeon (*Columba livia*). In *Neural mechanisms of behaviour in the pigeon*, Brain Behaviour and Evolution Symp. Edit.

Maturana, H. R. and Frenk, S. (1963). Directional movement and horizontal edge detectors in the pigeon retina. *Science* **142**, 977–9.

—— Lettvin, J. Y., McCulloch, W. S., and Pitts, W. H. (1960). Anatomy and physiology of vision in the frog (*Rana pipiens*). *J. gen. Physiol.* **43**, Suppl. **2**, 129–71.

Mauchline, J. and Fisher, L. R. (1969). The biology of Euphausiids. *Adv. Mar. Biol.* **7**, 1–454.

Mayr, I. (1972). Verteilung, lokalisation und Absorption der Zapfenölkugen bei Vögeln (Ploceidae). *Vision Res.* **12**, 1477–84.

Menzel, R. (1975). Colour receptors in insects. In *The compound eye and vision in insects* (ed. A. Horridge), pp. 121–53. Clarendon Press, Oxford.

Merrett, N. R., Badcock, J., and Herring, P. J. (1973). The status of *Benthalbella infans* (Pisces: Myctophoidei), its development, bioluminescence, general biology and distribution in the eastern North Atlantic. *J. Zool. Lond.* **170**, 1–48.

Mertens, L. E. (1970). *In-water photography.* John Wiley, New York.

Meyer, D. B. (1977). The avian eye and its adaptation. In *Handbook of sensory physiology*, Vol. VII/5 (ed. F. Crescitelli), pp. 549–611. Springer-Verlag, Berlin.

Meyer, D. L., Heiligenberg, W. and Bullock, T. H. (1976). A ventral substrate response. A new postural control mechanism in fishes. *J. comp. Physiol.* **109**, 59–68.

Michael, C. R. (1968a). Receptive fields of single optic nerve fibers in a mammal with an all-cone retina. I. Contrast-sensitive units. *J. Neurophysiol.* **31**, 249–56.

—— (1968b). Receptive fields of single optic nerve fibers in a mammal with an all-cone retina. II. Directionally sensitive units. *J. Neurophysiol.* **31**, 257–67.

—— (1968c). Receptive fields of single optic nerve fibers in a mammal with an all-cone retina. III. Opponent colour units. *J. Neurophysiol.* **31**, 268–82.

Middleton, W. E. K. (1952). *Vision through the atmosphere.* University of Toronto Press.

Miller, W. H., Møller, A. R., and Bernhard, C. G. (1966). The corneal nipple array. In *The functional organization of the compound eye*, pp. 21–33 (ed. C. G. Bernhard), Pergamon Press, Oxford.

Moon, P. (1940). Proposed standard solar radiation curves for engineering use. *J. Franklin Inst.* **230**, 583–617.

Morel, A. and Caloumenos, L. (1974). Variabilité de la repartition spectrale de l'énergie photosynthétique. *Tethys* **6**, 93–104.

—— and Smith, R. C. (1974). Relation between total quanta and total energy for aquatic photosynthesis. *Limnol. Oceanog.* **19**, 591–600.

Moreland, J. D. and Lythgoe, J. N. (1968). Yellow corneas in fishes. *Vision Res.* **8**, 1377–80.

Morin, J. G., Harrington, A., Nealson, K., Krieger, N., Baldwin, T. O., and Hastings, J. W. (1975). Light for all reasons: versatility in the behavioural repertoire of the flashlight fish. *Science* **190**, 74–6.

Morris, V. B. and Shorey, C. D. (1967). An electron-microscope study of types of receptor in the chick retina. *J. Comp. Neurol.* **129**, 313–39.

Morton, R. A. (1972). The chemistry of the visual pigments. In *Handbook of sensory physiology*, Vol. VII/1 (ed. H. J. A. Dartnall), pp. 33–68. Springer-Verlag, Berlin.

Moskalkova, K. I. (1971). Adaptive changes of the retina in autogeny of *Gobius melanostomus* (Pall.). *Dokl. Akad. Nauk. SSSR* **198**, 1225–7.

Munk, O. (1966). Ocular anatomy of some deep-sea teleosts. *Dana Rep.* **70**, 1–62.

—— (1970). On the occurrence and significance of horizontal band-shaped retinal areae in teleosts. *Vidensk. Meddr. dansk. naturh. Foren.* **133**, 85–120.

—— (1977). The visual cells and retinal tapetum of the foveate deep-sea fish *Scopelosaurus lepidus* (teleostei). *Zoomorphologie* **87**, 21–49.

—— and Frederiksen, R. D. (1974). On the function of aphakic apertures in teleosts. *Vidensk. Meddr dansk naturh. Foren.* **137**, 65–94.

Muntz, W. R. A. (1972). Inert absorbing and reflecting pigments. In *Handbook of sensory physiology*, Vol. VII/1 (ed. H. J. A. Dartnall), pp. 529–65. Springer-Verlag, Berlin.

—— (1973). Yellow filters and the absorption of light by the visual pigments of some Amazonian fishes. *Vision Res.* **13**, 2235–54.

—— (1975). The visual consequences of yellow filtering pigments in the eyes of fishes occupying different habitats. In *Light as an ecological factor* Vol. II (ed. G. C. Evans, R. Bainbridge, and O. Rackham), pp. 271–87. Blackwell, Oxford.

—— (1976). On yellow lenses in mesopelagic animals. *J. mar. biol. Ass. UK* **56**, 963–76.

—— Baddeley, A. D., and Lythgoe, J. N. (1974). Visual resolution under water. *Aerospace Med.* **45**, 61–6.

Munz, F. W. (1957). The photosensitive retinal pigments of marine and euryhaline teleost fishes. Ph.D Thesis, University of California, Los Angeles.

—— (1958). Photosensitive pigments from the retinae of certain deep sea fishes. *J. Physiol.* **140**, 220–5.

—— and McFarland, W. N. (1973). The significance of spectral position in the rhodopsins of tropical marine fishes. *Vision Res.* **13**, 1829–74.

—— —— (1975). Part I, Presumptive cone pigments extracted from tropical marine fishes. *Vision Res.* **15**, 1045–62.

—— —— (1977). Evolutionary adaptations of fishes to the photic environment. In *Handbook of sensory physiology*, Vol. VII/5 (ed. F. Crescitelli). Springer-Verlag, Berlin.

Murton, R. K. (1965). *The wood pigeon.* Collins, London.

Neill, S. R. St J. and Cullen, J. M. (1974). Experiments on whether schooling by their prey affects the hunting behaviour of cephalopods and fish predators. *J. zool. Lond.* **172**, 549–69.

Newton, I. (1730). *Opticks: or a treatise of the reflections, refractions, inflections and colours of light* (4th edn), London.

Nicol, J. A. C. (1962). Animal luminescence. *Adv. comp. physiol. Biochem.* **1**, 217–73.

—— (1965). Migration of chorioidal tapetal pigment in the spur dog, *Squalus acanthias. J. mar. biol. Ass. UK* **45**, 405–27.

—— (1967). Luminescence in fishes. In *Aspects of marine zoology* (ed. N. B. Marshall), pp. 27–55. Academic Press, London.

—— (1974). Studies on the eyes of fishes: structure and ultrastructure. In *Vision in fishes* (ed. M. A. Ali), pp. 579–607. Plenum, New York.

—— Arnott, H. J., and Best, C. G. (1973). Tapeta lucida in bony fishes (Actinopterygii): a survey. *Can. J. Zool.* **51**, 69–81.

Nilsson, N. A. (1963). Interaction between trout and char in Scandinavia. *Trans. Am. Fish. Soc.* **92**, 276–85.

Northmore, D. P. M. (1977). Spatial adaptation and light summation in the goldfish visual system. *Nature (Lond.)* **268**, 450–1.

O'Connel, C. P. (1963). The structure of the eye of *Sardinops caerulia, Engraulis mordax*, and four other pelagic marine teleosts. *J. Morph.* **113**, 287–330.

O'Day, W. T. and Fernandez, H. R. (1974). *Aristostomias scintillans* (Malacosteidae): a deep-sea fish with visual pigments apparently adapted to its own bioluminescence. *Vision Res.* **14**, 545–50.

Ogneff, J. (1911). Ueber die aendurungen in den organen der Goldfische nach dreijährigen veibleiben in Finsternis. *Anat. Anz.* **40**, 81–7.

Orlov, O. Yu (1974). Coloured spectacles of animals, *Priroda, Mosk.* August, 35–41.

—— and Gamburtzeva, A. G. (1975). Dynamics of corneal colorations in fish, *Hexagrammos octagrammus. Biofizika* **21**, 362–5.

Papageorgis, C. (1975). Mimicry in neotropical butterflies. *Am. Sci.* **63**, 522–32.

Parker, G. H. (1948). Animal colour changes and their neurohumours. Cambridge University Press.

Partridge, L. D. and Brown, J. E. (1970). Receptive fields of rat retinal ganglion cells. *Vision Res.* **10**, 455–60.

Payne, R. S. (1962). How the barn owl locates prey by hearing. *Living birds* **1**, 151–9.

Peiponen, V. A. (1964). Zur Bedentung der Öikugeln im Farbensehen der Sauropsiden. *Ann. Zool. Fenn.* **1**, 281–302.

Pennycuick, C. J. (1972). *Animal flight.* Arnold, London.

Pickens, A. L. (1930). Favorite colors of humming birds. *The Auk* **47**, 346–52.

Pijl, L. Van der and Dodson, C. H. (1966). *Orchid flowers: their pollination and evolution.* University of Miami Press, Coral Gables, Fla.

Pilleri, G. (1974). Side-swimming, vision and sense of touch in *Platanista indi* (Cetacea, Platanistidae). *Experientia* **30**, 100–4.

Pirenne, M. H. (1943). Binocular and uniocular threshold for vision. *Nature (Lond.)* **152**, 698–9.

—— (1967). *Vision and the eye* (2nd edn). Chapman & Hall, London.

—— and Crombie, A. C. (1944). White plumage of sea birds. *Nature (Lond.)* **153**, 526–7.

Pitcher, T. J., Partridge, B. L. and Wardle, C. S. (1976). A blind fish can school. *Science* **194**, 963–5.

Popper, A. N. (1970). Auditory capacities of the Mexican Blind cavefish (*Astyanax jordani*) and its Eyed Ancestor (*Astyanax mexicanus*). *Animal Behaviour* **18**, 552.

Post, C. T. and Goldsmith, T. H. (1969). Physiological evidence for colour receptors in the eye of a butterfly. *Ann. ent. Soc. Am.* **62**, 1497.

Proctor, M. and Yeo, P. (1973). *The pollination of flowers*. Collins, London.

Protasov, V. R. (1964). Some features of the vision of gshes (in Russian). In *Skorosti Dvizheniia I Nekotorye Osobenosti Zreniia Ryb*, pp. 29–48. (Ed. D. V. Radakov and V. R. Protasov.) Akad. Nauk. SSSR, Inst. Morfologii Zhivotnykh, Moskva. Nauka (Translation by Z. Kabata, DAFFS, Marine Laboratory, Aberdeen, U.K., Translation 949.)

Pumphrey, R. J. (1950). Hearing. *Symp. Soc. exp. Biol.* **4**, 3–18.

Purkinje, J. (1819). *Beiträge zur Kenntnis des Sehens in subjectiver Hinsicht*. J. G. Calve, Prague.

Ratliff, F. (1965). *Mach bands*. Holden Day, San Francisco.

—— (1972). Contour and contrast. *Sci. Am.* (June) 91–101.

Rayleigh, Lord (Strutt, J. W.) (1871). On the light from the sky, its polarization and colour. *Phil. Mag.* **41**, 107–20.

—— (1930). Absolute intensity of the aurora line in the night sky and the number of atomic transitions. *Proc. roy. Soc. Lond.* A **129**, 458–67.

Richardson, E. A. (1969). Contrast enhancement imaging devices by selection of input photosurface spectral response. *Adv. Electronics & Electron Phys.* **28B**, 661–75.

Ripps, H. and Weale, R. A. (1976). The visual stimulus. In *The eye*, Vol. IIa (ed. H. Davson), pp. 43–99. Academic Press, New York.

Roaf, H. E. (1933). Colour vision. *Physiol. Rev.* **13**, 43–79.

Roberts, B. L. and Russell, I. J. (1972). The activity of lateral line efferent neurones in stationary and swimming dogfish. *J. exp. Biol.* **57**, 435–58.

Robson, J. G. (1975). Receptive fields: neural representation of the spatial and intensive attributes of the visual image. In *Handbook of perception*, Vol. 5, Academic Press, London.

Rochon-Duvigneaud, A. (1943). *Les yeux et la vision desverté brés*. Mason et Cie, Paris.

Rodieck, R. W. (1973). *The vertebrate retina*. W. H. Freeman, San Francisco.

Rothschild, M. (1975). Remarks on carotenoids in the evolution of signals. In *Co-evolution of animals and plants*, (ed. L. E. Gilbert and P. H. Raven), pp. 20–51. University of Texas Press, Austin.

Rozenberg, G. V. (1966). *Twilight—a study in atmospheric optics*. Plenum Press, New York.

Rushton, W. A. H. (1972). Visual pigments in man. In *Handbook of sensory physiology*, Vol. VII/1 (ed. H. J. A. Dartnall), pp. 364–94. Springer-Verlag, Berlin.

Russell, I. J. (1976). Amphibian lateral line receptors. In *Frog neurobiology*, pp. 513–50. (ed. R. Llinás and W. Precht). Sprinter, New York.

—— and Sellick, P. M. (1976). Measurement of potassium and chloride ion concentrations in the cupulae of the lateral lines of *Xenopus laevis*. *J. Physiol.* **257**, 245–55.

Sadoglu, P. (1957). Mendelian inheritance in the hybrids between the Mexican blind fish and their overground ancestors. *Verh. Dtsch. Zool. Ges.* 432–9.

—— (1975). Genetic paths leading to blindness in *Astyanax mexicanus*. In *Vision in fishes* (ed. M. A. Ali), pp. 419–26. Plenum Press, New York.

Sasaki, T., Okami, N., Oshiba, G. and Watanabe, S. (1958). Spectral energy distribution of submarine daylight of Kii Peninsula in relation to the investigation of oceanic productivity. *Rec. Oceanogr. Works Jpn.* **2**, 119–28.

Sastri, U. D. P. and Das, S. R. (1968). Typical spectral distributions and colour for tropical daylight. *J. opt. Soc. Am.* **58**, 391–8.

Schagen, P. (1977). Some recent developments in remote sensing. *Nature (Lond.)* **266**, 223–8.

Scheffer, V. B. (1964). Deep diving of elephant seals. *Murrelet* **45**, 9.

Scheich, H. and Bullock, T. H. (1974). The detection of electric fields from electric organs. In *Handbook of sensory physiology*, Vol. III/3, pp. 201–256. (ed. A. Fessard). Springer-Verlag, New York.

Schmidt-Nielsen, K. (1964). *Desert animals*. Oxford University Press.

—— Taylor, C. R., Shkolnic, A. (1972). Desert snails: problems of survival. In *Comparative physiology of desert animals* (ed. G. M. O. Maloy), pp. 1–13. Symposia of the Zoological Society of London **31**. Academic Press, London.

Scholes, J. H. (1975). Colour receptors and the synaptic connexions in the retina of a cyprinid fish. *Phil. Trans. roy. Soc. B* **270**, 61–118.

Schwartz, E. (1971). Die Ortung von Wasserarellen durch Oberflächenfische. *Z. vergl. Physiol.* **74**, 64–80.

—— (1974). Lateral-line mechanoreceptors in fishes and amphibians. In *Handbook of sensory physiology*, Vol. III/3, pp. 257–278. (Ed. A. Fessard). Springer-Verlag, New York.

Schwemer, J., Hamdorf, K., and Gogola, M. (1971). Der UV-Sehfarbstoff der Insekten: Photochemie in vitro und in vivo. *Z. vergl. Physiol.* **75**, 174–88.

Shichi, H., Lewis, M. S., Irreverre, F. and Stone, A. L. (1969). Biochemistry of visual pigments I: Purification and properties of bovine rhodopsin. *J. biol. Chem.* **244**, 529–36.

Siegel, A. and Fletcher, D. E. (1969). *Guide to aircraft in-flight camouflage*. Applied Psychological Services Inc., Wayne, Pa. Report No. NADC-AC-6904, March 1969.

Silver, P. H. (1967). Spectral sensitivity of the white rat by a training method. *Vision Res.* **7**, 377–83.

Simmons, K. E. L. (1972). Some adaptive features of seabird plumage types. *Br. Birds* **65**, 465–79, 510–21.

Sirovich, L. and Abramov, I. (1977). Photoproducts and pseudo-pigments. *Vision Res.* **17**, 5–16.

Sivak, J. G. (1973). Interrelation of feeding behaviour and accommodative lens movements in some species of North American freshwater fishes. *J. fish Res. Bd. Canada* **30**, 1141–6.

Sliney, D. H. (1977). The ambient light environment and ocular hazards. In *Retinitis pigmentosa* (ed. M. B. Landers, M. L. Wolbarsht, J. E. Dowling, and A. M. Laties.) Plenum Press, New York.

Smith, R. C. and Tyler, J. E. (1967). Optical properties of natural water. *J. opt. Soc. Amer.* **57**, 589–601.

— —, — — and Goldman, C. R. (1973). Optical properties and colour of Lake Tahoe and Crater Lake. *Limnol. Oceanog.* **18**, 189–99.

Spence, D. H. N. (1972). Light on freshwater macrophytes. *Trans. bot. Soc. Edinb.* **41**, 491–505.

——, Campbell, R. M., and Chrystal, J. (1971). Spectral intensity in some Scottish freshwater lochs. *Freshwater Biol.* **1**, 321–37.

Starck, W. A. and Davis, W. P. (1966). Night habits of fishes of Alligator Reef; *Florida Ichthyologica. the Aquar. J.* **38**, 313–56.

Steeman Nielsen, E. (1974). Light and primary production. In *Optical aspects of oceanography* (ed. N. G. Jerlov and E. Steeman Nielsen), pp. 361–88. Academic Press, London.

Stiles, W. S. (1948). The physical interpretation of the spectral sensitivity curve of the eye. In *Transactions of the optical convention of the Worshipful Company of Spectacle Makers*, pp. 97–107, Spectacle Makers Company, London.

Stone, J. and Fukada Y. (1974). Properties of W, X- and Y-cells. *J. Neurol physiol.* **37**, 722–48.

Sutter, David (1880). Les phenomenes de la vision. *L'Art* **20**, 216–20.

Swift, E., Biggley, W. H., and Napora, N. A. (1977). The bioluminescence emission spectra of *Pyrosoma atlanticum*, *P. spinosum* (Tunicata), *Euphausia tenera* (Crustacea) and *Gonostoma sp.* (Pisces). *J. mar. biol. Assoc. UK* **57**, 817–23.

Swihart, S. L. (1970). The neural basis of colour vision in the butterfly, *Papilio troilus. J. Insect. Physiol.* **16**, 1623–36.

—— and Gordon, W. C. (1971). Red photoreceptors in butterflies. *Nature (Lond.)* **231**, 126.

Talling, J. F. (1970). Generalised and specialized features of phytoplankton as a form of photosynthetic cover. In *Prediction and measurement of photosynthetic productivity* 431–45. Centre for Agricultural publishing and documentation. Wageningen.

Tansley, K. (1964). The gecko retina. *Vision Res.* **4**, 33–7.

—— (1965). *Vision in vertebrates*. Chapman & Hall, London.

Thayer, G. H. & Thayer, A. H. (1909). *Concealing-coloration in the Anima-Kingdom*. New York.

Thurston, M. H. (1976a). The vertical distribution and diurnal migration of the crustacea Amphipoda collected during the SOND Cruise, 1965, I. The Gammaridea. *J. mar. biol. Assoc. UK* **56**, 359–82.

—— (1976b). The vertical distribution and diurnal migration of the crustacea Amphipoda collected during the SOND Cruise, 1965, II. The Hyperiidae and general discussion. *J. mar. biol. Assoc. UK* **56**, 383–470.

Timofeeva, V. A. (1974). Optics of turbid waters (results of laboratory studies). In *Optical aspects of oceanography* (ed. N. G. Jerlov and E. Steeman Nielsen), Academic Press, London.

Tyler, J. E. (1959). Natural water as a monochromator. *Limnol. Oceanogr.* **4**, 102–5.

—— (1960). Radiance distribution as a function of depth in an underwater environment. *Bull. Scripps Inst. Oceanogr. Calif.* **7**, 363–412.

—— (1968). The Secchi disc. *Limnol. Oceanogr.* **13**, 1–7.

—— and Preisendorfer, R. W. (1962). Transmission of energy within the sea. In *The Sea* 1 (Ed. Hill, M. N.), pp. 397–451. Interscience, New York.

—— and Smith, R. C. (1970). *Measurements of spectral irradiance under water.* Gordon and Breach, New York.

Tyndall, J. (1869). On the blue colour of the sky, the polarization of skylight, and on the polarization of light by cloudy matter generally. *Phil. Mag.* **37**, 384–94.

Underwood, G. (1970). The eye. In *Biology of the Reptilia* (ed. C. Gans and T. S. Parsons), pp. 1–97. Academic Press, New York.

Vandel, A. (1964). *Biospeologie.* Gauthier-Villars, Paris.

Vakkur, G. J. and Bishop, P. O. (1963). The schematic eye of the cat. *Vision Res.* **3**, 357–82.

Vilter, V. (1947). Dissociation spatiale des cones et des batonnets dans la rétine du callionyme et ses relations avec l'architectonique neuronale de l'appareil visuel. *C. R. Seanc. Soc. Biol.* **141**, 346–8.

—— (1950). Adaptation biologique de l'appareil visuel et les structures rétiniennes de la sardine. C. R. Séances Soc. Biol. **144**, 200–3.

Vries, A. L. de and Wohlschlag, D. E. (1964) Diving depths of the Weddel Seal. *Science* **145**, 292.

Waelchi, G. (1883). Zur topographie der gefärbten Kugeln der Vogelnetzhaut. *Arch. Ophthal.* **29**, 205–23.

Walcott, B. (1975). Anatomical changes during light-adaptation in insect compound eyes. In *The compound eye and vision in insects* (ed. G. A. Horridge), pp. 20–33. Clarendon Press, Oxford.

Wald, G. (1958). The significance of vertebrate metamorphosis. *Science* **128**, 1481–90.

—— (1960). The distribution and evolution of visual systems. In *Comparative biochemistry*, Vol. I. Academic Press, New York.

Wales, W. (1974). Extraretinal photosensitivity in fish larvae. In *Vision in fishes* (ed. M. A. Ali) pp. 445–50. Plenum Press, New York.

Walls, G. L. (1934). The reptilian retina. *Am. J. Ophthal.* **17**, 892–915.

—— (1942). *The vertebrate eye and its adaptive radiation.* Hafner, New York.

—— and Judd, H. D. (1933). The intra-ocular colour filters of vertebrates. *Br. J. Ophthal.* **17**, 641–75, 705–25.

Ward, F. (1919). *Animal life under water*, Cassell, London.

Waterman, T. H. (1954). Polarization patterns in submarine illumination. *Science* **120**, 927–32.

—— (1955). Polarization of scattered sunlight in deep water. *Deep Sea Res.* **3**, Suppl., 426–34.

—— (1972). Visual direction finding in fishes. In *Animal orientation and navigation* (ed. S. R. Galler, K. Schmidt-Koenig, G. J. Jacobs, and R. E. Bellerille), pp. 437–56, NASA, Washington, D.C.

—— (1974). Underwater light and the orientation of animals. In *Optical aspects of oceanography* (ed. N. G. Jerlov and E. Steeman-Nielsen), pp. 415–43 Academic Press, London.

—— (1975). Natural polarized light and e-vector discrimination by vertebrates. In *Light as an ecological factor* (ed G. C. Evans, R. Bainbridge, and O. Rackham), Blackwell, Oxford.

—— and Westell, W. E. (1956). Quantitative effect of the sun's position on submarine light polarization. *J. Mar. Res.* **15**, 149–69.

Wehner, R. (1975). Pattern recognition. In *The compound eye and vision in insects*, pp. 75–113 (ed. G. A. Horridge). Clarendon Press, Oxford.

Werth, E. (1915). Kurzer uberblick über die gesamtrafage der Ornithopholie. *Bot. Jahrb.* **53**, 314–78.

Wheeler, A. (1969). *The fishes of the British Isles and north-west Europe*. Macmillan, London.

White, W. J. (1964). Vision. In *Bioastronautics Data Book* (Ed. P. Webb). NASA, Washington D.C.

Wickler, M. (1968). *Mimicry in plants and animals*. (Trans. Martin, R. D.), Weidenfield and Nicolson, London.

Wilkens, H. (1971). Genetic interpretation of regressive evolutionary process: studies on hybrid eyes of two Astyanax cave populations (Choranidae, pisces). *Evolution* **25**, 530–44.

Willmer, E. N. (1953). Determining factors in the evolution of the retina in vertebrates. *Symp. Soc. exp. Biol.* **7**, 377–94.

Woodhead, P. M. J. (1966). The behaviour of fish in relation to light in the sea. *Oceanogr. mar. Biol. ann. Rev.* **4**, 377–403.

Woods, J. D. (1971). Micro-oceanography. In *Underwater science* (ed. J. D. Woods and J. N. Lythgoe), pp. 291–317. Oxford University Press.

Wright, A. W. (1972). Psychometric and psychophysical hue discrimination functions for the pigeon. *Vision Res.* **12**. 1447–64.

Wunder, W. (1925). Physiologische und Vergleichend – anatomische untersuchungen an der Knockenfischnetzhaut. *Z. vergleich. Physiol.* **3**, 1–61.

Wyszecki, G. and Stiles, W. S. (1967). *Colour science*. John Wiley, New York.

Yentsch, L. S. (1960). The influence of phytoplankton on the colour of sea-water. *Deep-sea Res.* **7**, 1–9.

—— (1962). Measurement of visible light absorption by particulate matter in the ocean. *Limnol. Oceanogr.* **7**, 202–17.

—— and Reichert, C. A. (1962). The interrelationship between water-soluble yellow substances and chloroplastic pigments in marine algae. *Bot. Marina* **3**, 65–74.

Yura, H. T. (1971). Small-angle scattering of light by ocean water. *Appl. Opt.* **10**, 114–18.

Author index

Subject index

DATE DUE